I0212041

OVER THE RANGE

*SUNSHINE AND SHADOW
IN THE KIMBERLEYS*

ION IDRIESS

ETT IMPRINT
Exile Bay

ETT IMPRINT
PO Box R1906
Royal Exchange NSW 1225 Australia

First published by Angus & Robertson 1937. Reprinted 1937 (three), 1938, 1939 (twice), 1941, 1942, 1943, 1945, 1947, 1948 (twice), 1949, 1951 (twice), 1956
First published by ETT Imprint in 2021

First electronic edition published by ETT Imprint 2024

ISBN 9781923205611 (pbk)
ISBN 9781922473790 (ebk)

Cover: Aboriginal tracker Pannican

The Publisher would like to thank Terry Birthisel for his help with this book

Design by Tom Thompson

FOREWORD

THIS book may interest Australians in one of the wildest areas left in their continent—that north of the King Leopold Range. And it may reveal a little of a most interesting man—the stone-age man of thousands of years ago. If it should influence Australians to do something towards curing his ills and allowing him to retain his liberty, I shall be glad.

Time is a leviathan of apparent inconsistency; yet it seems to be regulated by laws similar to those that rule the tiny seed which one day bursts into full flower. Time has allowed the aboriginal to roam undisturbed for thousands, possibly millions, of years. Now—not in a thousand years, or ten, but almost in months—Time is wiping the aboriginal from the face of the earth.

The patrol whose story is told in the following pages was carried out in 1933. I have before me a letter from a northern mounted policeman who recently patrolled that, very same country. The letter staggered me. In that: short time a surprising number of the aboriginals I met: there four years ago have died. And this in an area of country where the white settlers can be counted on the fingers of both hands; while to the north of that area, there are no whites at all. And despite the fact that those whites are doing all in their power to save the remnants.

So, if we really do mean to save the last of the stone-age men we must race Time.

ION IDRIESS

AUTHOR'S ROUTE

CONTENTS

CHAPTER

1. "OVER THE RANGE"   6
2. JUST TRAVELLING ALONG   9
3. MOUNT HART   14
4. FRONTIER LIFE   19
5. FELIX'S WILD CHILDREN   25
6. THE CHASE BEGINS   32
7. TOOLWANOR SLIPS AWAY   38
8. TOOLWANOR IS CAUGHT   43
9. SEEKING UNGANDONGERY ALIAS CHARCOAL   48
10. THROUGH A LONELY LAND   56
11. IN THE FRONTIER LANDS   64
12. THE MESSAGE-STICK   70
13. THE CAPTURE OF CHARCOAL AND OOMA-CUN   75
14. CHARCOAL, MY FELLOW AUTHOR   85
15. BURRIN'S SPIRIT WALKS   91
16. IN AGE-OLD COUNTRY   98
17. CHAROO   104
18. DEAD MEN'S BONES   112
19. THE WITCH-DOCTOR'S CURSE   119
20. WALCOTT INLET   125
21. HOME IN THE WILDERNESS   134
22. LIFE IN PIONEER LAND   139
23. "WHO WILLED THE WARRIOR TO DIE?"   146
24. LIFE IN ABORIGINAL-LAND   152
25. THE HERMIT IN THE WILDERNESS   157
26. TRIALS OF A PIONEER   163
27. THE UNGOODJU STONE   168
28. THE ESCAPE OF ALLBOROO   173
29. ON THE MARCH AGAIN   160
30. A FEAST FOR THE TROOPS   183
31. THE LEPER'S RIDE OF MISERY   187
32. DONKEY IS CAUGHT   192
33. THE SPIRITS COME AGAIN   196
34. INTRIGUE   202
35. DERBY   206
36. FINALE   210

1
"OVER THE RANGE"

ROMANCE; visions of untamed country; of wild men. Mountain barriers; an almost unknown coastline.

"He smells the breeze," they say in Derby, "coming over the range, as they watch some brown-faced man quietly riding away, his eyes turned dreamily towards the north.

The parallel barriers of the King Leopold Range for years defied penetration, even by the finest bushmen on earth. To the south they wall off the West Kimberley, of which Derby is the little cattle-port. To the east stretches the East Kimberley. For a thousand miles south of both stretches the remainder of the great State of Western Australia. Beyond the King Leopolds the extreme north-western corner of Australia is vaguely known as the Nor'-west Kimberley.

Probably not more than twenty white men live "over the range." Of the nine who have perished there, eight died "with their boots on." The tenth staggered into his hut muttering: "I won't die with my boots on." He fell on the bunk and gasped to the black boy: "Unlace boots belonga me!" Then he kicked his boots to the hut roof and sighed: "Now I won't die with my boots on."

Farther north, inland from the coast, there are no white men except a dingo-poisoner or two. After leaving Derby, while riding through the Pindan we passed one such, Jack Wilson, the "Little Iron Man." He had "smelt the breeze coming over the range," and with his unsmiling face and direct eyes was following the lure.

"You could never kill him," Dr Hodge had said to me in Derby.

At the end of the road is Kimberley Downs station, only sixty miles north of Derby. Brilliant sunlight, sweet air. A million acres of grassy plains stretching among low, scrubby hills lightly timbered, with glittering lagoon and billabong and tree-fringed watercourses stretching far away. We unsaddled as Barney Timony came strolling across from the men's quarters.

"Good day, Laurie."

"Good day, Barney."

"Old Felix will be happy to-day. Smell the breeze coming over the range?" the stockman added as he looked towards the north.

Old Felix Edgar on his Mount Hart station was fifty miles farther out.

The bullock-paddock of Kimberley Downs is a hundred miles around. The white-washed homestead and outbuildings stand on a gentle rise facing Mount Marmion a quaint hill standing straight up out of the plain with a flat top and dwarf trees sky-lined on its summit like scraggly hair on a giant's pate. That wind-blown eyrie has been sacred ground from time immemorial, its clefts guarding native bones. Fronting the homestead, to the left, is the ridge where Duncan speared young Clabby dark trees of the Leonard can be seen plainly from the homestead. Rising beside the latter is the rocky "Hill of the Spirits." From this hill Mrs Thompson watches for her husband as he comes riding home across the plains. Two lubras always trail fearfully after her to guard against the "evil that bad spirits might do!"

These lubras belong to a local tribe of which hardly a dozen survive. Influenza and leprosy are mainly responsible.

The big bell rang. From the garden we walked through to the back veranda with its wired mosquito-netting. In the pest season, one can lounge and eat in comfort here. An irascible cockatoo raised a laugh as he came screeching across the yard to ride a big fat duck. He nipped her on the leg. Obediently she squatted, and he climbed on her back. With a "quack, quack" she staggered up then waddled to the kitchen. The house lubras pretended they were too busy to attend to the bird on her back. His crest rose and he abused them with aboriginal swear words they had taught him.

As the lubras went along the veranda carrying lunch, Cocky screeched in final abuse, savagely nipped the duck's neck and away she waddled. In the middle of the yard she paused to puff her feathers and shake herself. Cocky scolded her unmercifully.

Away downhill towards the men's quarters she waddled, Cocky screeching an insult as they passed the trackers cleaning saddlery near the wagon shed. At the men's quarters Cocky nipped his steed. She squatted down and he climbed off. Then with crest erect he strode into the quarters screeching "Barney! Barney!"

Immediately the terror had disappeared the duck stood up, hastily fixed her feathers and waddled away. About the same time Cocky emerged half-flying, half-jumping out of the door, apparently impelled by a boot. His screeches awoke the hill-side. What he screeched to his runaway steed almost reduced the household lubras to hysterics.

Constable Laurie O'Neill was in charge of the patrol. And I was riding with the patrol to cross the range and see the "Wild Lands."

"How is Rosie behaving?" inquired O'Neill.

"A little worse than usual," sighed Mrs Thompson.

O'Neill laughed.

"Heaven help your visitors next time then."

Rosie was the big lubra with disdainful walk and insolent eye. Recently, she had given away new dress after new dress until Mrs Thompson refused to give her any more. Rosie stubbornly refused to water the garden until she got a new dress. One gala day several car-loads of visitors came out from Derby. The lubras appeared for their rations when the veranda was crowded with nice people. They received their rations and walked giggling away. Rosie stood there, insolently eyeing everyone.

"Take your rations away to the camp, Rosie," ordered Mrs Thompson.

"Won't go. No got dress."

"You are wearing a dress now," reproved Mrs Thompson. "Go away."

With a brazen glance at the company Rosie slowly turned and waddled away. There was no back to her dress. And she weighs sixteen stone.

Mrs Thompson is a fine type of the far-out bush woman. She has need to be. Apart from the tiny port of Derby, there are hardly a dozen white women in the West Kimberley. There are more in the East Kimberley. In the Nor'-west there are no white women at all inland, and only half a dozen isolated along the coast. The Kimberleys, owing to their extreme isolation, are essentially a man's land.

The rare station woman thus gains unusual experience in the ways of men working on the lonely places in a lonely land: their moods, their quietness, at times their jealousies of work and custom; above all, the idiosyncrasies of the cooks! A station "poisoner" in his own kitchen is a dictator indeed. The station woman must be: tactful; never interfere in the slightest with the work of the men; allow them to keep their quarters sacred to themselves; seldom visit their mustering or other camps unless riding around with her husband; and not ask too many questions concerning their work unless her opinion or suggestions are invited. Above all, she must not tell the boss of any little irregularity she may see. This is the golden rule. The men will do anything for the woman who learns it quickly.

Kimberley Downs is very "modern." Though the road from Derby ends at the homestead door there is a private telephone to the little town. And that means many things.

2
JUST TRAVELLING ALONG

NEXT morning the patrol, to a cheery farewell, filed out of the station yard, Slippery the mule doing his snorting best to buck his packs off, Mandy tying herself in a knot. Larry and Davey, the trackers, rode ahead followed by the twenty odd packhorses and mules, then Constable Laurie O'Neill and myself. Before us, under a bright sky, stretched the Nor'-west Kimberley.

Old Larry had grown grizzled in the service of the Western Australian Mounted Police. During a skirmish with the armed native outlaws, Pigeon and Captain, he had been shot in the leg when a child. The police picked him up, reared him, and he had been a tracker ever since, except for periodical walk-abouts. Davey was a smart young aboriginal who, only three years before, had been a munjon (wild bush blackfellow).

Each horse and mule was truculently showing its own personality: its liking for certain mates, its kickable dislike towards its own breed. Mules and horses were individually plodders, or "flash," or rogues. Several of the mules were "blackfellows' mules"—they would allow only the trackers to handle them.

Laurie O'Neill was a fine type of the Western Australian Mounted Police. Tall and strong with the long swinging walk of the bushman, his boyish face and read smile hid a determination that was alertly quick to swing into action. Not yet thirty, he had already twenty thousand miles of patrolling to his credit; and his quick chase and arrest of an armed lunatic who had shot a man was but one proof of his gameness.

The object of this patrol was to see if all was well with the few scattered settlers over the range, and to arrest half a dozen native murderers whose killings had frightened their own tribesmen into soliciting "white pleece" protection.

The authorities interfere as little as possible with the customs of the semi-wild and wild tribes, believing it the better, policy to allow them to to settle their own disputes. But when a native appeals for assistance action must be taken: he is a British subject and has a right to the protection of the Law.

I had seized the opportunity to see those practically inaccessible lands.

To an alarmed screeching of cockatoos we rode among the big trees of the Six Mile Lagoon, vocal with the trumpeting of brolgas and the whistling and squawking of wildfowl. Among the yellow lilies baby ducks were bobbing up tiny heads only to bob down as the horses plunged in for a drink. With whip and voice the trackers drove the mules from this animal paradise and we headed across a lightly timbered plain where wheat grass waved in patches already seven feet high. For this was the end of the wet season and everything was vibrant with life. The rejuvenated earth under the warmth of the sun was replenishing all creation.

The rogues among the horses and mules sought every chance to break the line and hide under shady trees where sweet grass grew; the calls of birds gradually faded into the chirrups that persist on a hot midday. A big tree-frog croaked hoarsely as we rode under a hollow limb; native bees tickled us as they sought to extract the salt from the sweat on our foreheads and chests; plain turkeys watched curiously, their heads on long necks just topping the grass.

We slithered down a steep-banked creek, and the mules bogged. Despite shouting and stockwhip they simply lay down. "Now do what you like about it!" said their cunning eyes, while their ears twitched defiance. The old grey horse stood patiently, one ear rakishly cocked. Cunning old Mandy, sticking in the mud just a wee bit, with a long, contented sigh flopped down leaving me foolishly standing astride her, up to the knees in muddy water The trackers laughed although their stockwhips cracked unavailing^ in an effort to prevent Kate and Pussycat from waddling farther out.

Up to our knees in mud we were forced to unsaddle the mules, carry the packs across on to solid ground, haul the mules out, then saddle them again.

"Patience does it," said Laurie. "There's nothing else for it when a mule flops down in the mud."

We camped at twenty miles, gloriously tired, gloriously hungry; ready for a smoke and a yarn then a sleep under golden stars twinkling through mosquito-nets. A bird called from the trees on the Lennard nearby. He whistled hoarsely and low, then instantly imitated the call on a high note that swept triumphantly along the river. The fire glowed lower and lower; old Larry was snoring; there came the subdued tinkle of horse-bells; again the peculiar bird-call; then – sleep.

The Leonard was in swirling flood, angrily submerging the branches of leaning trees. A nervy sight for a poor swimmer. All hands unsaddled the mules; then then fashioned a boat out of the canvas tent-fly, building it into rough shape with the pack-saddles and tying the two ends. When the swags were stowed aboard she floated well. Stripping, we pushed her out at an angle upstream. Soon the water was above our waists. We strained against it when chest-deep, struggling to retain foothold. Underbelow, it was sucking at our ankles, sucking the gravel away from under our toes; as it pressed against our chests we heard plainly the hissing and sobbing rising from the rippling brown surface. The trackers laughed boisterously when the current swept me off my feet and I clung desperately to the boat. They kept on their toes for a surprising time; then all hands were swimming and clinging to the boat, battling to push her upstream, swimming sideways to the current while edging up into it. My legs were swept straight out and entangled the tracker behind. He laughed as at a great joke, although it was a pretty desperate swim for all in midstream.

I was thankful at last to feel rocks underfoot; we had landed just above a tangle of snags and branches. During the return swims for the remainder of the gear and the horses I gladly remained ashore to mind the camp.

A few miles farther on a low range of hills appeared, peculiar crests and spires and hump-backs and walls of purple-grey above the plain. In late afternoon we rode among the fine trees of the Barker, which was "up" too but not so strongly as the Lennard. Repeating the crossing performance, we were surprised to see black boys unsaddling pack-animals, and others starting a log fire.

A short, strongly-built white man, with close-cropped beard, was filling his pipe as we rode up.

"Glad to have company. Come and have a drink of tea. The cattle are coming up behind."

It was the gruff, deliberate voice of Scotty Saddler, chief actor in one of the great mystery dramas of the bush. Surmises about the facts of that strange case are voiced at every campfire in the Kimberleys.

The pack-animals rushed the ready-made camp, knowing well the day was done. Gratefully we unsaddled.

Through the timber Scotty's cattle appeared, quietly feeding their way into camp. An art that, timing them naturally to arrive on camp as the sun is going down. Thus, unhurried and well fed, they camp contentedly all night. These bullocks camped in front of the big fire, with the black line of river trees facing them. The first watch rode out, singing a native lullaby. By the fire the billies were boiling, the tucker of both camps spread out on tarpaulins. The trackers were were yarning with the native stockmen, and judging by their inquisitive glances I was a tit-bit of gossip. As a tracker is supposed to know everything old Larry assured them I was an "inspector." The trackers themselves were puzzled as to what position I held with the patrol, but they were not going to admit that.

Scotty chuckled: "Black fellow telegraph will spread the news all over the range that an inspector is coming out on patrol. The boys will wonder their heads off. They'd never expect a sergeant to ride over the range, let alone an inspector."

"They will probably connect it with the Royal Commission on the leprosy question," said Laurie.

Ah, yes," growled Scotty.

The trackers, while satisfying others' curiosity, were satisfying their own concerning friends and tribesmen over the range, recent initiations, the latest corroboree, fights, feuds, and the movement of game. And working too. For the Australian tracker takes his job seriously. He is no fool. He loves to be a tracker; the job lifts him above his fellows, and gives him great authority in the eyes of all aboriginals. He is especially suited for that difficult job.

His previous wild life has been lived in a hotbed of native intrigue, where life is a constant fight against the wild, where human life is often a match of wits against wits, endurance and strength waring against nature and superstition. So our trackers, with all their friendly inquiries, were also shrewdly fishing for scraps of in-formation; ears open for any voluntary hints, or any guarded reference that might put them on the tracks of the men the patrol was seeking.

Well behind the fire were the pack-saddles and a dark mob of feeding horses, those of the night watch being loosely hitched to trees. Quick womanish laughter told of the trackers' gallantry, for several lubras rode with Scotty's stockboys. A lively little lubra of twelve years was all done up in stockman's pants and shirt. Scotty had saved her life when a baby and had reared her. He was droving this mob of fats into Derby, to ship by the southern boat for Fremantle.

After a hearty meal he yarned in a voice that after a life-time in the country still retained a trace of his Scottish accent. His shrewd eyes gazed steadily from a well- conditioned face. Men whisper that Scotty has defied the "Third Degree." Certainly his eyes show strength of purpose, his face unhurried daring. He had come to this country as a penniless lad, had eventually worked his way over the range and had hewn a station out of the Wild Lands.

The life-story of any man who has done that would fill an exciting book.

Laurie and Scotty had lots to yarn about: shipping space, steamer sailings, mobs of cattle from other stations on the road for Derby; mutual friends amongst station- owners and stockmen, dingo-shooters and other nomads of the bush; transport feats in a country that has not one road. They yarned of country already found and surmised, of lagoons and billabongs, of over the range, niggers, scrubbers, tracks, "wets," bush-fires, floods, fever and stampedes; of droving feats through gorges and across trackless ranges; and all the other colourful phases of frontier life in the Kimberleys.

The night voices grew quiet; the cattle were quiet too. Once there was a snort, a patter, then a rumble of hoofs as uneasy beasts lurched up, but they steadied immediately top the watchman's reassuring call and Scotty's steady "Whoa Bullicks! Whoa Bullicks!" While talking he had his ears and his mind on the bullocks. The relief mounted and rode into the darkness, slowly singing around the outskirts of the mob. The night watch must sing nearly all the time: the beasts are reassured by the sound of the human voice.

We turned in and fell asleep quickly. Once I awoke, and stared at a little bright red light among the branches of the trees. But it was a star, very low down. Out in the night the watch, as he rode around the cattle was singing a native lullaby.

Young Dick the Mascot.

3
MOUNT HART

NEXT morning we gave Scotty a hand to drive his cattle across the Barker. Quite a manoeuvre to patiently keep a mob of beasts unflurried while urging them across a swollen stream. Scotty, calling in calm, confident voice to the leaders, as if they were personal mates, urged them to step into the water and take the lead across. It was a pleasant sight in the sunrise, with the flanking horsemen riding down the steep banks among the trees; then splashing out into the swiftly flowing stream.

But our mules had seized their opportunity. When we rode back to camp Pompey and Carrie had hidden in the long grass and Pussycat and Rosie had quietly nosed away in the opposite direction. It took Laurie two hours to track them. Eventually we saddled the team; then Slippery, with a snort, started pig-rooting and bolted amongst the trees, with the trackers hanging to him. That started the horses: the old grey indulged in a middle- aged root; Mandy put her head down and sent her packs flying. The animals were all bucked up. It was in the air. Everything was filled with the vim of life.

We rode away at last and presently drew close to the Napier Range that loomed abruptly like broken turrets along the sky-line. Laurie, with a nod, said:

"That little range is not high, but it stretches from well east of us right west to the coast. And it's impassable except here and there.

Davey suddenly jumped from his horse and ran after a big old-man bungarra. That goanna had arms like a bear. Rearing up it showed teeth and tongue and claws, and hissed balefully. Larry engaged its attention while Davey attacked from behind. It put up a great fight, but its six-foot length was soon swinging from across Davey's saddle.

With the steady squelch of hoofs plonking in and out of mud, the patrol found firmer ground among the outliers of the Napier Range that unfolded new pictures every few hundred yards as we wound in among them. Hills of dull red, bold bluffs of heavy purple, bastions of bluish-grey rock rose from lawns of wheat grass rippling under an afternoon breeze.

We camped in a world of fantastic shadows at Fletcher's

Camp. This lonely waterhole among queer hills had been a favourite camp of Fletcher's patrol; before he was stabbed to death by a Malay in Broome.

Despite the dark, Davey was energetically washing his clothes.

"That young tracker of yours seems exceptionally clean for a black fellow," I remarked.

"Don't you believe it," laughed Laurie. "It's only flashness. Whenever you see that dandy washing his clothes you'll know we are nearing a station or a tribal camp. Davey likes to cut a dash before the young lubras."

We pushed on for Mount Hart, seeing no sign of man, and rode into the outlying foot-hills of the King Leopolds, down into a grassy valley with a hill-side rising sheer by the left stirrup, and a pink bluff like a wall of Gibraltar to the right. Weird baobab-trees clung to it like fat grey spiders clutching a wan.

The first men to penetrate these frontier lands must have lived wonderfully as well as hard. We realized what battling Alexander Forrest must have done in 1879, his tiny party crawling along the foot of the great barrier, trying to poke in here and there, but beaten back again and again. Long years were to pass by before the range was penetrated.

Davey was clinging to his horse's neck as he began climbing a sharp spur to the left, the pack-animals scrambling behind him, digging for toe-holds as they zigzagged up and up. Then down into another valley and another climb with vistas of range after range stretching into afternoon shadows vague in misty colouring.

"How on earth is the patrol going to find and catch the wild men away out there?" I wondered. Like silhouetted camelmen the patrol crept along the divide till we looked straight down into a great hollow completely rimmed by small hills. From the grass haze that covered it gleamed the white roofs of Mount Hart homestead, the Kumumbullabulla of the blacks. It was dark before we were greeted by a rush of furious dogs, the bull-roar of a man's voice calling them off. The owner of the voice came to meet us. Once a giant of a man, his shoulders now were somewhat bent; his great arms with gnarled hands hung almost to his knees. Starlight shone on an almost bald head and heavily wrinkled face. With relieved welcome in a gruff, rumbling voice he invited us to: "Come right inside for a pannikin of tea. Was just sitting down to dinner. Let the niggers look after the packs. Laurie, I'm downright glad to see you."

Old Felix Edgar's face beamed with rugged pleasure as he

shook the hand of the young policeman. Then he greeted me, his eyes steady and friendly above a grizzled moustache. He led the way into the homestead: a big, barn-like room, its earthern floor carpeted with stiffly dried goatskins and bullock-skins that rattled as one walked over them and through to a bough shed under which rough food was spread upon a table of planks with seats of sawn-off logs. There an inquisitive-eyed lubra brought a massive kettle of tea from the kitchen across the yard. We could not have enjoyed a meal more had we been dining in a palatial hotel.

"How is Bunch-'em-up, Laurie ?" growled Felix.

"Holding the fort in Derby."

"Aye. He'll hold it until he can't stand on his legs He s been sick though, lately. I don't want him back here until he is a well man."

"He has had a nasty touch of fever. But he wouldn't stay in hospital," Laurie explained.

"I suppose not. They'd have to rope him like a steer to hold him in a hospital bed. Just fancy a nurse trying to handle 'Bunch-'em-up' Gardiner! He sickened at an awkward time though. I've got to muster and get a mob away. And to load in a few weeks' time. And the bush *munjons* are all around the place. I've been at my wit's end. All IS ready for mustering, but the *munjons* will come down from the hills and raid the place as soon as my back is turned. They were plentiful as crows up in the hills all yesterday and early to-day. When they disappeared I guessed they'd sighted a patrol. Glad I was to hear your horses."

Bunch-'em-up Gardiner was Felix's overseer. We had left him away back in Derby, enjoying a somewhat hectic holiday after a long spell over the range.

"I'll see you well started on your mustering before I carry on," promised Laurie. He paused while a black stockman walked noiselessly by, then glanced around among the shadows. "We'll give you a hand," he resumed quietly, "and ride with you a few days to your boundary. Our presence will keep your station-boys in order and the bush natives will be puzzled. When you begin mustering in country near my first objective I'll leave you suddenly."

Felix breathed his relief.

"That puts my mind at ease. If you ride with me until I get a start I'll be set. And when you do say farewell, line up the boys and give them a tongue banging. Big Paddy is nearly out of control."

"I'll have a word with them," promised Laurie, "sufficient to keep them under control until you get your cattle into Derby anyway."

"I wish you could drive away the leprosy as easily as you scatter the *munjons*. When are they going to find a cure for that leprosy! It will wipe the poor devils out if it isn't soon checked."

"Is it among your boys?"

"I don't know. Can't see well enough to detect it. But I'm suspicious. I catch a whisper from the house gins when they don't think I'm listening."

"I'll examine the whole camp in the morning."

"Good. When I saw you come along with a stranger I thought for a moment he might be a doctor come to investigate. I did hear a rumour about a Leprosy Commission."

"That's correct," said Laurie. "The commissioner, Mr H. D. Moseley, is in the Kimberleys now."

"Best news I've heard for a long time."

"Got any milking cows left?" inquired Laurie.

"Not one. I gave up after they speared that last lot. Thirty-six fine beasts they were. No, you can't keep a milker here. A beast has to be half wild to stand any chance."

"Do you lose many cattle?" I asked.

"Not many—and less every year. The natives are dying out fast. What with disease and birth-control and continuous feuds there won't be a nigger left in the country in a few years. We'll miss them, although they do spear a few cattle."

It was late when Felix yawned prodigiously. We unrolled our blankets upon bunks of stretched bullock-hide luxurious after nights of sleeping on the ground. Sleep came quickly.

Next morning Laurie lined up all in the native camp for medical inspection. Patrols seek out the sick and help them if they will allow themselves to be helped. Most bush natives run for the hills if they suffer from the dread complaints the treatment of which means they must leave their own country to receive the medicine of the white man.

"Their eyes are nearly sticking out of their heads" said Laurie with a smile. "They have never seen an Inspector before."

"They don't seem very awed."

"No, they're consumed by curiosity. It's a bigger sick parade than I've seen here for a long time."

Mount Hart is a frontier station; hard to realize that such still exists in Australia. The homestead was really one big shed, bare walls, open doors placed so that at a glance any one moving in the country behind or in front can be seen. The only window has a heavy wooden shutter that at a touch drops into place. The timbers are tough squared logs Everything is rough, strong and serviceable. Shelves around the walls hold the inevitable bottles, tins and boxes. Handy on the walls are guns and rifles; the needed belt with heavy revolver is slung across the table. The solid table is of hewn boards. All chairs are sawn-off blocks from trunks of trees with bullock-hide nailed over the "fashionable" ones. Four shelves of well-thumbed books, without covers, form the library. Up above are beams of hardwood, and across these lie rolls of station necessities: leather, rolls of saddle-making material, new straps, chains and saddlery. The other furniture is made of strong cases on legs. The only ornaments are two pictures of racehorses cut from some paper and a quaint cloth duck with silky yellow head and feet. Under back and front verandas are spare bunks of bullock-hide.

Lovely poinciana-trees shade Chalmers's grave. He had been Felix's partner, and was once known as the uncrowned king of Derby. He met a tragic end, the fate of all who have "gone west" over the range.

At the back of the homestead is the low-built storehouse, cart-shed and eating-shed, opposite the kitchen and meat-house. Near by are strong tables on rough-hewn legs, and beams supporting station gear and saddlery for a hundred horses. Rows of hobble-chains and branding-irons, bells and whips and halters are arranged on stands built in the form of a courtyard. At the back of these and outside the fence is the blacksmith's shop and harness-room of bark, with a wagon under a bough shed. Farther back still is the strong stockyard. And to the left of this are the huts of the native stockboys.

Encircling all is the rim of the everlasting hills.

4

FRONTIER LIFE

THE station was all bustle: stockboys riding away seeking fit horses for the muster, others working at the saddlery, the household lubras lackadaisically busy packing several months' tucker, old Felix overseeing all. From medical inspection, Laurie came striding along, taking in at a glance and with a smile the activities around.

"The patrol can move off in twenty minutes. But our friends will be a day getting ready to move. I'll leave the trackers with them to give a hand and liven up the stockboys. Come for a stroll."

As we moved away, Felix came lumbering across and in a hoarse rumble meant for a whisper inquired anxiously:

"How did the inspection go, Laurie?"

"Very well. They're the healthiest bunch I've seen for some time. But a dozen men and women took to the hills last night and I can't guarantee them."

"So long as my own people are healthy, I'm more pleased than I can say." And Felix turned to his supervising.

We climbed the basalt hill rising right behind the house. "I want to see if there's anything fresh up at the native hide-outs," explained Laurie.

"Are any of the men you are seeking hiding in this locality?"
"No, they are all farther out. There are several men though in this vicinity that I'd like to lay my hands on just the same. Possum and Wallaby in particular. Seeking them is like chasing shadows. They are night travellers, and any native who is game to travel at night is exceptionally hard to catch."

The main hide-out was a mass of black rocks between two hill crests. From here, we looked right down upon the homestead and over all the open country in that huge hollow. We could see right down in between the trees; a kangaroo hopping across a bare patch looked like a rabbit. The white shirt of old Felix, the stockmen (looking like boys) working in the station yard and walking down from the stockyard, the horses, the smoke from the chimney, two stockmen cantering behind a mob of horses a mile away, the huts and gunyahs of the native camp and fight his trouble out. But the young lubras fires - all were plain to see. And yet from the house, even with glasses, it would be impossible to see natives lying upon these black rocks, peering between the cracks and through the peep-holes.

"It is a perfect outpost," I agreed admiringly.

"Yes," said Laurie, "the settlers in these parts can bless their lucky stars that the Aboriginal is not of the aggressive Red Indian type, and that they prefer the spear to the rifle. Otherwise, no white men could live in this country Not until settlement took place in greatly increased numbers."

"The aboriginal is not the type who would repeatedly attack and fight as a tribe," I suggested.

"No. They are bands of hunting nomads who, when they shed a little blood, cease fighting to dance and sing about it. Otherwise, they live their own lives and don't care how the white man lives his. That is how we have been able to settle the country so easily."

The big form of old Felix in his white shirt was standing in the middle of the yard.

"One solitary sniper from here could make that homestead untenable."

"There are very few 'Pigeons' among the natives," answered Laurie grimly, as he gazed around seeking fresh tracks.

Pigeon was an aboriginal outlaw who in the early days had kept the West Kimberley in a state of constant excitement. He shot four white men before he paid the penalty.

Behind us vision was clear; anything that moved in the wild country back there could be seen. No chance of a look out up here being surprised from the rear. The hill sloped back to a steep little waterfall. Among the rocks were the ashes of often-used fires; beef bones were lying about.

"This looks as if they have speared even the homestead cattle at times, cut them up, then cooked and eaten them up here while still watching the homestead."

"They do that while old Felix is away," said Laurie, "if Bunch-'em-up also has to ride away for awhile."

"Is this where the wild chaps come when they stir up trouble in the camp below?"

"Yes, they climb the waterfall behind us in the night, then slip straight down the hill here into the stockboys' camp. They have carried off young lubras from right beside the house—even when Chalmers was alive and he and Felix and Bunch-'em-up were sleeping inside. The stockboys are too frightened to seize the *munjons* lest they stop a spear. There's only one stockman there that the bush natives are scared of, Big

Paddy. The trouble is that Big Paddy himself reverts to a *munjon* when the periodical mood seizes him."

"It's a perfect setting for a wild nor'-west drama."

"Yes, only life down there is fact, not fiction. And no wonderful heroine either: there's not a solitary white women over the range."

From a peak across a valley behind us rose a snaky wisp of pale blue smoke. As it climbed into the still air it swelled stronger into a black column almost stationary.

"Bad signalling country," nodded Laurie. "Too many ranges limit the vision. All the same, in a few hours the abos for a hundred miles around will know that the patrol is still at Mount Hart."

"How on earth will you catch your men when they will be warned of your approach?"

White wits against black. Our going mustering with old Felix will fluster them. They won't know in what direction I am really heading; and they won't know when m going to leave Felix, or whether I am going to leave him at all. They don't know who I'm after; they don't now what I know; above all, they are confident there are a few particular killings about which I know nothing."

"So that those particular killers won't even bother to cover their tracks?"

"That's so."

"The old stone-age man is no fool."

"The stone-age man," said Laurie definitely, "is no fool in anything that touches his own line of life and that interests him. But he is chained to the primitive by a mental chain that he will never break; he seems to have been born a million years ago with a brain that could not expand as the rest of humanity developed."

We returned to the homestead. The trackers were busy, cheerily lending a hand while taking pride of place among the stockboys and slyly joking with the coming and going young house lubras.

Davey, smart in clean shirt, riding-breeches and leggings, was in his element, his quick eyes everywhere, fancying himself too as a lady-killer. Old Larry with his shrewd grizzled face was invaluable among the horses, with quiet efficiency and a joke now and then helping to sort out some tangle that the undisciplined horse-boys had got into. And all the time those two trackers were seeking information, learning things; working with tactful diplomacy, playing off tribal feeling against feeling, fear against fear, jealousy against jealousy, cunning against cunning. Sorting out the grain from the chaff, putting two and two together.

The Australian aboriginal could probably defy the white man's laws, if he were not, to our point of view, disloyal to himself. He is distinctly a group man within a tribe. He will betray his fellow with an easy conscience if his own particular tribal or group law will allow him, and if he believes that swift vengeance will not overtake him.

If the trouble is a near tribal one, he must give his information by stealth, for he too is watched, and his enemies with equal pleasure will betray him to the betrayed man's enemies, Hence, at every camp we came to, whether of station blacks or a wild bush camp, the trackers indulged in their own particular sleuthing, and enjoyed it.

Only under certain circumstances will a group of aboriginals stick together through thick and thin.

Big Paddy (Windigil), sombre of face, six feet of tough manhood, was boss boy here. Taking his time, he scowled as he worked, for he was itching under the urge to throw off his clothes, snatch his spears and take to the bush.

A few years previously Big Paddy's delight was his merry little son Kitchener, favourite of homestead and camp. Kitchener's passion was horses, and he would always ride at the gallop, scorning constant warnings. After repeated pleadings, he was allowed to travel with the musterers. Again and again he was warned against galloping his horse down the stony hills. Each time he laughed merrily and promised never to do it again. One day while riding out on the flank he shouted that he wanted a drink and galloped his horse to a nearby creek. Potts, the then overseer, thought the lad was a long time returning, but he could see the horse standing there quietly in the grass. Becoming uneasy, the overseer reined away from the mob and cantered back to the waiting horse. Kitchener was lying there, blood dripping from his mouth, the horse had propped at a hole and the lad must have shot over its head on to the rocks.

The camp was horrified, Jinny the mother went crazy. Big Paddy nursed his grief in a quiet, mad fury. Then he urged the Old Men to "sing out" those responsible for the death of his son.

Straight to the primitive.

Two wild bush natives, Danmarra and Bullidon were hunting up in a mountain creek. The Old Men declared that these strangers had "willed" the lad to his death.

Big Paddy took the overseer's rifle, stole away, and shot both those innocent men.

Time passed. Native intrigue and jealousy began murmurings that reached even to the distant white-man town of Derby. None dared speak outright.

Constable Hawse came with trackers Larry, Mick and Cherubim, who found the remains of the bodies. They chopped a hand off each as proof of the finding. Big Paddy did a few years in jail. He broke jail twice. The second time the police let him go; he travelled day and night until he reached his own beloved country. Starved by his people, he arrived at the homestead lacerated and wolfish-eyed. He "sat down" for days, regaining his strength, quietly sizing up his little kingdom.

His wife had taken to the bush with a wild bush black; Bungeri, a solidly built, sulky black and a fighter, had usurped his place not only as boss boy at the station, but of the tribe as well.

While Big Paddy was quietly growing fit he mused on the white man's law. He did not want to go back to jail again—not yet. So he went softly to Chalmers and asked permission to give Bungeri a hiding. Chalmers thought a thrashing would do the savage boss boy no harm, so he said:

"All right. Go and get into him but—don't kill him!"

Big Paddy almost killed him. They fought with fighting-sticks, but the duel developed into a melee in which Big Paddy laid out three others who came to the usurper's assistance.

He cowed the camp. Grimly then he threw off his clothes, disdained his wounds, but ochred and oiled his body. Then seized the spears that had been purloined during his absence, and took to the bush. He found his wife, brought her back to camp and thrashed her unmercifully. "Civilizing" her, he called it. Then resumed his place as boss boy of the stockboys and camp.

What Big Paddy did to the man who stole his wife is unknown. He had learned from experience: he left no tracks, no trace; neither did he boast.

And now Big Paddy scowled as he worked.

It was amusing—to any one looking on. Old Felix, pipe seldom out of his mouth, "roaring up" his large, devil-may-care family. He roars at fat Judy who waddles yawning to her duties. He livens the loafing stockboys, then strides away to the stockyard to see how matters are progressing there. His roars come floating down to the house. The lubras laugh, the boys, supposed to be busy rolling swags, grin in chorus.

Then young Weeda is missing, or Dolly or Bolva, or some boy who had been detailed for a particular job.

Weeda is a naughty little lubra; an adept at stealing Felix's sugar and tobacco. She can pick the kitchen and storehouse locks with a piece of wire. Dolly is nearly as cunning. Bolva is Weeda's young sister. She steals the hens' eggs and knows how to sneak into the meat-house even though it is wired all around and the door padlocked. Hardly more than children to our standard, but, long since, women according to their own. Weeda, with steadfast gaze, assures me in halting pidgin that she is a "straight woman!" But then the stranger does not know Weeda. Her shock of wild hair she combs should occasion prompt; her slim body is gracefully rounded; her skin is of smooth, dull copper. All enlivened by two large slumbrous eyes. Her mate Dolly is slimmer. Dolly looks even more childlike and bland but is a tigress when aroused.

Before the stranger, Weeda and Bolva and Dolly behave like three shy little black angels.

Weeda and Bolva, Wild girls of the hills.

5

FELIX'S WILD CHILDREN

POSSUM is one of the wild men of the hills. When they took Big Paddy to jail Possum swooped down, snatched Weeda in the night and dragged her screaming away. Weeda fought like a wild-cat. Savagely he clouted her, then pointed up towards the hide-out. She bit him. He kicked her, then pointed again and they were away, Weeda jumping with his spearpoint jabbing behind her. Thus, very early in her young life, Weeda met her master.

Possum is a little man with the savage pluck of a giant. He will tackle any man, will even walk into a wild bush camp and fight his trouble out. But the young lubras who, m good condition from an easy life and eating white man's food, live in the native camps attached to these few lonely homesteads are his speciality. Possum swoops down and takes one away to the ranges and months of quick moving, hunting and fighting. His conquest is his carrier, his beast of burden. He carries only his fighting gear, she follows carrying everything, stumbling after him over the ranges when he flies by night after some particularly daring escapade. When he .as worn er out he calmly abandons her and swoops down on another — something young and strong that can travel.

When Possum had worn Weeda into a tottering scarecrow he left her to find her own way home. Then he swooped down again on Mount Hart and carried off young Bolva, Weeda's child sister.

Had Big Paddy been in camp Possum would not have replenished his harem so easily. But Paddy was far away in jail. Despite the sarcasm of old Felix and Chalmers, the remaining natives were too frightened of the wild fighter to seize him when he came boldly into their camp. "You pack of white-livered curs! Why don't you hold him and sing out for us," roared Felix when yet another young lubra had been dragged screaming away.

But the sulky stockboys had seen more than one man transfixed by the spears of Possum

Wallaby is a woman-stealer who raids differently He is an excellent stockboy—when he chooses. He spies out a station where there are plenty of young lubras. Then he hides his spears, washes the ochres and ashes from his body, from a "plant" he produces a pair of trousers, and one night quietly appears in the stockboys' camp. In the morning he saunters up to the station and asks the boss for a job. He works well too; the station-owner or manager congratulates himself on having secured a willing boy. Wallaby works — but at the same time makes his choice of a bride.

Then, one morning Wallaby is missing, and one of the young station lubras, and anything handy Wallaby can lay his hands on.

Wallaby, though not so recklessly game as Possum, is brave for all that, and dangerous because of his cunning and knowledge of the white man's ways. If these two woman-stealers were to combine they would make life interesting in the Kimberleys. As it is, many a young lubra goes nightly to sleep with a fluttering heart, wondering if she will awake to feel Possum's claws in her hair.

However, Weeda and Bolva were now back at Mount Hart m smiling mischief again, their scarred bodies well fed and plump—but with a sudden hunted look in their eyes should anything startle them. Big Paddy was back in camp too.

Night came with sudden peace. Old Felix stretched with a tired groan of thankfulness. We were all ready to leave for the mustering in the morning. Through the open doors came a quick drumming of feet, rhythmic clicking of wommeras, wild chant of approaching farewell.

"Been long in this country, Felix?" I asked.

"Aye, lad. I don't know how long. I came with young Tony Cornish and fourteen hundred sheep and a small mob of horses and cattle for the Kimberley Pastoral Company that had taken up land on the Fitzroy. In eighty-one Brockman's party and the Murray Squatting Syndicate party landed at Beagle Bay, a few months before. We came the four-masted brig *Harnar*. A storm knocked s about in King Sound and left us high and dry where Derby now stands. We pushed the horses and cattle overboard and left them to battle for themselves. They trailed straight out into the Pindan, mad for water. Poor old horses! Most of them pulled through, and we got them long afterwards. All but poor old Nobby. He got his hobbles caught in a root and perished within fifty yards of the water. Nobby's Well, where you watered your own horses, is named after him. It was a native soak in our time. We landed the sheep. Then came a desperate struggle to locate water. But we pulled through. The Yeeda station people had come first; then the K.P.C.; then Meeda station was formed. Gradually we crept up the Fitzroy, settling the West Kimberley here and there: Blythe and Rose and others of us gradually pushing out, either on our own or acting for big companies formed down south. Cornish and I took those sheep across the river and formed Lulugui station, opposite Yeeda. The niggers speared our best boy, Willie, a few days later, and came within an ace of getting the lot of us. They soon killed Tony Cornish too—farther along the Fitzroy."

Felix lay staring at the stars till the stamp of feet and savage song and shrill chant of lubras broke his reverie.

A fitting accompaniment to memories of settling the Kimberleys.

"It was a grand job settling the Fitzroy," Felix rumbled. "Some good men went west in the doing. Then it was a man's land. Not that I mean anything against the women; they were wonderful; but there was only one here and there. Farther south they followed their men in greater numbers."

"Do you mean to say there are no women across the range, Felix?"

"No. No woman has ever crossed the range from this side. But there has been one here—the farthest out."

His old face wrinkled into a smile.

"Who was she?" I asked curiously.

"A barmaid from Derby. A game young woman, and used to having her own way. She'd heard talk of 'over the range' and got curious: wanted to be the first woman to cross the range. The more the boys laughed at her, the more she swore she would. I think the boys chiacked her a bit. Anyway, she arrived here one night riding with the mailman, and gave Chalmers and me the shock of our lives. But she couldn't go any farther. We put her up here while the mailman went on to Blythe's place at Mount House, his farthest out. He picked her up on the return trip and she rode back to Derby."

"I should have liked to see you doing the host to a white woman." This with a laugh and a glance at the goatskins on the earthen floor, the log chairs, and the bullock-hide bunks.

"I could do it better now," growled Felix proudly. Didn't have this new house then. We felt a bit awkward but she was no trouble."

"When did the first cattle come over the range?"

"Not until years after the West and East Kimberleys were settled. Time just dreams on in these places, and as the years go by you don't remember dates very well. If my memory is right, the first mob to cross the range was somewhere about 1903. I remember Bob Brown and Tom Cole bringing one of the first mobs to these parts somewhere about 1910. But it was a great job finding the passes into the country before that. We are still finding them."

Old Felix lapsed into memories. And what a host must be his! For a living man to have gone through that full pioneering life and still be actively engaged is a surprise in these days of settled civilization. He carries the scars of three wounds, one spear ripped across his huge chest. In the days of Pidgeon and Captain he experienced lively times too. Pidgeon had shot Constable Richardson, then hurried through the bush to Wingina Gorge where the Lennard cuts through the range. Edgar was out with a mob of cattle, travelling through wild bush to settle a new station. Brother Fred, Burke and Gibbs were travelling with five hundred cattle and a dray. On that morning unpleasantness had occurred between Fred Edgar and Burke and Gibbs, because the two latter refused to carry fire-arms of any sort. Burke and Gibbs, with Edgar's native stockman Nigger, rode on ahead with the cattle, while Edgar and Jumbo with the dray followed more slowly. In the afternoon the cattle reached the water-lined gorge and immediately drank. Pigeon and Captain fired from the rocks and killed the white men. Stockboy Nigger wheeled and galloped to warn Edgar as Pigeon rushed Burke's horse which luckily proved hard to catch. The stockboy reached Edgar and screamed his warning: "Pigeon he gallop behind! He kill you! Then he going kill Lukin!"

In haste Edgar unyoked the bullocks and snatched a Winchester. Giving a gun to Jumbo and a revolver to Nigger, he shouted: "Quick! look after yourselves!" Then mounted and rode for his life to warn Lukin at his station.

Pigeon kept to the hoof-beats of the galloping man for mile after mile, but Edgar had the blood horse and it lasted longest. Lively days. Pigeon afterwards shot Jasper dead, and when Blythe galloped at him with drawn revolver blew Blythe's thumb off. It was the trigger guard that saved Blythe's life. Felix had been in the little scrap in which our tracker Larry was wounded while a lad.

Pigeon had been a police tracker. He understood quick moving and quick thinking; could put initiative into action; understood horses and fire-arms and the white man's ways, and was both a hero and a feared man amongst many hundreds of wild tribesmen. It has been fortunate for the settlement of Australia that very few crack aboriginal riflemen have taken to the bush against the whites. A few such have livened up the Kimberleys at times.

Although the East and West Kimberleys are now settled the country over the range is not. Although the tribesmen are fast entering the "iron age" (and alas fast vanishing under disease) old

Felix always has a revolver handy—must never be without one when he leaves the house; for some of these aboriginals are "sulky feller." The danger is aggravated when the *munjons* come down from the hills, Felix, now, can hardly use the gun, even if there were time, for his eyesight is failing. But the mere fact of the weapon being at his belt has saved him again and again.

Dozing under the back veranda that night I wondered if the station blacks, spurred on by the *munjons*, would ever tackle old Felix again. Their naked black forms noiseless as shadows, would be invisible in the tiny yard invisible too among the black shadows of the buildings. Just then there sounded a low growl, followed by the fluttering pad of a hulking dog as he came across the goat-skins inside, then out on to the back veranda. His eyes were glowing. Soundlessly he prowled on into the yard.

I understood then. These savage dogs were ceaselessly patrolling: round the yard, in through the always open back door and out through the front, all through the night No sooner would one lie down than the green eyes of another glowed as he came prowling through the house to the eerie fluttering of the hard, goatskin mats. Those dogs must have saved Felix's life numbers of times.

I wondered whether, if the station natives came and stood motionless, the dogs would recognize them by smell and do nothing. I hardly thought so as another huge brute like a shadowy lion came from the eating-shed. Now and again one would turn on another with throaty growls. From the camp still came snatches of wild song and the stamp of feet. No, it is doubtful if even Big Paddy and Possum together would be game to tackle Felix at night.

On the front veranda old Felix was groaning and roll¬ing uneasily. Laurie was sleeping like a log. The long- drawn, mournful howl of a dingo came echoing from among the starlit hills. White fangs gleamed instantly and heckles rose in reply. Again the dingo howled; and then came sleep.

Dawn broke softly, cool and beautiful. Sunrise came stealing up over the hills. A bird called; another whistled from up in the shadowy range. A few moments later old Felix groaned, yawned like one of his great dogs, and rolled heavily from his bunk. He dragged on his trousers, then one boot, grunted as he flopped the shod leg down,' drew on the other boot, stood slowly erect, then came heavily stamping over the goatskins out into the yard. At the back gate he roared towards the camp for the house lubras to come and light the fire. He was roaring like a hoarse bull before Weeda deigned to shrill reply. Grumbling and protesting he trod heavily back to the tin dish on the block of wood. The day had begun.

Walking smartly, the trackers were first into the yard. "Get the horses and mules, Davey," ordered Laurie. "And keep an eye on Felix's boys; see they bring up his horses without leaving any behind. Run your eye over the packs, Larry, and make sure that nothing is forgotten."

The line of police saddlery was all ready for mounting in a moment. Not so the station packs. Felix was already discovering broken girths and surcingles not reported the day before. He roared. The lubras were making a great display of getting breakfast ready; the stockboys were bending over pack-bags, strings of hobble-chains, tucker for two months for a dozen hands, tarpaulins, gear of all descriptions. Felix roared here, roared there. All was being sorted out as a thunder of hoofs announced the coming of the horses. Big Paddy, bridle over his arm, went scowling towards the stockyard with his stockboys.

The lubras brought breakfast across to the eating-shed. Felix wiped his forehead to pause and roar at young Weeda who had forgotten the mosquito-net and was "poking about like a mule!" Then at Boghole Willie, most willing but the most stupid. His face wore a perpetual grin, half his lip with the right side of the moustache pointing slantwise to the sky. A terrible wound that had been. Fortunately, a police patrol under Pollett happened along. Willie implored Pollett to shoot him when he was stitching up the wound.

"Rats!" said Pollett as he pushed the needle through. "You'll live to get into lots more mischief yet, Willie. A live black man is better than a dead one."

Breakfast over, all hands trooped to the stockyard. Three lubras in trousers and smiles, with bridles over their arms, followed the laughing stockboys. Horses and mules scurried around the yard as each man waited his chance to dash in and corner his animal. Old Felix sat his big bay like a field marshal, his whip every now and then curling around a fractious mule.

Cornered in the big yard, all the animals were soon sorted out, saddled and packed. As each animal was set free it plunged away to join its own particular mates, jostling and lashing out at any stranger in its path. Just before we mounted, Felix issued his final instructions and handed over the keys of the kitchen to the natives left in charge. The house, store, and outbuildings were pad-

padlocked. Then he signed for the cavalcade to move off.

As we moved away, Laurie reined behind. Quietly he gave the station natives orders to guard Felix's homestead during his absence, warned them against listening to the *munjons* should they come down and suggest a raid on the station.

The trackers and Big Paddy were in the lead, followed by the pack-animals with stockboys evenly placed for the first few miles, alert to wheel the fractious ones anxious to break the line.

Old Carrie's two mulish specialities were to flop into every waterhole we came to then wait for us to whip her out, and to surprise any horseman who swerved aside to drive her back to the mob. She would amble along until that particular horseman was directly behind her then simply lift her rump and lash out.

Weeda, with a shock of hair sticking out from below an old felt hat, and thin legs in dirty pants thrust straight out, adorned the back of a little mule that once belonged to young Don Regan who was killed by the blacks or drowned while crossing the Lennard—no one knows which. Boghole Willie looked funnily good humoured, for all his twisted lip. Brandy, son of Whisky, rode with tiny hunched shoulders on a little donkey. Brandy, with old felt hat and stockwhip, is aged ten.

A glorious day. Vision so clear that shadows of the trees away up on the hills were perfectly distinct. As we rode through kurrajong and coolabah, box and gum, musical with birds, and over miles of waving grassland, it was good to be alive.

Old Larry and Davey in undress uniform.

6
THE CHASE BEGINS

THE first wall of the Leopolds early barred the way. The trackers vanished apparently into the cliffs before the mouth of Gardiner's Gap opened for us in the rear. We clambered on in single file straight through the heart of the range, bluffs of pink rock rising on either side, succeeded by steep grassy hills scantily timbered. The silence of the hills was broken by the laugh of a rider well ahead, the slithering of hoofs over rock, the occasional call of a bird, the tinkle of a rivulet that soon grew into tree-lined rock-pools. For some time the cavalcade splashed its winding way down the pass, then unexpectedly rode out from between towering walls into a grassy valley that stretched away to where the Precipice Range runs parallel with the Leopolds. To the north towered Mount Chalmers.

"That Bluff looks like a mighty castle split in halves," I remarked to old Felix.

"Yes. Bunch-'em-up and I were camped near here one night when a meteor fell with a blinding flash, and a crash that made horses and men spring to their feet. For minutes afterwards you could hear rocks falling away like heavy trucks rumbling over loose stones. They heard it away at Fairfield station and over at Mount House forty miles away. Something like that might have struck the Bluff ages ago."

Bunch-'em-up Gardiner had found Gardiner's Gap, or rather the natives showed it to him. Men had ridden right past it seeking for such a path.

It was the gradual finding of these passes that, in the main, has made the Leopold lands accessible. The ranges run approximately from east to west, ending in a hopeless tangle at the rugged coast. To the man riding north they, as a rule, appear in turn before him like parallel walls, their summits usually rimmed by sheer cliff faces. The majority are flat topped.

Straight "through," a range may only have a width of three, five or ten miles, then will appear a grassy valley, often stony, from three to ten miles wide and twenty or more long. And across this valley looms another range, another wall-like barrier. By narrow passes through these ranges the traveller passes into valley after valley. Some ranges, however, are a series of steep, rounded hills.

These are crossed by riding up a negotiable spur, then over a divide and down into the lower country. The ranges seldom rise more than two thousand five hundred feet, with isolated peaks up to three thousand feet. But the entire country has a grandeur peculiarly its own.

"How far from here to Derby, Felix?"

"Two hundred miles, and the road rough as the hobs of hell. By the time I get my footsore beasts to Derby the cream of the fat is off them. Then they must travel over a thousand sea-miles to market. When they get there they will have cost me a fiver a beast in transport and fees. It takes me three to four years to grow a fat beast, and by the time I get him to Perth I'm lucky to receive a tenner for him. Some shiploads have hardly paid their fare down. That's our trouble: cost of trans-port kills this country."

"Do our friends the abos give you much real trouble?"

"Oh, they've speared a good many of my cattle, especially down in the Isdell gorges. But it's not so much the beasts they spear that we worry about, it is the constant fear they put into the herds. These split up into small, half-wild mobs, ready to gallop at the smell of a black-fellow. To grow fat, cattle must be restful and contented."

"How about pests ?"

"Ticks are the worst over the range; they cling to the cattle, sometimes, like bunches of grapes. Cows with calves suffer most. In the dry time the cow is suckling a calf while the ticks are sucking her blood. Then we have trouble sometimes with the stock-horses; they're liable to die of 'walk-about' disease—eat some weed, and walk and walk until they die. It will all come right in the end I suppose, after I'm pushing up the daisies."

We travelled a few days with Felix. When a small mob of cattle was seen, stockboys would drop out from the flank and turn them down the valley facing the way we had come. The boys, singing and laughing, would later catch us up. When Felix came to his boundary he would turn around and muster straight back down the valley, picking up all the little mobs that had been turned into it. So with succeeding valleys, until he had mustered a mob large enough from which to select the number of fats he wants. We rode parallel with the Precipice Range, its red cliff-edge, like a newly built castle wall, six hundred feet high, stretching for thirty miles. The three big humps of Mount Edgar loomed in the distance. We off saddled at Saddlers Springs, a sweet waterhole fed from a spring on the Isdell Range.

The impression of a "new" country was strengthened by these landmarks, mostly named after men still alive, or not long dead. At

Saddlers Springs the mules raised the welkin braying for their horse cobbers that had been unsaddled before them. Here Bill Connell awaited us. A very heavily built man in the pink of health, brown moustached, "just dying for a yarn," he seldom sees a white man. His place is two days' ride away back in the hills. There he lives with two very old natives and two big dogs for company. Having no means of transport he lives largely on native game and foods. Nigger smoke-talks had told him of the patrol and of Felix's mustering plant. Once he had absorbed the "outside" news the night's conversation developed in earnest. Reminiscences of buckjumping horses and cunning mules, of riders white and black who could "stick like a flea in glue"; quaint stories of birds and furry little animals that at some time or other had attached themselves to his camp for tucker and company; and a weird story of a "crying voice" that wailed at night from a lagoon.

Stories of good and "bad" niggers brought up the redoubtable Possum who a week ago had raided a distant homestead and carried off a favourite young lubra. "Skin and hair will be flying soon," added Bill, "according to the smoke-talk. A couple of the Old Men wanted that young lubra and they've spurred on the bucks to chase Possum and cut his liver out. Possum will eat their livers'; I'm thinking. Did you hear about Murphy?" he asked Laurie.

"No."

"He's been found dead in the West Kimberley. That'll be a job for the Fitzroy Police Patrol, I suppose."

"Yes, it is out of my district. No news had come through when I left Derby."

"You can't beat nigger smoke-talks. Only wireless could beat 'em; but then we've got no wireless out here. I often hear news away out in the hills that Derby doesn't hear for a month. The trouble is, they only pass on news that interests them."

Laurie smiled: "I suppose you knew all about me?"

"Of course. You've got 'em a bit puzzled though travelling with the stranger. They don't know what to make of Mr Idriess here; now, they reckon you must have come out to give Felix a hand with the mustering."

"So I have," said Laurie.

Bill Connell was still talking after I'd stretched out on my blankets and was dreamily staring through a green lattice at a blue sky speckled with golden dust. The branches of two trees intermingled directly overhead formed the lattice. . One could almost swear those trees were sleeping, so drooping, so motionless were the leaves. The voices of the natives around their fire passed from laughter and chatter to lazy groans and yawns. They just sprawled back and curled up as sleep took them. Then silence.

A day later we rode over a low divide and down on to a blacksoil plain well grassed with bundle-bundle, Mitchell, Flinders and ribbon grasses, with occasional patches of spindle grass amongst which stood up the sweetly edible grey mimosa bush.

Felix had bought 130,000 acres of this country from Kidman the Cattle King when he was abandoning Glenroy station. The transport problem, aggravated by cattle-spearing, had here defeated the greatest cattleman the world has known.

Land is cheap out there. Without market and transport land is of little use. Then, the great amount of rough hilly country lessens its value still further. Away to the south-west Felix sold one block of 100,000 acres and another of 80,000 acres for £100 each, thirty-four years' leasehold.

One half the stockboys with packhorses rode away towards the distant limits of this plain. At twenty miles they would separate and, turning, drive all the cattle they could find towards the centre of the plain where Felix, mustering from the other end, would pick them up on his return muster. Mustering in that unfenced country is a bushman's job. In late afternoon we rode towards a thick line of bright green trees.

Nodding towards them Laurie said:

"The Isdell River, Jack. Felix's boundary. We leave him to-morrow. We've helped him to a good start. From the Isdell he will turn and muster his country in a face right back towards the homestead, and from there take his selected mob to Derby. The country of the first man I want is a short day's ride from here. He took to the hills for a certainty when he learned that the patrol was coming. But I'm counting on him believing we are only out to help Felix muster. If so, he will return to his camp and I'll surprise him."

"What has he done?"

"Oh, killed a few natives. That wouldn't count so much if it was all 'tribal'; but he's 'gone cheeky' and slaughters more."

"He sounds a bit of a Tarzan."

"A wild man right enough is Toolwanor, but from his size you'd never imagine he was a killer."

"You know him then?"

"Yes. I arrested him three years ago when he was running wild with Davey. They both did a stretch in jail. I secured Davey for a tracker when he was released; the bigger the outlaw the better the tracker you know. The *munjon* is much the best bushman. He knows all the native tricks, and if of the intelligent type can soon be trained. Toolwanor took straight to the bush again when he was released from jail. I suppose he'll be the harder to catch after that little experience of the white man's ways. He is a bit of a boaster, and a great hero now among his tribe for having been in the white man's jail."

Laurie's anticipation of Toolwanor's tactics was vindicated that evening. For when Laurie was issuing the trackers' meal old Larry quietly told him that the stock- boys had ridden on a hunting party that day. One of them mentioned that Toolwanor, confident the patrol would continue with Felix, had returned to camp at Grace's Knob.

Next morning, after all hands were saddled up, Laurie called the stockboys quietly aside and emphasized their duty to Felix while they remained in the old man's employ. His remarks were particularly addressed to Big Paddy.

Saying *au revoir* to Felix, the patrol rode away. We felt sorry for the old pioneer, after a life-time of hard battling. Alone in the wilds, his eyesight failing, he was forced to depend on his outfit of carefree aboriginals to muster this huge run. He must manage his station, manage his stockboys, and find transport and food and keep for them and their tribe as well. While he is planning and worrying of evenings, they are playing and laughing; lucky beings with not a thought for the morrow, unless the individual happened to be under some tribal taboo. Swayed constantly by such a leader as Big Paddy, or one less dependable. As Felix musters, he must ride behind with the plant well out of sight of the musterers. Whether they do their work, or ride their horses lame after kangaroos and let the cattle go hang, depends entirely upon their mood of the moment—and on Big Paddy. If Felix does not get his yearly mob of fats to ship south.

Riding parallel with the Isdell, its thick wall of trees screened the patrol from sharp eyes on distant low hills. Laurie sent the trackers out on the plain to ride separately and cut the tracks of any hunting party. If successful, we would then hunt the hunters.

The pack-animals followed Laurie in single file, each behind its particular mate, all contented now and broken into the trail. I rode behind on the old grey, keenly interested in that most interesting of all hunts, a man-hunt. It hardly seemed possible that wild men in their own country, with all its natural resources allied against the opponent, could be captured by one solitary white man and two trackers. My job was simply to mind my own business.

36

It being warm, I was wearing a short-brimmed city hat with a handkerchief fastened to the rim at the back to protect my neck. This innocent handkerchief subsequently created the greatest curiosity among the natives of the Nor'-west Kimberley.

The day wore on but no tracks were found. A chain of lagoons beautiful with pink and blue water-lilies and noisy with wild duck broke the monotony of the river's long, dark pools lined with tall cadjuput, Leichhardt pine, and screw palm. All the rivers we were to see were lined with almost a forest of trees, much thicker and larger than in the open and the mountain country. In the after-noon the river took a huge boomerang sweep to the left, then directly right again towards two round knobs standing out boldly across the plain. That was Grace's Knob. Just below them was the pioneer hut of Maxted and Smith, two young men starting a station on the pick of the country the Cattle King had abandoned. By the river there was the native camp and in it should be Toolwanor.

Laurie halted. Soon afterwards the trackers appeared. They had seen no sign of a track, no smoke, heard no distant call of hunters. Evidently the hunting parties had worked across some other part of the plain or, on this day, had sought the tribal food amongst the sandstones. Laurie ordered Larry and Davey to make quickly a great circuit to the left, and in the shelter of the river trees. When a few miles below the native camp, they were to cross and ride up-river among the low hills the patrol could just see. When in behind the camp they were to judge their time and ride towards the camp and hide. At sundown, Laurie would gallop straight at the camp. Toolwanor, and others wanted, would see him but would take their time and slip across the river and into the hills behind. But the two trackers were to rush the camp from behind. If Toolwanor was already running, he would run into them.

With an appreciative grin Larry and Davey trotted away. We waited until late afternoon when all native hunters would be trudging back to camp. Then we rode out across the plain; we would ride into camp right on the heels of the hunters.

A look out was unlikely now. The aboriginal is alert when he knows there is definite danger, but soon loses caution, becomes, indeed, surprisingly careless when he believes that danger is not definitely near.

As our file of packhorses streamed out across the plain not one warning smoke arose from the Packhorse Range.

7

TOOLWANOR SLIPS AWAY

THE raid was perfectly timed. A thin belt of trees between the oncoming patrol and the river screened us in the waning afternoon light. Just at sunset we rode past them. Across a small plain ahead thin wisps of camp smoke were rising by the river trees. Laurie leaned forward and was away at full gallop. Old Kate pricked her ears: she was attached to Laurie's horse. She snorted, hunched her back, then set off at a lumbering gallop after her favourite. Pancake twitched his ears and hurried on; several animals followed Kate at the trot. I had visions of the packs and swags and equipment being scattered all over the plain. In a few minutes Laurie was right on the camp, and the trackers' horses came plunging through from the opposite bank. Men, women and children stood or squatted in comical attitudes of surprise. Then the dogs started howling. But Toolwanor was gone. Convinced that the patrol was mustering he had returned, but had left at midday for the flying-fox camp.

While the women, children, old people and dogs all crouched staring from the gunyahs or campfires, the tribesmen lined up when the packhorses came along: shaggy bushmen, heavily scarred, deeply wrinkled of face, their eyes wary as the pack-animals come snorting beside them. Several gingerly offered to lend a hand at unpacking, grunting their offer with waving of arms. But the mules snorted at the grinning faces and lashed out at the unpractised hands. I was the centre of the closest scrutiny, never dreaming that the handkerchief at the back of the hat was mainly responsible. The trackers were to be bombarded with questions as to what a man who wore a hat like that could possibly be.

Laurie, through Davey as interpreter, was questioning a bearded group. They had admitted to Toolwanor in the first shocks of surprise, but now grinned blandly or looked stony of face and simply knew nothing, understood nothing, cared nothing. Laurie shrugged philosophically and turned to greet old Peter Bextrum who came strolling across from a neat hut near a huge baobab-tree; a slightly built man with pale blue eyes, likeable face, and that bristly hair that weathers many summers before turning grey. He invited us to the homestead; both Maxtcd and Smith were away mustering. We strolled towards a new bark hut on the river-bank.

While the billies were boiling and during the meal old Peter talked in a soft drawl while his eyes were scrutinizing a man.

He had been one of the early men over the range Grace's Knob was taken up by J. A. Game. Sid Kidman eventually bought it but was forced to abandon it. And now Maxted and Smith were "giving it a go." The first cattle had come here in 1903, Peter in 1905. The country, still a bit wild, was utterly primitive then. He knew many of the local aboriginals from childhood He loved the country. With nothing but his own labour and a great heart he had made sufficient to retire simply, though isolated from even the rudiments of civilization. Peter's life-story is a lesson in the ways of a quiet man in a wild country.

Provisions to Grace's Knob, since a track had been found, came by Blythe's wagon to Mount Hart or Mount House (named after the naturalist Dr House) thence by packhorse. No wheeled vehicle had yet rolled along here. Sometimes Blythe's wagon could not get through to Mount House; then all the stores had to come by pack-horse two hundred miles from Derby. Not long ago the mail used to arrive once in four or five months. Now a packhorse mailman goes as far as Mount House once a month and a station-boy brings the mail on to Grace's Knob.

"Time is flying," mused old Peter. "It looks as if the country is really going to be opened up."

The aboriginals have many staunch friends among the whites throughout all the Kimberleys. But Peter is a counsellor of the blacks and can merge with their mentality to the point where the most understanding of white men are checked by that baffling bar which separates their reasoning from ours. He doctors the blacks, too, particularly as regards the dread disease that is so fast wiping out the aboriginal. His knowledge, unfortunately, only holds the disease in check; still, he must have given untold relief to many an aboriginal. In worried tone he asked Laurie particulars of the "big sick"—the sudden virulent outbreak of leprosy. Peter had noticed no symptoms at Grace's Knob, and was very proud of the health of "his blacks."

Night fell suddenly. As the hurricane lamp was lit a quick wild chanting broke out down on the river-bank.

Laurie was packing a little food in an easily carried bag. Old Larry appeared noiselessly at the hut door, his grizzled face expressive, then turned away without a word. Laurie picked up his bag, took his hat with a smile that said: "I'll be seeing you later," and strode out.

Peter continued smoking, gazing at the velvet night framed in the open door. "He's gone after Toolwanor," he said quietly.

"To-night?"

"Yes. He knows that immediately after dark a runner will leave to warn him. And once Toolwanor knows the patrol is really after him, he'll take some catching."

"Will Laurie take horses?"

"No. The country is too rough. Where the flying foxes are is a labyrinth of gorges."

"Won't the runner get there before him?"

"No. Davey the tracker's country is away in there, and he knows where the flying foxes camp. He has hunted in that very gorge with the man he is now hunting. No, they'll arrive first, and creep up close to Toolwanor's camp, then wait and seize the runner when he comes, before he can signal with the hoot of an owl. At dawn they'll rush Toolwanor. Laurie will have the walk of his life in that labyrinth."

Peter talked on and on about the blacks. It is a fact that upon many bushmen who live farthest out the aboriginal gains a strong hold. It may be that, living among primitive surroundings, the dormant primitive deep within the white man is drawn towards the absolute primitive in the aboriginal.

Lying there listening I thought of the striking similarity of stone-age belief and ritual in tribes thousands of miles apart. What Peter was saying of their more guarded rites here describes those practised on Cape York Peninsula three thousand miles east, before the two great influenza plagues practically wiped out the north-eastern tribes. From the Peninsula, straight west across Queensland to the Territory and into the farthest Kimberleys the life, customs, and beliefs of these scattered but self- contained tribes were identical, and had been so for thousands of years. Yet each tribe regarded the other as a foreigner; few even spoke the same language, though they are physically and mentally the same.

It is an entrancing puzzle: From whence did the stone- age man originally come? Who taught him to think? How far under more favourable conditions of life would his undoubted brains have developed and raised him in human life? And from what men, and in what time and under what circumstances, did he inherit and develop his "sacred" beliefs and signs and customs. The origin of these is unknown even to the Old Men who have been the tribal guardians since antiquity; or else, the knowledge has been handed down in the "secret language," while an evasive reply or a very different explanation is given to any inquisitive white inquirer. There is sometimes a suggestion of ancient Egypt.

Some custom, some belief, some sign, some totemic carving, will flash a man's memory back to something seen in the tombs or museums of Egypt. Although no reasoning can very well connect our aboriginals with the intelligent giants who built the Pyramids four thousand and more years ago.

Dawn brought ear-splitting screeches from thousands of cockatoos coming to water at the river, their wings sounding like wind beating low down over the roof of the hut. In the trees by the lovely river-pools the noisy white birds would feed and play and quarrel all day. Old Peter was quietly smoking by the hut door waiting for me to wake up. A fat, favourite piccaninny was playing outside with the dogs, giving Peter cheek in laughing voice. Quick-eyed lubras were laughing and gossiping by the galley. A high-pitched yell followed by a long-drawn tirade of native language came piercingly from the bush blacks' camp down on the river. Old Culwaddy the "king," squatting by the galley fire, looked up questioningly —old Culwaddy who has realized that his tribe has run its time, who sees the evening of extinction coming, who advises his warriors not to fight.

After breakfast, we strolled up the Isdell to where it has cut through little rocky hills. Avenues of the tallest paper-bark and lanes of pandanus palm threw a golden colour upon the water where it runs over brown sand. Grey- limbed fig-trees showed heavy clusters of fruit among their dark green leaves. Where Woollybutt Creek junctions is a quiet, deep, dark green pool densely lined with foliage, in which many fish warily avoid the long black snouts of the small river crocodiles motionless upon the water. There nature has provided for her wild children no matter what the season might betide. For there grew the poison-bark tree. In the dry season, when the river vanishes into a series of permanent pools, the natives crush this bark and throw it into the pool. Juices from the bark mix with the water and suffocate the fish which come floating to the surface. The aboriginal, a botanist of a naturally perfect order, utilizes numerous plants, bulbs, creepers, bark, leaves, berries, juices, for the same purpose.

Everywhere was prolific vegetable life: yams were in season; lily-bulbs were just becoming edible in the lagoons; all along the sandstones were plum-trees, the green and black fruit of which ripened in that order; the rosella bush was coming in; the cricket-ball nuts on the baobabs were ripening. Along the apparently barren sandstone ranges particularly, berry, fruit, bulb, herb, root and vine were plentiful. On the plains, too, and in the closed-in valleys, vegetable life by lagoon and billabong and creek was prolific. The aboriginal secures far more food out of the ground than he does of moving life upon it. Strange that he has never dreamed of planting and improving vegetable foods to tide him over drought times. He has made Mother Earth feed him throughout the ages without an effort to nurture her in turn and thus help her to feed him more bountifully. No wonder he has never progressed in culture.

Wallabies and 'roos come down from the sandstone at night to feed on the plains where wild turkeys and ducks, water-hens and geese were breeding in the lagoons. Though animal and bird life was plentiful only in favoured localities, rich plant life that supplied the aboriginal with food was everywhere. After the long, soaking wet the country was bursting with life.

From the soaked ranges water would keep trickling down the ravines into the creeks to keep the rivers supplied for months to come; while the waterholes, the billabongs and lagoons would draw water from the soaked plains. No wonder that the aboriginals in such country are physically and mentally stronger and happier than their brothers in the more arid interior of the continent.

Old Peter was intrigued by a missionary, a decent chap named Street, who had recently come into the ranges. Apparently from no organized missionary body, he was a freelance in battling circumstances. He must have been a sincere man, for he had a hard job ahead of him. Peter said the natives so far had turned him down because he would not give them tobacco. It was against his principles to buy them with tobacco.

TOOLWANOR, ALIAS NIPPER

8
TOOLWANOR IS CAUGHT

THE aboriginals' chief craving is for tobacco. I doubt whether they would even work on the stations, though riding to muster is a work that many love, without that lure. Tobacco first; then iron. For both, they will walk surprising distances; even some among the *munjons* will work for a time. Over the range the "iron age" is fast coming—indeed has come. Stone axes have been thrown away for a horseshoe which, cut in halves and sharpened within a hafted handle, has made an immeasurably superior tool. Any old lump of iron will be fashioned into axe-head or spearhead, in preference to stone. Glass too is eagerly sought and transformed into spearheads with surprising efficiency and artistry. I watched them at it, for the trackers had managed to secrete a few empty beer bottles and scraps of iron in the pack-bags. And so throughout the patrol they managed a little quiet trading.

Three men squatted on the ground beside a fire, in which was heating a long wire. When red hot this was twisted round a bottle end until it dropped off; then round the shoulder until the neck dropped off; then in four places lengthwise along the tube until the bottle fell apart in four equal lengths. These were to be fashioned into four exceptionally long spearheads. Each worker squatted on one heel, with the other leg loosely stretched out. On the ground between his legs was a flat stone on which was a piece of paper-bark. This soft cushion was to take the vibration, otherwise the glass would crack when pressure was applied to chip it. By the worker's hand were his tools, three eight-inch-long pieces of fencing-wire with diamond- and chisel-shaped edges, sharpened so by vigorous rubbing on the stone. Each man worked seriously, pleased to have an audience. Piccaninnies squatted around absorbing the lesson. The fashioning of spearheads represented a most serious aspect of life to the boys.

A worker picked up one of the pieces of glass, squinted at it, turned it over in his hand. The glass was thick, and definitely concave. He must work out that depression, shorten and thin the glass before he commenced the actual spearhead. With his left fingers he held the glass flat on the bark upon the stone. His right hand held the wire tool (as we might hold a stick tight in the hand) with its edge projecting from the finger side of the palm and pointing towards the worker's body. Pressing the tool edge firmly against one-half the width of the edge of the glass, he levered downward with a quick, short thrust, and a long, deep flake of glass flew out. This action he repeated all round the glass edge, each downward thrust of the tool from the thumb and palm and arm giving a great leverage. The jar was absorbed by the bark cushion. The glass had now a rough, serrated edge all round it. This was rubbed on the stone and it split and powdered away. He then reversed the glass and repeated the operation, but with shorter, sharper, and less powerful leverages; thus smaller flakes of glass flew out. The larger chips were taken from the convex side of the glass, in order to eventually gain the desired flatness. Working with surprising quickness, he repeated the operation again and again, the glass rapidly assuming the rough shape of a spearhead. The right length had now been attained, the glass materially thinned and made perfectly flat.

During the process the craftsman constantly sharpened his wire tool by vigorous rubbing on the stone. He now carefully studied the glass and the position and thrust of the tool before taking each chip; it had to be a sure, long thrust to take out a long flake, and a well-placed, quick one to take out a small flake; and now the chips were not only considerably lessening the thickness of the glass and fast bringing it into the desired shape, but each stroke was working it into what would be the point and cutting-edges of the spearhead. The tip of the spearhead was now being roughly formed; the cutting strokes were more deliberate and alternate, the glass being turned after each stroke and an opposite chip taken. This left a saw edge of teeth completely around the shaping spearhead. These teeth were rubbed on the stone—but gently, lest the glass teeth instead of powdering should snap away and crack the glass.

Thus the coming edges and tip were formed and worn down to fineness. Now, a new and finely-pointed tool was taken up. On the now thin glass this tool was used gently and the final shape of the spearhead immediately began to form under the black fingers. Each gentle scratch, each careful sawing left a tiny needle-point along the razor edges of the glass. All terminated in the delicate point of the finished spearhead, the serrations producing a truly terrible cutting instrument. As the craftsman held it out for inspection, pride was in the movement. It was a beautifully made thing, worked as beautifully as a machine could do it. Quick work too. In an hour these three men turned out twenty spearheads.

Each spearhead lasts only for one throw: if it hits the game it splinters, If it misses and hits the earth it splinters and breaks. But glass is much easier to work than stone, and the aboriginal does not consider work or time if the subject he is engaged upon interests him. Their similarly shaped stone spearheads break easily enough and, though the delicately made, serrated cutting edges are very sharp they do not cut as glass does; hence a larger proportion of game escapes.

The last of the stone-age men will walk any distance, go through any privation, to secure an old lump of iron: once they possess an iron spearhead they have a weapon of great killing power and one that can be used for years.

Back at the camp, the bushmen were squatting among the trees. According to native etiquette they allowed us to get settled, then old Mungilla alias Rattler came striding across, the rugged creases of his face supposed to be set in an amiable grin. Six feet two of skin and bone and sinew, he stood on one leg with his other foot crossed behind the knee of his standing leg, his hands behind his back, one hand clasping the wrist of the other. A favourite attitude of the aboriginal.

In slow gutturals of very indifferent pidgin he grunted for "tabac." His tribesmen, squatting some distance away apparently doing nothing in particular, were really awaiting the result before following his example.

Rattler and his mate Yangulla had long been killers.

Among the people here were a few feared ones who occasionally burst out into killing, almost without check, apparently for the sheer love of killing. Rattler not long before had added two victims to his tally. Brelnor and Ungun had gone hunting to Plain Creek twenty-five miles away. Rattler allowed them time to become intent on the hunt, then he set out on their tracks—hunting the hunters. He speared them both for the sheer lust of killing and left them lying there. Later, an ethnologist was a guest at Kidman's station, and Rattler sold him the skeletons for a stick of tobacco each. Delighted with such an easy market Rattler asked if he could deliver more of the goods.

"Yes," replied the ethnologist, "especially if they are new specimens and not old ones from caves."

Rattler, with a knowing leer, promised they would be "new" ones.

"There must be a number of people dying," remarked the ethnologist, "if he can get clean skeletons like that."

"No more man die!" explained the interpreter.

"Rattler kill him new fellow man sell belonga you!"

Plain Creek is their appointed killing-ground. Here they have retired from time immemorial to fight their duels, to complete "vengeance killings" whether outright by the "law" that makes the business known to all, or by the treachery that invites the unsuspecting victim to a pleasant hunting trip and then slays him with the ferocity of a mad beast.

This tribe is especially cruel in that they are noted women-killers. Old Charlie had killed three of his; the last a very young lubra the preceding summer. It was an exceptionally hot day. Old Charlie was sitting under the shade of a cadjuput-tree while his girl-wife ran back¬wards and forwards from the river, and with a small jam- tin poured water over him. But she was too slow to keep him cooled down: in a rage he leapt up and cracked her skull.

Though the aboriginal is capable of faithfulness and affection he is prone to sudden and violent outbursts, far more so than the white race.

A black shadow hangs over this little crowd so far out in the wilds. Their women are no longer bearing children: an occasional piccaninny only emphasizes the fact. This writing on the wall spreads through nearly all the aboriginal tribes; only a few primitives in the wildest area are not so affected today. When this thing comes to them they know it means the beginning of the end.

Shortly after midday Laurie and the trackers came into camp with —Toolwanor. They had clambered down rocky ravines, pushed through thorny scrub, along a rock-filled creek into a gorge, over a rough hill-side and down into a further gorge. Quick travelling so as to beat the runner; no word above a whisper even though a man fall or scrape his shin on rock or log; no smoking. In the small hours came the fetid smell of a flying-fox colony. Davey hissed a warning—dull coals glowed in a sandy creek under a clump of giant paper-barks. They crept back and waited for the runner. He came like a shadow. They sprang and silenced him; Laurie stared into his eyes and hissed a warning. They crept back towards the glow. A shadow blotted out the coals as it glided among the white tree-trunks to stand and listen, then returned to the fire and sleep again. They rushed the camp at dawn.

Bushmen lay sleeping there, but Toolwanor had vanished. They were quickly on his tracks. Davey set off at a swift, circling run, guessing Toolwanor's destination to be a hide-out down in a gorge. He and Toolwanor had used that hide-out before. Davey outdistanced his man and waited among the boulders. Almost immediately he heard the excited voice of Toolwanor coming close, calling something to his woman. As Toolwanor appeared Davey leapt and had him down with one handcuff snapped on his wrist, but the little savage fought like a wildcat, his lubra staring amazed. -Davey forced the man's head under a rock and slipped on the other cuff in time to jump, erect and face the threatening lubra.

Once her man was cuffed, she stood there glaring, gripping his spears, uncertain whether to run or stand. Toolwanor pleaded with his one-time companion in misdeeds to let him go. Davey sat back panting, shaking his head: he was a police tracker now. When Laurie came along, the gin Chalba followed the patrol back to camp.

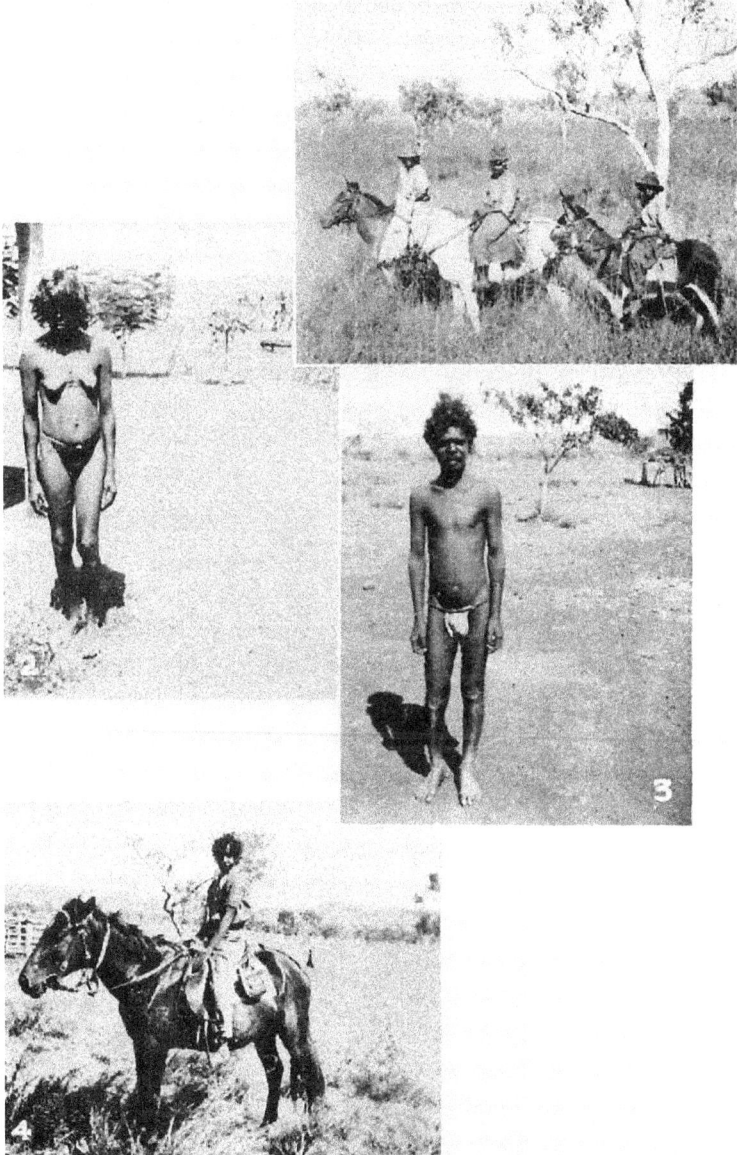

1. KIMBERLEY STOCKMEN
2. JUST DOWN FROM THE HILLS
3. BUT HE CAME TOO
4. SHE'LL RIDE ANYTHING

9

SEEKING UNGANDONGERY ALIAS CHARCOAL

TOOLWANOR explained that his tribal name was Coodo-gedogo, then impressively assured us that his "white- feller name" was Nipper. Alert of eye, with big black moustache and tangled hair, he was a well-built sinewy little chap holding himself perkily upright, a serious, determined expression on his rough-hewn face. A double hero now that he was again in the hands of the "white Pleece, the tribesmen crowded admiringly around him, old Rattler chuckling appreciatively. With aplomb Nipper took a scarlet handkerchief from the neck of a stockman and clothed himself with it as a sign that he was once again civilized. Similarly, his tall lubra calmly took a dress from a station lubra and covered her athletic body.

Nipper was accused of having killed a certain man, to wit, Burrin. Nipper admitted it with a throw-out of his chest, then pointed to Chalba and declared that Burrin had tried to steal his wife. With no malice, he accused a certain Ungandongery, white-feller name Charcoal of having helped him in the killing. This complicated matters; it meant that now the patrol must chase this Charcoal if a case could be proved against him. Nipper was asked where Charcoal was. "Hunting," he replied and vaguely jerked his chin out towards the wilderness.

He was asked then where Burrin's body lay. He grimaced more definitely, though somewhat in the same direction. He was ordered to guide us to the body in the morning. He agreed wholeheartedly; but more than one morning was to pass by before we stood at Burrin's grave. Meanwhile, the patrol would be on the look-out for Charcoal.

This Ungandongery alias Charcoal sounded interesting.

"You and Charcoal will have something in common," drawled old Peter to me—"not physically perhaps; Charcoal is a six-footer, a man killer, a 'proper' wild man. But he is a 'playwright,' 'actor,' and 'author' famous throughout stone-age land," added Peter with a twinkle in his eye. "His latest play with its new songs caught on and has been all the rage for the last two years."

Laurie smiled:

"You'll be meeting a fellow author—if we can catch him."

Old Peter smoked quietly, watching both of us. Then drawled:

"You will be meeting a mining man too. . . . You've done a lot of prospecting in your time?"

"A fair bit."

"Well, Charcoal is a prospector too. He mines his corroboree and war paints from the native ochre mines away in the Synnott Range. For an aboriginal he is quite a miner, all done until recent years by stone-age tools."

"That makes Charcoal doubly interesting."

"Yes. They were interesting days when I first met him at Synnott Creek. I was prospecting. Thought I was the only white man within hundreds of miles. And there was Charcoal, prospecting too with a stone pick, looking for ochres to paint his body. He was only a piccanin then. And along came Brockman on his exploring expedition to north of the Glenelg; Charlie Crossland the surveyor was with him. I've been one of many appreciative audiences applauding Charcoal's plays since that day."

The Australian aboriginal is a natural mimic, very keen on his own chanting songs, initiation rites, dances and corroborees. Some of these last require thought and con-siderable time to organize and sometimes days to perform. The blacks tell their stories in pantomime, the dressing up for which requires no little taste and ingenuity. And there is a great deal of symbolism throughout that to the white man who does not understand may seem in the main childish.

The services of any tribesman who is an artist at dressing the actors for a corroboree are always in keen demand. But the author of a new corroboree that catches their imagination is famous throughout the land, because the corroboree is copied and passed on from tribe to tribe.

Thus Charcoal was a well-known man in country where he never had been and dare not go. And beyond those tribal areas his plays were "stolen" by ambitious ones who slightly altered the corroboree to suit locality and local conditions and calmly pirated all credit. I felt quite keen to meet my fellow author.

The natives, now that Charcoal's name had been men¬tioned, were ready to give details of the murder—details they previously had denied all knowledge of—and of Charcoal's whereabouts. To all old Larry listened. Then he came to Laurie, his wrinkled face in a knowing grin.

"These fellar all about liars! he said with a shrug.

"Know everything all a time. Now know *too* — much!"

"Keep your ears open," ordered Laurie. "And tell Davey keep his eyes open everywhere about for Charcoal's tracks."

With sundown, the cockatoos down at the river, having drunk their fill, flew heavily up to the tree-tops, screeching conversationally. In flocks they flew to the giant baobab, till its great limbs and spreading foliage became a snowy mass flowered by the yellow of constantly rising crests. In a deafening din, they waited until the last straggler came flying up from the river, then with a roar like an express train they took the air and went screeching away to their camping-ground across the plain. Campfires flared up down by the river. A long-drawn cry rang out as some late hunter approached camp.

Next morning the patrol forded the river and wound on among the hills. A beautiful day, the long grass moist and silvery with spider-webs that might have been the hair-nets of fairies. The trackers rode seriously, glancing to right and left. For long grass betrays tracks. No actual foot track as on soft ground; but ride with the sun at a certain angle and a man's imprint on moist grass can be followed at the canter. A cunning native fearing pursuit always tries to plant his foot under the grass, should he be forced to cross a tell-tale patch.

This invisible yet visible imprint is difficult to explain; it is somewhat similar to the visible-invisible track left by a foot on a stretch of hard, bare rock. Manoeuvre until the sunlight is behind you at a certain angle and, if you have learned the secret of connecting your eyesight with the rays, you probably will see that vaporous ghost print upon the hard rock. It depends on a favourable combination of natural laws. A good tracker may thus under certain weather or atmospheric conditions track a man over hard bare sandstone; he gets a "line" on the broad surface of the rock so that the sun shines on it in a certain way. The track may be only a film partially remaining here and there, but he will work it into his vision until he gets another line straight in the direction the track appears to be going. Sooner or later he will come to rock that is weathered and on the sand grains there will identify the plain track. A track on moist grass is somewhat similar even though the resilient grass, hours later, shows no sign of pressure.

Nipper stepped out, obviously proud of himself. His hefty spouse strode behind, carrying her lord's spears. Chalba had a face hard as crinkly bark, but shrewd eyes. How men could fight to death over her, civilized man would be puzzled to understand. But one glance at her athletic body explained all. Chalba could work. And to the aboriginal, work and endurance is beauty in a woman. The long grass incommoded Chalba so she whipped off her purloined dress and stuffed it into her grass-plaited dilly-bag. Obviously relieved she strode on, a virile figure of primitive womanhood. Straight as a gun-barrel, endurance and speed in every line of her, she was fit to be the wife of any primitive. Chalba proved to be a great "smeller out" of yams, an expert in the finding of any edible root or bulb or fruit or vegetable, or of wild-fowl eggs. A keen smeller out too of birds, lizards, possums, native cats, water rats, and all manner of small game. Not a grumbler; practically tireless on forced marches; a fighter too, if Chalba was a prize that any primitive man might envy and fight for.

Davey suddenly spurred his horse to a canter; presently dismounted, hitched the rein on a tree, then, crouching low, disappeared in the grass. The patrol rode on. Soon came the sharp crack of a rifle. Davey had shot a kangaroo; he rarely missed. I sometimes wondered whether this smart, crack rifle-shot would ever take to the bush. If so, he would be familiar with every point in the game. He knew all the police methods in pursuing the quarry that he once was, and soon would know all the tricks by which the primitives sought to shake off the patrols. He was learning the handling of mules and horses, the geography of a great area of country over which he would not have dared to roam when he was a *munjon*. He knew Derby; knew the scattered white men and their life over the range; was being brought into personal contact with all the "bad" blacks. If ever Davey takes to the bush with a rifle he will make another Pigeon, probably a more dangerous one.

About midday we heard a faint, whispering sound, like a sighing silver song. Nodding towards the Phillips Range, Laurie said:

"That might be a waterfall."

"Then again, it might be the wind sighing in the tree-tops down the valley," I suggested.

"Feel like exploring? It is nearly dinner-time anyway."

"Right-oh."

Laurie called and beckoned and the trackers veered in towards the left. Soon a tree-shaded cleft appeared in the range. We rode up this tiny gorge which widened between cliffs of pinkish rock in pyramidal slabs one upon the other. Along a ledge high up hopped a strange little wallaby like a cat with a furry tail. He sat back on his tail and stared down at us, Baobabs and palms graced a silver stream that linked water-pools covered with lilies. Farther on, from the sandstone rim, a water-spray sang over a cliff and down into a dark green pool in which swam blue-grey fish. Horses and mules eagerly sank noses into lawns soft as clover.

"A great place to boil the billy," said Laurie as he dismounted.

"*Bongin*," nodded Nipper towards the waterfall as he slung off the kangaroo he had been carrying for Davey.

Leaving the waterfall we rode up a wonderful valley, red sandstone walling one side, black basalt the other: towering bastions to which baobabs clung with strange effect. Far up on a crag a black sentinel stood, his spears like needles set in a toy hand. As we looked he cupped his hand to his mouth and a long-drawn cry went floating away.

The horses pricked inquisitive ears, the trackers gazed speculatively, Chalba went to her lord and whispered. He nodded and again and again his eyes turned to that little statue in ebony.

This craggy valley is a great hide-out and favourite hunting-ground. Beautifully grassed, with a sparkling stream running down its centre among park-like trees. The baobabs gave a weird touch to the beauty. The squat bulk of these elephantine trees will flourish in sand or loam or clinging to a precipice. This craggy valley and its distant waterfall would make a wonderful setting for a romantic story. In fact it has been so used. There is the story of a big mob of cattle driven there to be held quietly by four white men until a hue and cry for them had died down. But the natives, wonderfully quick to sense something unusual, began harrying the herd. The whites, their packhorses well provisioned, could apparently, merely by camping at the mouth of the valley, hold the herd secure indefinitely. But the *munjons* crawled among the cattle at night "belly stabbing" them, thus stampeding them again and again, in the dark confusion cutting up the slaughtered beasts and carrying them up to the crags to be cooked. There they would light fires on the cliff-edge and dance in triumph as the meat cooked, hurling sneering defiance into the black valley below. But rifle-shots taught caution to the wild dancers outlined by the flames. Thereafter they made their fires farther back, leaping to the black cliff-edges in jeering corroboree while waving hunks of meat.

Very few of that herd ever reached a market.

Laurie pointed to a small tree growing prominently upon a grassy knoll.

"I passed here just twelve months ago," he said, "and won't forget that tree in a hurry. For a month I had been hot on the tracks of an abo called Cowalor, but was encumbered by having half a dozen native murderers on the chain. There was an old witch-doctor in particular (responsible for the trouble and numerous other killings) with Mooraroo and Spit. The remaining killers were connected with another case. The witch-doctor, Mooraroo, Wyacketu, Cowalor and Spit had sung and killed Winidot away up north near Vansittart Bay. They speared him while he was up a tree getting a 'sugar-bag' (wild honey). I had them all except this Cowalor; he had led me a merry dance. I struck his tracks here fresh, apparently making towards Russ's. I decided to take a chance; to leave the prisoners around that tree and ride on swiftly with the trackers. I'd probably surprise Cowalor at Russ's then. If I came on with the prisoners he would be warned and take to the hills. So I padlocked the chain around the tree and searched every man for the umpteenth time to make certain he had neither file nor wire concealed. I chose that particular tree because there is soft loam underfoot with not a stone in it. After making sure that the prisoners had not the faintest chance of breaking that chain, I left them plenty of water and food, and rode for Russ's for all I was worth. Cowalor had gone. But his lubra was there: she said he had gone away on some devil-devil business. I cut his tracks making for Mount House. Missed him there; followed his tracks to the Barnett River and nabbed him. All hands were done in and the horses exhausted; we'd travelled one hundred miles with only four hours' spell. When I returned here the prisoners were gone."

"What had happened?"

"A lubra had been trailing the patrol for days, maybe weeks. She cut the chain with a tomahawk."

"Stiff luck."

"Yes. That was a twelve-hundred-and-fifty-mile patrol, and those prisoners had taken some catching. The old witch-doctor was a particularly bad egg, responsible for some very cowardly killings. In Winidot's case they waited until he was up that tree helpless, his spears lying at its foot."

In late afternoon we clambered up a steep rocky rise then up on to the Phillips Range. Always on these flat tablelands the grass is scraggy, the trees smaller, the country much poorer. Next morning's awakening was glorious. The brightness of the spreading colours of the rising sun slowly dimmed the morning star. Bird voices broke out everywhere. The bush was like a free and happy aviary, birds calling, chattering, gossiping near and far; cheeky ones were interested in old Larry lighting the fire and putting the billy on. These birds seemed to camp at midday, for when travelling we saw comparatively few.

We travelled on, seeking a skeleton, while seeking Charcoal. Evidence soon appeared of the wild man's cunning, of his bushcraft and organization when tackling anything dear to his heart. It was a narrow valley; a natural trap for cattle. Between the sandstones, spreading lawns of short green grass covered treacherous bog beneath. All around here the spearmen would hide, armed with those terrible shovel-bladed spears that will kill a bullock at seventy yards. Miles out on the plain, and spread out for miles like slowly converging beaters, men, women, children and dogs would gradually start the cattle towards the valley. They might be so distant that it would take a day, even two days, of crafty driving to get them there. At any point where the converging mob would be likely to break away natives lay hidden ready to leap out shouting and so keep the uneasy beasts travelling always towards the valley mouth. When they entered the valley, the beasts would be a mob terrified of the odour of black men. These would suddenly appear yelling and screaming behind them, dogs would come yelping at their heels. The beasts, already half winded, would break into a lumbering gallop necessarily straight up the valley. Presently, ahead and at their flanks, howling figures would appear. As the bewildered beasts paused others would suddenly rush from the trees straight at them. The beasts would then swerve and plunge head-long into the bog. In the lust to kill that followed the broad-bladed spears would slice the bellowing beasts plunging in the morass. Thus our primitive forefathers slaughtered wild beasts—human packs driving even mastodons into bogs.

In this lonely place some time ago the tribesmen had enjoyed a great kill, but the tracks in the mud were of none of the men wanted by the patrol. Bending over their horses' necks Larry and Davey pointed out tracks of men they knew. Nipper eagerly pointed out strangers' tracks, laughing at their success as he pointed to the heaps of bones by the burned-out fires and detailed the names of the men. Keenly, too, Chalba prowled around, calling attention now and then to the churned up mud, a broken spear-haft, a broken-off horn, plainly telling of some prolonged struggle between men and some particularly fight- able beast.

To most aboriginals, a track once seen is memorized for all time. Davey knew Charcoal's track, for he had seen it when he was a *munjon* spearing cattle in company with Nipper. The tribesmen even remember the police horses when once seen, and recognized them when still far away.

There was nothing to do but follow Nipper to Burrin's burial place, meanwhile seeking all hunting-grounds where Charcoal might be surprised or where he might have left his track. Mother Earth is the fingerprint department of the mounted police in the wilds.

We rode across a tableland that eventually seemed to break over the rim of the world. Just then two dogs hot on a scent came loping from the trees. They leapt back in silent surprise almost from our horses' hoofs. The dogs were followed by a huntsman, his woman close behind.

They stood as surprised as the dogs. The man, upright and fearless, was daubed with ochre bars of red and white, his forehead band brilliant with tufts of parrot feathers. He carried a wommera and two excellently made shovel-bladed spears; a stone knife was shoved through his human hair belt. His wild woman stared fearfully from behind him; after one quick glance at Nipper her eyes were concentrated upon Laurie's face.

The huntsman spoke Davey's lingo. Craftily Davey inquired of the nearest white-men settlers, then of tribesman friends, then casually mentioned Charcoal's native name. He learned that Charcoal with his friends was hunting his way across country to white-man Dave Rust's. After friendly inquiries in which Charcoal's name did not recur, we left them dazzled by the gift of a pocket-knife, and rode on.

"If Charcoal knows we are after him, that man doesn't," said Laurie, "unless Nipper talked to him in sign language. They are not tribesmen so they may not have. Anyway, I've got a line on Charcoal's direction now. I'd ride straight for Fred Russ's, only Bob Muir is away down here close by Mount Caroline. I must make sure all is well with him."

"Is he a settler?"

"Well, yes. A lonely sort of chap, somewhat similar type to Anderson and the Little Iron Man and other wanderers. Has a good plant. Wanders around on his own doing a bit of dogging (dingo-hunting). Sometimes he takes up a bit of country, and sells it if he can. If not, he just rides away and leaves it."

He must be jolly lonely on his own, right out here in the wilds."

"Some of the few men out here prefer to travel and live like that."

"Do you visit every one when on patrol?"

"If I possibly can; there are not many of them. Invariably I visit all the settlers, but the dozen nomad whites might be anywhere."

"Do any get speared by the blacks?"

"Occasionally. Bob Muir's brother was speared in the Territory. Bob is a very quiet, cautious chap, and kind to the blacks. But they get that type of man too sometimes." The Drysdale River natives have speared Bob Anderson since these lines were written. And Jack Wilson, the Little Iron Man, has had a narrow escape. A black youngster put strychnine in his kangaroo-tail stew, anticipating the "fun" of seeing Jack throw fits "all a same poisoned pup."

10
THROUGH A LONELY LAND

FROM the edge of the tableland we gazed out over a grassy plain that merged into a hazy range. Dark lines of creek timber meandered across it. It looked a lonely land out there. We led the horses along an animal pad that zig-zagged down the one accessible descent. The mules were nearly standing on their noses, old Kate and Mandy snorted at foothold after foothold, fussily making sure before they would trust their precious bodies to the stepping rocks below.

Bob Muir's home was poked away between range and creek and plain. It was a new humpy of bark and saplings, quaintly impressive of white man's defiance of the wild. A fearfully lonely place. How a solitary human can exist without going crazy in a place like that puzzles me. Bob must live hard too—very hard. The hut door was chained and padlocked. Surprised blacks down at the creek told the trackers that the white man had gone to Fred Russ's to give him a hand with his yearly muster. Mumbling from under glowering brows they grunted that Charcoal had been there but had left for Ambudda (Mount Barnett). From there he was going to hunt his way across to the white-man Russ. They added venomously that Charcoal's fighters were taking what they wanted as they travelled.

Across the plain swarming with kangaroos we rode to the Barnett River. So far, we had only seen 'roos occasionally. Here big old "red men," six feet high, bounded heavily along to sit back on their tail-tips and gaze at us, ears a-twitch, nostrils sniffing, big eyes alive with curiosity. The plain was not so sweetly grassed either; great patches were covered with coarse grass ten feet high in which the pack-animals vanished to old Pancake's delight. Laurie's hat was only visible when a murmuring wind bowed the giant stalks aside. Those stalks were now a brown sea of curling grass seeds whose sharp points would have made life unbearable but for the canvas trousers we wore to guard against them.

Throughout the patrol, the distances we covered with no sign of a white human, and the quietness, were almost awe inspiring.

Under such conditions the trees seemed alive, impressing us with a far greater sense of life than is generally believed of trees. Many trees under a warm sun murmured contentedly with their leaves open to the breeze; on a hot, windless day their leaves grew very still and half-curled up. Other trees stood motionless with shrivelled leaves drooping like a still horse with hanging head on a hot day. Thus they prevented the sun from robbing them of their precious water. Some protected their leaves with a film of wax as a young girl might protect her cheeks with cream; others, like wild men, grew hair on their leaves; still others, with delicate leaves, only opened them in the early morning, closing them up for the remainder of the day until sunset, when they uncurled in delight to the caress of the cool evening breeze. Some trees grew only on the basalts, others on the sandstones; the haughty ones with beautiful foliage clung to the river- banks or sentinelled with their white trunks the green edges of lagoons. But all were actively alive and fighting to grow and expand, and in flower and seed give life to other trees.

We saw very few cattle—none at all for several weeks at a time. We could have ridden for weeks, possibly months, and never have seen a white man had it not been that Laurie was riding from scattered white to white.

"How far Ambudda?" asked Laurie of Nipper.

" Little bit long way," answered Nipper with a jerk of his chin out into the distance ahead. It was a day's ride, but that meant all the same to Nipper.

Mount Barnett had been abandoned for some time. More's the pity. The unreliable cattle-market and worse transportation problem are killers out here. A lonely grave on the river-bank tells a story of unbreakable courage and human loyalty. The deserted homestead was built of roughly squared pine and roofed with tea-tree. An awesome loneliness hovered around the place. To the thud of our horses' hoofs a big black cat, of all things, started meowing, and came running out, almost frantic for human company. It made itself a perfect nuisance until nightfall when a large ginger cat appeared. I was sorry to see them. Their increase will take to the bush and cause havoc to bird life. Modern man, wherever he goes, plants the seeds of disaster among all things primitive. His horses and cattle carry ticks and strangles and pleurisy; his sheep carry pest seed; and his vessels, when wrecked, carry rats and disease which devastate lovely islands that have never known a pest.

There was no sign of natives recently in the Mount Barnett locality. We cleared a couple of snakes out of the mouldy house and had the billy on by nightfall.

"We must have sat down on a kangaroo camp when we boiled the billy at midday," I remarked irritably. Laurie laughed while

while I burned three kangaroo ticks from my legs.

"They can dig in some," he said. "They're ugly little pests. If you get one in your ear you'll know all about it."

I changed the subject:

"We've seen no smoke-talks for some days."

"No. It's difficult country for long-distance 'smoking'; too many ranges of equal height bunched close together. Smoke-signal visibility is best across plain country from distant hill to hill. Anyway, they don't bother to signal unless they wish to warn somebody, and the few aboriginals we've met recently don't seem anxious to warn Charcoal."

"Has he definitely made for the hills do you think?"

"I hope not. It will mean a long chase if he has. Most likely he is at Fred Russ's. At this time of the year the cattlemen are mustering and it is the native harvest time. The bush *munjons* come in to the homesteads, anxious to give a hand in a clumsy sort of way—keen for tobacco and the chance to pick up any odd scraps of iron. The station men don't need them; but they welcome them; kill a beast for them now and then, and try to impress on them that if they want a beast while out in the bush, to kill only one as they want it—not run a mob into a bog and slaughter the lot. The *munjons* know there is always plenty of easy tucker for them at mustering-time and, what means a lot more, tobacco and iron. They can mix with the station blacks and not be under suspicion that they have sneaked into camp to steal lubras or cause worse trouble. After the mustering, the *munjons* return to the bush with insides well lined and enough scraps of iron for quite a number of tomahawks and spearheads. It won't be long before every native over the range has an iron tomahawk of some sort or another. Charcoal, probably, will be at Russ's, slinging his weight about. If he doesn't know I'm after him I may take him by surprise."

One day we splashed across the shallow Hann and in late afternoon neared Fred Russ's. Laurie sent the trackers to surprise the bush camp from the rear. We rode on at a swift walk, the trackers craning their heads over the long grass to right and left seeking hunting parties, their eyes ceaselessly roving, ears listening, faces alert with the hunter's instinct.

We struck a faint, dusty pad. Larry pointed—a bare footprint in the dust. Away over the long grass a depression lined with sweet young grass showed faintly visible among the trees. The trackers broke into a canter, but no blacks were digging yams in the depression. Larry rode swiftly to the left, Davey straight ahead, slowing down and standing in his stirrups before each little depression or shady gully or any low ground that might harbour animal or plant life; then at the gallop he was on the spot swifter than natives could have heard his hoof-beats. Again and again he timed his rush so that, had natives been there, they would have been just too late to crouch in the grass or hide. But we saw no natives.

Suddenly Davey galloped all out. Across open country a wisp of smoke showed, then gunyahs, and in a moment more we were right in the bush camp. One startled glance and then lubras were snatching for some old dress, men snatching at a pair of trousers, piccaninnies climbing to the gunyah roofs, dogs crouching uneasily. Most of the lubras squatted in the dust and ashes, looking strangely like monkeys. One old crone was alternately pinching a pretty child's cheeks and lousing her hair. A very old woman who had been hamstrung was dragging herself across to a gunyah on her hands, one skinny leg up under her chin. A pretty young lubra smiled proudly when Davey noticed her piccaninny, and held it up for him to feel how fat it was. Tousled-headed tribesmen, their chests deeply cicatrized, stood scowling or staring silently. All had eyes for the handkerchief on my hat. Some hundred yards away towards the homestead were the far better built huts of the station blacks; a crowd of them were watching while over by the goat-yard excited voices called. No wanted men were in camp We rode across to the homestead, prettily set in a circle of natural grass¬land with the bush trees half a mile away. Every leaf was swept clean for yards around the homestead. The "old place" was a huge log shed. Close by it was the new little house of iron, green painted, the feathery leaves of a poinciana shading its veranda. An old Jack donkey came galloping and hee-hawing in great excitement at sight of the horses and mules. To the barking of the dogs a white man came from the kitchen to greet us; a heavily built man with open countenance and a sharply trimmed beard turning grey. Behind him toddled a fat little piccaninny, her big black eyes rolling from curiosity.

"Jack Calahan," explained Laurie, "and Gibb River station. Hullo, Jack!"

"Hullo, Laurie, I was expecting you."

"Why so, Jack?"

"The natives knew yesterday you were coming—might have known before for all I know."

"That explains why Charcoal isn't in camp then." "No, he left with his crowd before the message came through, went to Dave Rust's place. Dave will be glad to know you're here—especially if by any chance you're going out his way."

'Why, particularly?"

"Because he's away with Fred giving him a hand to muster. That new place he's started up on Mount Elizabeth has only Jack Campbell in charge. Jack is as good as a white man; but he's got to come down here in a few days and help Dave take his little mob of cattle back. That will leave the hut and all Dave's possessions, including those ten acres of peanuts, all alone."

Hmm, said Laurie, "a fine chance for the bush natives under a leader."

"Yes. But come inside, I'll liven up the lubras and we'll have the billy boiled in no time. All the men are away mustering. Bob Muir came across to lend a hand too."

As we off saddled, Jack shouted to the house lubras who were busy taking stock of the strangers. They giggled. He then swore at one in particular; but the more he swore the more she giggled.

'   'Having trouble with the lady, Jack?" called Laurie. Yes, Laurie, I always have: only it doesn't do to swear at them before strangers, they get too conceited." When Jack walked towards them however they all dived into the kitchen, the little toddler following Jack like a pet puppy.

This pioneer homestead was comfortably and neatly built for strength and coolness; through its centre ran an open passage as wide as a lane, big open windows with iron shutters opened on a veranda surrounding all. The kitchen fireplace was large enough to roast a bullock. It needed to be; when all hands were preparing for the muster there was a big crowd to feed. Fred Russ had made a success of this place despite the rough country, transportation, and distance from market— two hundred and fifty miles from Derby, rough going. After mustering, it takes a month to drove a mob into Derby. After a wet season cattle hoofs are tender. Any beasts that become footsore must be abandoned, the cattle steamer will not wait. Even if it would, sore-footed beasts cannot travel; they merely knock the condition off themselves. From Derby the cattle are shipped on their thousand odd miles sea trip. To market a beast from Derby costs just on £6. The cattleman must receive at least £11 a beast to make a profit for keeping it and looking after it for four or five years. Unfortunately, cattle have been shipped to Fremantle and met such a bad Perth market that the owner has had to send a cheque after them to pay for expenses. Stores come from Wyndham two hundred miles north-east, by camel. An occasional Afghan makes a good bushman. These rare birds, with the help of natives, found that by winding in and out over the soft ground of the valleys they could bring a camel-train where no wheeled transport could go. Cartage per camel-team costs £15 10s. per ton; from Fremantle, landed here, £20 per ton. A ton of material often costs more in transportation than its value.

A lonely life with just the satisfaction of carving a living out of the wilderness, and the pleasure of looking forward to the yearly visit of a police patrol—and the mail. In the dry season they get this once a month now by sending a black boy across to Mount House, only seventy miles away. Still, life out here, despite its worries, flows along wonderfully smoothly. The worries of city life and the troubles that torment the world are far from them. The far-away world seems a fool, worrying its time away. Some things that the cities are seething over are not even known out here.

But then, the man who likes city life would go mad in this quiet loneliness.

After a hearty meal we lit the pipes out on the veranda. "Will Bob Muir return with the musterers?" inquired Laurie.

"Yes, " said Jack. "That was the arrangement." Then: "Maudie! When Bob Muir come back?"

"Nother one to-morrow," answered a voice from the kitchen. Which meant not tomorrow, but any old morrow after that.

"Where's my pannikin?" called Jack.

"Might be somewhere!" came the answer.

"I didn't puttem anywhere," yelled Jack. "Who puttem?"

"No good askem me! Might be self!"

"I tell you I didn't puttem anywhere!" yelled Jack "No good summons (accuse) me!" shrilled the voice. Might be you put yourself!"

She's trying to be smart just because strangers are here, fumed Jack as he rose to find the pannikin.

"They've actually washed themselves and combed their hair m front of a cracked looking-glass. Those infernal trackers of yours get the gins all social when they ride along this way."

Old Jack was a very decent, quiet sort, a great cook. A dingo-shooter, travelling on his own: a month here, a month there. Just another of the nomads who lead the lonely life but will not settle down even on a lonely station. He might visit Derby once in every two or three years. Some dingo-shooters will work for no man; others accept a short-time job now and then. We heard Jack issuing the household lubras their rations, then away they went, heavily loaded shadows in the night, back to the distant campfires where hungry ones awaited them. The toddler, nearly asleep, clutched home-made cakes in each grimy fist.

For every stockman employed on Kimberley stations, at least four other people have to be kept. His father and mother, sisters and brothers, or uncles and aunts — any he can possibly make dependent on him. Aboriginal labour is by no means as cheap as it is believed to be.

Old Larry appeared. One glance at his face showed that he had been doing secret-service work. "Charcoal go longa Dave Rust's. Sit down longa bushmen. He not know yet police look longa him. He help kill Burrin all right; kill other man, woman too. He say he not afraid police, he say he spear tracker quick. Spit out there somewhere too."

Laurie raised his eyebrows, and I thought immediately of this Spit who with others had escaped when chained around the tree.

"Spit say he big man now," went on Larry. "He say he can spear any cattle, can take any lubra from any man. He raid Mount Barnett; he grab one man's lubra. Man fight; Spit hit him over head; jump out and tell tribe, 'Me proper man now. Pleece can't catch me; me proper man! White man he say me proper hard — man!' "

Laurie laughed:

"I would have just loved to be behind him," he said "Go on."

"Oomagun he out there too! Alla man here too prighten say much, Oomagun he fight too much; too strong." There was grudging admiration in the old tracker's voice. They say Oomagun only kill man tribal, not against police law. But me spicious. 'Nother feller mob been here too; Dave Bryce's Willie, Dick, Mundy, Long Willie, Short Ahck, Martin. Steal plenty young gin; fight; go longa Walcott Inlet."

"All right," said Laurie. "Now you and Davey watch out camp. Find out how many men, women sick. Find out whether any man, woman, got 'big sick.' Whether any sick man run away, hide longa bush."

Larry nodded and was gone.

"How is their health?" inquired Laurie.

"Pretty good, thank heaven," answered old Jack. "There doesn't seem to be more than the usual amount of V.D."

There wouldn't be," said Laurie grimly, "when they go away into the bush and die."

"I'm afraid they do," sighed Jack. "We do all we can but what chance has our knowledge of medicines got against that! We try and send them into Derby for treatment, but the majority run away before they get there." Laurie nodded.

"It is a job that would tax the resources and ingenuity the Commonwealth," he said soberly. "Have you seen any signs of leprosy amongst them?"

"No, thank heaven, but we're watching every native that comes in from the bush. The trouble is we don't know how to pick a case. Unless a man's finger or arm has dropped off how are we to know whether he has leprosy or not? I hope you are not setting straight out after Charcoal. Fred is very anxious to see you. This leprosy problem has got us all bluffed."

"I don't know too much about it myself unfortunately," said Laurie. "We go through the Lazarette at Derby, and study every case we can. The old doctor points out the symptoms, and we've learned to detect a lot that we wouldn't notice otherwise. But it is a baffling disease." "It has the natives well bluffed too."

"No wonder, poor devils!"

"Any white cases yet?"

"None recent—which is surprising. The trouble is that symptoms may be a long time developing. There is uneasiness all over the Kimberleys."

A hullabaloo broke out down at the native camp. Shouts, shrieks, the clash of blows suddenly stopped by the authoritative shouts of old Larry.

"A bit of a rumpus," said Jack. "Just as well your trackers were there, I saw strange faces among the *munjons* today. Are you going after Charcoal straightaway?"

"No," answered Laurie slowly. "I'd like to see Fred first. I don't think they know I'm after Charcoal yet. If they do, and he has any close friends in camp, one will run and warn him. Anyway, a runner could reach Charcoal before I could. If I stay here awhile they won't move; and by the time Fred comes in with the bullocks they'll be less inclined still; they won't want to miss the feasts. Charcoal won't move either. If he is really waiting for Campbell to leave Rust's place and come down here he won't move until he is definitely warned we are close and are after him; and so far as I know none of his particular friends are in camp. If only I can keep him hanging around Rust's place I've got a chance of catching him."

We listened to a sudden wild song, wild voices joining in chorus, the sharp clicking of wommeras then the savage stamping of rhythmic feet. The waves of sound ceased abruptly; then again the song quickly swelled by throaty chorus, almost drowned by the thump of stamping feet.

Old Jack yawned:

"They're settled for the night ... going to be jolly cold too."

11
IN THE FRONTIER LANDS

NEXT morning Laurie strolled down to the native camp. Some active types among them, but only a few piccaninnies. The bush blacks shuffled while staring from shaggy brows, apprehensive, as the trackers lined them up for their first medical parade.

Laurie found one woman in a bad way from V.D., more terrible by far to the aboriginal than leprosy. Then came a man with thick, ridgy eyebrows. A rugged primitive, his grass-plaited arm-bands bit tight into bunched muscles. Laurie stared until the primitive's piercing eyes wavered uneasily. Laurie frowned at the man's forehead, his nose, his temples. The rugged face creased into an uneasy grin with flash of perfect teeth.

"Turn around," ordered Laurie.

Davey interpreted the order and the man shuffled around. Laurie stared at his shoulders. His muscular back was coated with ochre and the dust of ashes in which he had slept.

"Take him to the creek and make him bathe his back, clean now!" ordered Laurie. "And mind he doesn't run away." He proceeded carefully with the inspection.

When the trackers returned, the man's body was a picture, the sun glinting on muscles of copper bronze.

They had made him scrub himself with sand. He was smiling uneasily.

"Turn around!" ordered Laurie.

He did so, and there they were, dirty greyish patches, a little nobby lump here and there. The first leper.

We were to see others—too many for the patrol to bring in.

Old Larry's mention of Oomagun was intriguing, the real wild man invariably is interesting; but when he begins to loaf around white habitations he quickly loses both his strict tribal and individual personality. Oomagun rarely came near a white man, he just "ordered" his iron for spearheads, his tobacco from others who paid fleeting visits to the station-boys. We had heard whispers of him from camp to camp as a big wild man in the hills who could levy tribute and was both admired and feared. Laurie was curious to see him. He had nothing against him, though he knew he had killed according to tribal law; if he had killed otherwise the fear of his name had proved an effectual shield.

With expressive eyes the tribesmen assured us that Oomagun was as strong as three strong men, an expert with the spear, a ferocious killer when aroused. Oomagun attacked any enemy like a mad animal. They told of how he had once rushed a clever fighter who, being prepared, had with two lightning blows disarmed him. Oomagun slung his arms around the man, sank his teeth in his neck and tore his throat out. The working of their jaws as they explained, the gurgling growls with protruding tongue and bulging eyes, was ghastly pantomime.

For good reason tribesmen were frightened of but intensely admired Oomagun, while the children and women adored him. The wild native women are almost always that way, not that they receive much encouragement. Their men, generally, will be comparatively kind to them providing they remain uncomplaining beasts of burden, live to do his bidding, and not complain overmuch when he adds someone younger and stronger to his harem. The lubras are swift judges of character. After marriage, the first words, the first sentence, the tone of them tells her whether her man is going to he kind or not. While he is still in the first pride of possession she may begin to impose on his good nature and does so increasingly until, the sudden temperament of the aboriginal flaring up, he treats her roughly. And it is roughly. She crawls away, and her opinion of her husband translated into pidgin is an admiring, "My word, proper cheeky feller that one!" Thereafter, he seldom gives her an order twice, simply hits her across the head if near enough.

Still, there are cases in every tribe where man and woman really are united. When a blackfellow becomes a bit civilized he puts up with a nagging woman until his patience becomes exhausted. The more they are civilized, the longer their patience lasts. For instance, old Larry's present wife, Nancy (he gladly left her behind in Derby), is a vivacious young lubra with shrewd head and tongue as lively as a machine-gun. She follows Larry from place to place scolding, then screeching, until at last he wheels around and gives her the father1 of a thrashing. Then Nancy is peaceful and obedient—until she wants another.

This inborn love of trouble in native women lasts until they die. Often it is the old women who stir up trouble in camp, whisper suggestions for the ears of the Old Men, goad on the young men to mischief. Either they or the old witch-doctor or both are pretty sure to be at the bottom of most trouble. It gives them an interest in life.

The hunting-ground of the little crowd known as Dave Bryce's Willie, Dick, Mundy, Long Willie, Short Alick, and Martin lay between Gibb River and a section of the Leopolds west to the Coast as far as Walcott Inlet and from thence south to the hills of Oobagooma. Particularly rugged, in places practically inaccessible, country towards the precipitous coast. This band were actually native bushrangers amongst the natives, particularly mobile, and bound to a cunning leader. Fighters all, excellent spearmen and bushmen, wonders of physical endurance, cheekily confident because of their numerous escapes from the vengeance of white man and black alike. Here to-day and gone to-morrow, what they wanted they took: if a beast, it fell a victim to their shovel-bladed spears; if a young lubra, they simply took her and more; boldly entered any bush native camp, seized what they wanted, fighting any brave enough to protest. Such a band could not have terrorized native life before the beginning of the break up of the tribes; they would have been attacked *en masse* immediately they encroached on another tribe's territory. But detribalization is taking place even in that area now, and one result is this compact little band.

This was a police patrol and as such we passed the quieter native life by. The patrol was constantly seeking the renegades, the wild he-men of the tribes and sub-tribes and hordes, the men who were actively making life insecure for their fellows. Hence, this book deals particularly with this phase of aboriginal life.

Throughout the patrol, the natives were amusing in their anxiety to impress upon us their white-feller name. Any old name would do; if not given by a white man, then some lordly station black on walk-about is generally asked to suggest a name. Even though they did not work for whites, almost every aboriginal desired a white-feller name. Apparently it helped take away the taint of *munjon*. Fortunately so for identification purposes, because their own names were generally unpronounceable, let alone memorizable. In addition to these two names, every man, whether civilized or *munjon*, has a secret name; and this no white man will ever know, nor any other person except his own father and the Council of the Old Men. This is his spiritual, sacred name, the name that belongs to his spirit; it is actually he. He is never called by it; does not know it himself until fully initiated into manhood. Should any person, except the elders of the tribe, learn this name it is believed that that person can do the owner harm through magic. Through the witch-doctor an enemy can influence an evil spirit to do harm to the spirit within the living man.

Similarly, throughout Australia they have a secret language; and this is actually "they," the aboriginals, the sacred themselves within them all which is connected with creation. With this "secret" and thus "sacred" language they express their real beliefs, their feelings and mentality, their very selves, their "sacred life." And because of it the whites will never lift the veil that shades their mentality from ours.

I know of only one white man familiar with this sacred language; and he will never tell for the simple reason that he is a pure white native. His mother died when he was born; he was suckled at the breast of a native woman; his father sailed away and he grew up with the tribe as one of themselves. It is believed that in him is actually the spirit of a dead tribesman. At fifty years of age he is far more of a native than he is a white man. His "run" is on the north-eastern coast. There is another man three thousand miles west in the Kimberleys who was brought up amongst black piccaninnies and was initiated at manhood into the various degrees of the tribes. Few white men, indeed, know more of aboriginal life than he. But I doubt if even he has been initiated into their secret language, though he knows the secret signs. That secret language means the aboriginals' sacred life, the mental things that have been handed down to them by prehistoric fathers from tens of thousands of years ago, and that hold them fast to the universe as children of the universe.

Near sundown the musterers' packhorses came jingling towards the homestead, a tiny black boy sitting a huge black horse in the lead. Fearfully important he was with his sixteen-foot stockwhip. Thirty packhorses came jogging behind him, the stockboys with voice and whip-crack hurrying them to reach the homestead before sundown. The lubra goatherd was driving the goats into the goat-yard, and the old Jack donkey was trotting around in great excitement welcoming the oncoming horses with hee-haws like blasts from a siren. Around the kitchen a crowd of lubras and a few youngsters were receiving rations. The toddler insistently demanded "pumikin" which old Jack Calahan gave her in the form of watermelon. The quantity she could put away was amazing. In competition with the toddler, Jack's trained dog was sitting back with one paw at the salute, humanly expressive eyes begging his evening's supply of tit-bits. Jack can do anything with dogs.

As the pack-animals came jingling to the homestead there sounded a distant cracking of whips, lowing of cattle, faint shouting of men. The first stockhorses appeared hurrying amongst the timber, then the first of the mob; the lowing, the whip-cracking, the shouts rapidly grew plainer. The sun slipped down. The whole mob of cattle emerged on the plain, coming rapidly. Soon they were being yarded amongst a cloud of dust, horns clashing, rumbling of hoofs. Old Jack Calahan was rousing on the lubras to hurry with the evening meal. A half-moon rose in the sky. The stockmen, now a black group of horsemen, emerging from the stockyard came riding among the tall white gums and pandanus palms to the homestead. They had been in the saddle since before dawn. They dismounted with outstretched hand and heavy walk, jangling of spurs as each smiled greeting. The baby piccaninny toddled to Russ and demanded attention and "pumikin." Then a wash and the evening meal.

Fred Russ was the typical northern bushman, lean and wiry, brown as a berry, quiet and efficient: a type that has made a station in the wilderness despite all obstacles. Bob Muir was a thin quiet chap, seldom joining in the conversation unless spoken to. His knowledge of the bush in its lonelier aspects was uncanny. I used to wonder what his nightly thoughts must be when alone except for his dog, the birds and trees and natives. Dave Rust was a big, very strongly built, slow-smiling, big-hearted Scotchman. He was the type of man who can build a house from trees, make the harness for a team out of any old thing lying about, drove stock through little-known country, or develop a station out of the virgin hush. Farther north, he and Scotty Salmon had had a long struggle, and almost got on their feet when the big fall in cattle prices beat them. But only for a time. For three years now he had been working for Fred Russ, half his wages in money, half in cattle. Scotty Salmon was working as cook out on the coast at Munja, the Government Aboriginal Station at Walcott Inlet. Scotty's money was added to Rust's in aid of the new venture. Dave had taken up land at Mount Elizabeth only twenty-five miles away, built a hut and planted ten acres of peanuts in the wilderness. After this muster, he would take their little mob of cattle from here, to start definitely on the new venture. In like manner other stations have been started in the Kimberleys. The peanut venture was puzzling. Right out in the wilderness, the only transport by camel to Wyndham, then irregular steamer to Perth, all told nearly two thousand miles to market!

That evening saw a great meeting, six white men. Between us, we had covered much of the familiar world and been in little-known places besides. But, to the ceaseless roaming of a score of dogs, occasional tramp of heavy feet, jingle of spurs, the conversation eventually fined down to the cattle-market at Perth; then to little Derby the cattle-port for the West Kimberley, to jump away north to tiny Wyndham the only port of the East Kimberley; then to men and events "away over on the Fitzroy." Then came the unbreakable local chain, the men over the range, "walk-about" disease, the mailman, cattle, mules and donkeys and teams—and the aboriginal.

All six were both sorry and troubled at the aboriginal's rapid dying-out. These men saw it not only through their years in the bush, but here from year to year around them. I had seen the same thing throughout northern Australia, starting at Cape York Peninsula three thousand miles farther east. Across there, north of Cooktown, the population of whites had been barely one hundred. Here, over the range, there were hardly two dozen white men—none at all farther north. Both countries were well watered; game plentiful; plant life prolific; the natives over most of the country had no contact with whites. And yet they are practically gone in the Peninsula; were going fast here. They had quite gone in areas elsewhere. All hands were sorry, for almost all bushmen get to like the aboriginal.

We seemed hardly to have fallen asleep when there was stamp and bustle, spurs rattling on the hard earthern floor. Then Fred Russ's voice outside shouting to the station-boys to get up and go after the horses. It was jolly cold; the sun had not yet turned in his bed. Jack Calahan was rousing on the sleepy-eyed kitchen lubras who would far rather have slept than got the stockboys' breakfast. Stamping of boots on the earthern floor, jingling of spurs, sluicing of water in the dishes outside. Ugh! It was time I crawled out of bunk.

Then breakfast by hurricane lamp as shouts and crack of whips sounded away outside, hoofs thundering towards the stockyard. Then the native stockmen came shivering to the kitchen for breakfast.

The whites had saddled up and were ready to ride out at sunrise. Not so the aboriginal stockboys. To Fred's orders they saddled up in a lackadaisical way. With patience he had to repeat orders, watch every mule being packed, see that nothing was left behind, repeat instructions again and again, but never lose his temper. With white stockmen, a quiet "we will muster so and so tomorrow," would have been sufficient order the evening before. But there are no white stockmen over the range, each man works for himself.

12
THE MESSAGE-STICK

WHILE Laurie was doctoring Slippery the mule that through cussedness had lamed himself, I strolled with Larry down to the native camp. They were agog with curiosity, though obviously disappointed. I did not look nearly terrifying enough for an inspector, the trackers' description of whom had led all Aboriginal-land to picture him as breathing smoke and fire. Larry calmly announced that I was a "big doctor" come to cure the "big sick." Thereafter I moved freely amongst all the natives we met. No longer uneasy of the authority of the patrol, they believed that whatever business the constable might have with them would not concern me. This mental trait corresponds somewhat to their reasoning towards sickness. Sickness is a matter of "self," a peculiar personal state of the victim. It cannot affect nor concern any one else. This explains why a virulent and contagious disease may wipe out a whole tribe. To their reasoning, as I was not a policeman, nothing of a police nature would interest me. Because of this attitude, on several occasions during the patrol, tribesmen innocently let me into secrets sought by Laurie and the trackers. Laurie believed I "knew something" but he never hinted about the matter. 1 can see him smile as he reads these lines. Throughout the patrol of one thousand two hundred miles he never took unfair advantage of any native, just worked out his cases and made his captures fair and square.

However, I was indirectly responsible for putting the show away in one instance, and that this very morning. The tribesmen came crowding round, the *munjons* in particular all worried smiles through wondering what they could barter for tobacco. Laurie with Davey came strolling down from the stockyard. Presently, Davey introduced a grinning, bashful tribesman:

"This one man white-feller name Tommy," explained Davey. "He wantem sell you message-stick."

Message-sticks did not particularly interest me, but Tommy's beseeching grin as he thrust out the stick won the day, or rather the tobacco.

"Arright. S'posem Tommy tell me true what message-stick talk, I buy."

Davey translated, and Tommy nodded eager assent. In deep gutturals he explained the marks upon the stick while Davey, with his dirty finger pressed on mark after mark, translated.

"He say this message-stick from Grace's Knob mob. Stick tell men here, 'Pleece take Nipper. Don't tell pleece-man anything. S'pose you tell, we kill you.'" The message further warned against implicating any of the Grace's Knob tribe, adding that Charcoal would take vengeance too. It told that the patrol had found out nothing of Oomagun and Marmadu and others killing Worachi, nor of Oomagun killing "the woman."

It was a complete putaway. But the tribesmen did not realize it, not even Davey as he explained the message. It was merely a stick to them which was "dead" since its message had been delivered. They regarded it somewhat as we might a sheet of letter paper from which the rain had washed the ink. Only that to them, this message- stick before delivery had a personal thing about it, its message. After delivery the stick became merely a stick, and its message was "dead."

Tommy the runner had travelled with it ahead of the patrol. The Worachi mentioned was one of the very men Laurie had inquired about at Grace's Knob. Even his friends had assured us he was well, and was now absent with a hunting band. I smiled at thought of Marmadu and Rattler and Jack and the others crowding around the patrol after Nipper's arrest and so eagerly volunteering their "information" re Charcoal and the killing of Burrin. And yet, shrewd as they undoubtedly are, these aboriginals did not even now realize that the murder of Worachi was out! A good example of a queer phase of aboriginal mentality. I glanced at Laurie. He gave them all a fine sporting chance.

"If Oomagun and Marmadu have killed Worachi," he said, "I will catch them and take them to jail," and walked away.

It was yet another queer trait of aboriginal mentality that they neglected to warn Charcoal and Oomagun. Now that the police actually knew, they regarded the matter in a fatalistic vein. It had passed beyond concern of theirs; there would certainly be a chase and either Charcoal, Oomagun, and Marmadu would be caught, or they would not. But they took no active steps to warn them of this now imminent danger.

This stick thus proved that aboriginals do send definite messages by stick. It has been generally supposed that message-sticks are only "play-about," the pastime of an idle hour. These

THE stars showed only shadow branches like writhing black snakes, dead brambles, and coarse tussocks of buffalo grass. Then something sticks occasionally carry a distinct message as to the arrival of someone of importance, or to make arrangements between tribes for corroborees and initiation ceremonies, or from one man to another suggesting trade in such articles as ochres, pituri or weapons.

The characters, or rather markings, cut or burnt into the stick are not letters. They represent objects such as hills, lagoons, rivers, moon, stars, sun, days, men and women, with dates in days of time or "moons" or seasons. The messenger must memorize the message. The stick is his bonafides, his passport. When delivering the message he confirms it by pointing to each marking, giving its explicit memorized meaning. The message is meaningless to all but the man who marks it, the messenger who carries it, and the recipient when it has been delivered and explained. In other hands, a queerly shaped notch representing a familiar lagoon might be deciphered as to locality; the half-moon or sun mark might betray the time; the notches representing men and women could be distinguished, but the sense of the message would be missing.

For a special occasion only a stick may carry a message. You could visit almost any native camp and probably find a man idly cutting or burning notches in a play-about message-stick.

Thereafter I quietly collected real message-sticks wherever it was possible to get the man who had carried it to decipher. I learned that the tribesmen, in addition to smoke-signals, runner and possibly "thought" message, were also following and reporting our movements by message-stick from horde to horde, when group members in those hordes were tribally allied—not otherwise.

Being accepted as the "big doctor" who had come to cure the "big sick" hurt a bit; for no people in the world are more in need of widely organized medical attention. And yet their sick, if possible, fled at our approach, preferring to die in their own country rather than abandon it for a problematical cure in the white man's land.

The following day Laurie surprised the bush blacks' camp, intent on examining any sick ones who had evaded medical inspection. Shaggy haired strangers uneasily shuffled to the trackers' orders to line up.

"Line up!" ordered Laurie sharply to a sheepish looking stockboy squatting by a gunyah.

"He all right," advised Larry. "You bin see him before!"

"What's wrong with him then? He looks as dopey as last week-end."

"Oh, he all right," excused Larry, "he been mixem blankit!"

"H'm," growled Laurie, and ignored the bashful one.

The stockboy had married a *munjon girl* the evening before. Tribal preliminaries satisfactorily arranged he threw his blanket by his gunyah. She carried her blanket across and threw it down beside his. Thus the civilized stockboys marry in "white man fashion"; they "mixem blankit!" No other sick were found except a piccaninny. Laurie dosed it with salts. The patient was crawling about in the dust next day.

During the afternoon we noticed the old dog's ears twitching. When the musterers are away he sleeps daily in front of the homestead listening for the crack of a whip, the lowing of cattle. He hears the packhorses jogging home at last and then prick-eared he watches for the cattle. coming. But he never sees them. When the whips are cracking and the stockboys shouting and the hoofs rumbling towards the yard, the old blind dog walks out in front of the homestead, and stands there with outstretched head smelling in and hearing the life he loves. Fred Russ thinks the world of that old dog. The old fellow shivers though at the first growl of thunder; then he creeps inside and hides under a bed. He took a poison bait once and his nerves are ruined. He was listening now. There came the thud of hoofs approaching the back of the homestead. Then a score of horses, mules and donkeys with stockboys and several lubras, important and comical in trousers, came trotting to the stockyard. The outfit was in charge of Jack Campbell, Dave Rust's man. Campbell was a young half-caste, six feet two in height, a quiet, powerfully built man, obviously efficient and dependable. A little later and the musterers' whips sounded among the trees as another mob of cattle came lowing towards the homestead.

Fred Russ killed before sunset; killed a beast for the bush blacks too. They clustered around it like crows, eating certain parts raw; women pressing behind the men, stretching arms over their shoulders and snatching into the carcass; piccaninnies shrieking and climbing over the men; dogs snatching the fat from the hands of the women and children. A hawk came swooping down near tree-level to be immediately assailed by screeching pee-wits. He circled low over the native huts then planed towards the stockyard, chased by the screeching birds and cursed by the crows that swarmed the trees and stockyard rails taking every chance to swoop and steal a morsel of meat. The hawk dived straight down among a mob of crows. They scattered heavily, karking raucously while circling to get above him and swoop down with black, cruel beaks. One crow had snatched a lump of fat from the very jaws of a dog that had stolen it from a squealing piccaninny. The hawk chased it. The crow swerved almost into a stock-rail striving desperately to reach the shelter of the trees. But the hawk was on it, the crow dropping the meat and almost hitting the ground in its plunge to escape. The lubras were licking their greasy fingers then drying them on the dog's head and laughing as other dogs rushed the mongrel to lick off the grease. Some heads of the bush blacks' dogs are thickly matted where the lubras have wiped their hands after eating wild honey. It is surprising that the children, living in dirt, playing in dirt, sleeping in dirt, eating with the dogs, are so healthy. And their wonderful teeth! But when a flu epidemic comes along they die like flies while a white child would survive.

With the first golden sunlight all hands were in the saddle. The patrol then moved off, Davey in the lead; then Nipper, followed by his lubra Chalba; then the leper and sick woman; then old Larry, followed by the pack-horses and mules all full of mischief after their several days' spell. Slippery bucked, Pancake tried to hide, old Kate kept edging away into the timber; even my old grey was fancying himself. Jack Campbell rode back with us to his duties at Dave Rust's home. When out of sight of the homestead Laurie put the pace on, the animals being very willing for the first three hours; Nipper stepped out like a little Napoleon, but the leper and the sick woman looked woebegone. The way was among ridges that flattened out into a vague tableland of sandier country heavily grassed and timbered with yellow gum and pine and box and occasional sandalwood. Crossing the main headwaters of the Hann we did the twenty-five miles in a few hours. The trackers then trotted ahead. Suddenly they leaned over their horses' heads and, scattering, were away at the gallop. When I got up, they were interrogating three surprised tribesmen, all ochre painted from some recent corroboree. They were shepherding goats belonging to Dave Rust. They admitted that Charcoal and Oomagun with a "big mob" had just concentrated around Dave Rust's humpy.

13

THE CAPTURE OF CHARCOAL AND OOMAGUN

"WHAT luck," said Laurie. "Charcoal not flown yet, and Oomagun there too."

The patrol travelled quickly now that they were in danger of alarm from the dogs. At full gallop the trackers veered to right and left, Laurie galloping straight ahead. When I came jogging along with the packs they had the tribesmen rounded up among the trees, their rugged faces comically surprised, hastily snatched spears thrown at their feet. Two big bearded men watched by the trackers were obviously Charcoal and Oomagun. Tangle-haired women stood in wild-eyed alarm, children with snarling dogs crouched in gunyahs against which leaned weapons sufficient to arm a large tribe. Talking energetically to Davey was an open-countenanced, intelligent-looking aboriginal named Toby, with a particularly wide-awake little boy by his side. This Toby was obviously a "whiteman's blackfellow"; his laugh rang out loud and cheerily as he took command of the situation as know-all intermediary. It transpired that he was Toby the tracker, now on bush walk-about. He had been one of the trackers with Laurie last year in the Winidot case.

Near by was a neatly thatched hut walled with pine logs; a bough shed sheltering rough-hewn tables, and a bush forge. Farther along a chain of reedy waterholes stood out a bright-green patch of peanuts newly fenced. An air of utter wildness was over everything—the courage of a man to plant peanuts in such a place! This was Gnoungundooda—a pioneer's home with a vengeance. Crows started a lazy squawking from the tree-tops. Nipper commenced a conversation, a dog snarled and received a growl in reply, the horses and mules shook themselves and rolled as we slung the packs off, all hands drew breath and settled down. Larry came along with Toby.

"Toby wantem job tracking," he explained to Laurie.

"Hullo, Dick!" Laurie laughed. "I been see 'im you before!"

The pot-bellied urchin grinned widely, his big eyes dancing.

"Me wantem biff!" he announced.

"Still hungry! Well, we'll see if Larry can find you a feed of beef when the billy's boiled. I can't sign Toby on now," he said to Larry. "I'm full-handed."

Toby pleaded to be allowed to follow the patrol to Derby; he was tired of the bush and wanted to be civilized again, to see the sergeant and rejoin the police.

"Follow on if you like," agreed Laurie. "You can give a hand with the horses and any sick people we may find later."

So the patrol gained a willing recruit and a mascot. And couldn't that mascot eat!

Jack Campbell unlocked the hut. It smelt of a clean earthern floor. Little gecko lizards squeaked from the roof. Stores and saddlery, guns and tools and branding-irons were neatly in place— with Scotland on the walls.

Pictures of men in kilts, Scottish terriers cheeky in Scottish caps, Scottish lassies and castles and sword dancers and muscular men throwing cabers. Not to mention grey-bearded hearties gloating on a hoarded thirst before consuming large quantities of a national beverage. This Australian hut in the farthest back-blocks had plenty of Scotland inside it.

"Everything is all right," said Jack Campbell with relief. "I left several rifles here but no ammunition, and the stores locked in here are all we have to depend upon for the next three months. If the natives had made a clean sweep of the home it would mean that Dave would have to start all over again."

"He's had to do it before," said Laurie.

"Yes, it's unavoidable sometimes in this country, but it hurts all the same. These little places take a lot of putting together, and when once a man gets a place started he grows attached to it."

"How did Dave come to start here?" I asked.

"Oh, he and Scotty Salmon were driven out of Karunjie, an isolated place they started in the Nor'-east Kimberley. Dave then found this country, built a hut, worked meanwhile at Fred Russ's, taking his pay part money, part cattle. Scotty Salmon got a job as cook away down at Walcott Inlet. Scotty's money helps to buy cattle. Dave in between whiles planted these peanuts—Mr Reid at Walcott Inlet coaxed him to try. Dave made his own plough and harrow by straightening out horse-shoes. He made his harness out of greenhide and any old thing at all. He's got a few head of cattle now. After the muster he'll bring them up from Fred Russ's and start a home here in earnest."

A huntsman came strolling into camp and threw down a kangaroo; the women commenced making string from its fur. Out there in the primitive, white-man Rust had made his tools out of the primitive, as these stone-age people were making excellent string from the primitive. This was a female 'roo; the fur of the male is too stiff and hairy for making pliable string.

The women rubbed the 'roo with dust so as to take the "stickiness" out of the fur which was then quickly plucked and the body taken to the cooking-fires. The fur was placed in a hole in the ground then rhythmically beaten with a light green stick until it became fluffy, the hairs frothing up together. Squatting at ease, a low-browed woman with the finger-tips of her left hand took up some of this fluffy hair and twisted part between her fingers, the rest being held in her palm. Her twisting fingers produced the point of a thread. This she placed on her right thigh and with a strong downward pressure of her right palm rolled it along her thigh when it began to spin into a thread. As she worked, with her left finger-tips she fed the fluff from her palm into the growing thread. When she wished to replenish the fluff, she stopped the thread from untwisting by holding it between her legs. When the string was about two feet long the woman held it between her legs to prevent it untwisting then took up her spinner, a thin, well-polished stick like a big knitting-needle about eighteen inches long which fitted into a hole centred in a flat stick about eight inches long.

This short flat stick I thought of as the "propeller." The woman pushed the long thin stick through the hole in the propeller and jammed there the end of the thread, just twisting it around the upper point of the shorter end of the stick. Then with her right palm she twisted the long end of the stick along her thigh. The propeller softly hummed as it spun around. She now held her left arm straight out while the cord swiftly twisted around the stick as she fed the strand, continually bringing the long stick back to her thigh again immediately it had spun to the knee. Very soon her fluff supply was wound right up to her hand. At this stage she twisted the resultant thread end around the propeller, and taking another handful of fluff, rapidly repeated the operation. When the forming cord had twisted strongly around the stick until its "wind" was quite taken up she unwound it from the stick and wound it into a ball. More hair was fed and the operation once more repeated until in a very short time a large ball of strong kangaroo thread was fashioned. To make this into strong string three thread ends were jammed into the propeller, the stick was rolled on the thigh, and a strong string immediately began forming to the soft hum of the propeller.

It is strange that the aboriginals, although they have been expert enough to have perfected an efficient method of string-making from human hair, bark and fibre of trees, and animals' fur and hair, they yet have not thought a step further and evolved a method of knitting the string into cloth. Few indeed have thought of skinning the animal and using the skin as a cloak. Nor have they thought of the bow and arrow although they are expert at making numerous types of spears and weapons for land and water and air conditions, and have displayed remarkable ingenuity and skill in that highly specialized weapon, the returning boomerang.

Late that afternoon, Laurie "held court" under the bough shed. The natives squatted in front, keenly interested. Even the dogs lay quietly. Nipper wore the slightly bored but important air of the star actor who has been through all this before. Davey was interpreter, and a particularly capable one, for this district within a very wide radius was all his country. Toby was an important man for the tribesmen. He could speak good pidgin, had been a tracker and understood white-man law, had lately travelled with these tribesmen and was familiar with recent happenings from their point of view. He was constituted their Counsel for the Defence.

The charges were explained to those concerned. Then, preliminaries over, Davey stated that Yilboo, one of Charcoal's wives, had volunteered to give evidence. She stepped forward determinedly, a peculiarly set expression marking her sullen face. Well-built and slim she looked as wild as the hills, her unwavering eyes fixed on the constable, obviously inviting his questions. She spoke quietly. She said she was present with others in a hunting party when Ungandongery (Charcoal) her husband and Coodogedogo (Nipper) made a quarrel with Burrin over Chalba, Nipper's wife. Nipper did not like Burrin, but Charcoal had no quarrel with him. Burrin had no friends; he was a very quiet man and liked to hunt by himself. When Nipper made the quarrel Charcoal backed him up. Burrin walked away. Nipper speared Burrin in the leg. Charcoal then rushed Burrin and struck him on the back. Burrin died. Charcoal and Mallumbar and others buried him under stones while she watched. Asked if she fully understood that she was a witness in which her husband was accused of complicity in murder, she nodded viciously.

Then Allboroo was called up. A short, broad-shouldered, strongly-built man, his deep-set eyes were uneasy under beetling brows. A small moustache shielded protruding lips; his puckered forehead was half-hidden under a band of kangaroo fur dyed scarlet. Amongst these pure-bred primitives he seemed peculiarly out of place; the strong dash of

Malay in his features betrayed that he was a visitor from some coastal tribe. He corroborated the woman's statement, obviously relieved when the questioning was over. Nipper was called. He stepped forward smilingly, pleased to be the centre of all eyes in a silence only broken by a crow flopping into the tree-branches above. Nipper repeated his story with gusto, adding pan-tomime action to the straight-out story of how he and Charcoal had killed Burrin.

Ungandongery alias Charcoal was then called. He stood easily erect and stepped forward smiling, a rugged son of the wild, a six-foot savage whose direct-eyed stare was not easily abashed though his deeply corrugated face, if taken unawares, assumed a scowl of animal-like harshness. He looked just what nature had made him—an alert, intelligent animal-man, capable of knocking out a living with a stone-axe. Smilingly he told the same story as his wife, pointing to his leg to indicate where Nipper had speared Burrin, thumping his back to indicate just where he had struck the wounded man. Asked why he had helped to kill Burrin he hesitated, then, prompted by Toby, said because Burrin had made trouble with Nipper's wife. Asked why he interfered in the quarrel, he said because Nipper was his friend and so he helped him to kill the man.

Charcoal, though apparently quite satisfied with himself, betrayed by a crafty smile and uneasy glances that he was not mentally happy.

Then Oomagun was charged, in that he, with Marmadu alias Donkey and probably others, had murdered Worachi at Grace's Knob. Oomagun stepped forward, a living picture of the primitive: a six-footer, his tangle of shaggy hair fell to his beard; deep ridges lined his forehead above deep-set eyes whose momentary glare belied the softening smile that almost made pleasant his big face. He yawned and showed a cavernous mouth. With those horse-like teeth that lined it I could easily understand him tearing his enemy's throat out. Charcoal was taller and of a more athletic build; but Oomagun was broader, deeper, more rugged. He was sleepily wide awake, behind his friendly "I don't know I'm sure, but what is it you require of me" attitude. His black beard was Cut so that its sides appeared to be the ends of a gigantic moustache; his upper face was shaved; across forehead and nose was painted an unusual broad band of red, apparently mixed with transparent oil. With movement it gave the peculiar ap-pearance of a shining film from which his bloodshot eyes glared out. His deep chest and limbs, like the tribesmen's, were heavily cicatrized with the scars of warrior-hood. His half-closed paws suggested the gnarled roots of a tree. Altogether,

Oomagun was not the type of man a timid human would care to meet alone in the wilds. But now he spoke softly, with a quick, fleeting smile. He denied all knowledge of Worachi's death: would volunteer no information, no suggestion; did not seem to understand what it was all about; appeared to be slightly amused, but not interested.

Davey sharply called on Oombali as witness and in fact accessory. A powerful young buck rose uneasily. In low voice translated in turn by Davey and Toby, he described how the slayer party had planned to kill Worachi; how they had suggested that he should accompany them on a kangaroo hunt; how they had then treacherously lured him from his friends. How he, Oombali, at a signal, had suddenly flung his arms around Worachi while Ooma- gun, Marmadu white feller name Donkey, and Big Paddy (not the Mount Hart Big Paddy) had speared him.

Oomagun, although confronted by Oombali, neither denied nor admitted anything. Never speaking unless spoken to, and then answering in few words or else outdoing the "no savvy" Chinese, he seldom lost his slow smile. If all aboriginals had his mental as well as physical strength, Authority would have a hectic time in first catching the wrong-doers, and then in proving anything against them. He had taken precautions, though not aware that his own little murder was known, to disappear on the instant. When he received news that the patrol had arrived at and departed from Grace's Knob he had split up his own particular little band. One half he sent towards Walcott Inlet, the remainder to double back behind the patrol and return to Grace's Knob. A shrewd manoeuvre. But he should have sent Oombali too. He had also kept with him two wild young wives and several wilder cubs. But, while ready for instant flight, he had received no warning from the tribesmen at Fred Russ's.

The prisoners were put on the chain. Not a very impressive chain! Nipper had carried it a hundred miles and not noticed it; one day he had carried a kangaroo as well. The chain is strong but light. A loop of it is placed loosely around each man's neck and the loop padlocked. There is ample room between each man to allow them to walk, drink, or do anything in comfort —except run away. They could even do that, and swiftly, but they would become entangled around a tree, or else a man would fall and bring the others on top of him. Thus linked around the neck, equal distances apart along the long chain, their arms are perfectly free. This is absolutely necessary when marching through the bush. Hands must be free to brush away branches, grass and vines, and to allow them to carry native food which, if possible, they take delight in catching on the march. When climbing hills, clambering down into steep gullies, or winding along boulder-strewn gorges or down slippery banks or across deep streams, their limbs are thus free. They must have their hands free, too, to brush away flies and mosquitoes, to eat with, and to attend to themselves in a dozen different ways. The recent regulation in other areas (since revoked), that the chain must be discarded and prisoners handcuffed instead, does not seem humane.

We were part of a wild scene that night. The tall, thin trees scraggily growing above a misty film of grass tops; shadows of native gunyahs; prisoners squatting around a tree gutturally discussing the exciting events of the day; lubras lighting a circle of little fires around them The aboriginal loves his fire: it is his friend, his company, really his home. Behind the prisoners were the black shadows of the squatting tribespeople; a dog's eyes shone balefully luminous. The flames blazed up and threw the prisoners and their tree, the gunyahs, the bush shed, into flickering relief. A dog, with a naked piccaninny staring at us over its back, stood out like a cameo where before only two green eyes were visible. Rifles on the saddles piles of spears propped up near by, swags lying around. Tribesmen, lubras, a few children and many dogs squatted around other trees thrown into relief by other flames, while thin, snaky smokes coiled whitely up. Low gutturals came from around the trees; some night heron trumpeted harshly away down the creek. Old Larry with young Dick trotting after him came with the key of the chain to report that each man was secure. Laurie gave his orders for the night and the trackers turned away to sleep near their charges— Davey with sprightly step.

"He's spied some nice young lubra among that crowd," said Laurie. "He probably knew her when he was running here as wild as they. That gay young tracker will wake up with a shovel-bladed spear between his ribs one of these days. There you are!"

A gay laugh, shrill sarcasm from older lubras, came softly from among the trees as Davey squatted down— not by the prisoners. Old Larry spread his blankets beside the ring of hairy heads that gazed quizzically up at him. Charcoal growled something in sarcastic tones that won a low laugh, but Larry stretched out on his blanket with the quiet assurance of an old campaigner. A fine old sergeant-major was Larry.

"It must be a bit lonesome at times," I remarked, "when you are out alone for months with only the blacks for company."

"Yes," answered Laurie, "especially if I've got a bad bunch on the chain and we're in country where there might be an attempt at rescue. So long as the weather holds fine though it's not bad. A man has home to look forward to after the patrol is over."

Laurie had recently married. After three or four months of this life, home and a young wife would indeed be something to look forward to.

The patrol moved off next morning with packhorses loaded with meat, for Jack Campbell had killed a bullock. A considerably enlarged patrol. The lordly prisoners wanted their wives to come to "look after them." Laurie allowed Yunga to come, she was one of Oomagun's wives with a little daughter; the other he made stay behind to care for the younger cubs. Yilboo, Charcoal's wife, apparently anxious, stepped forward wanting to come "to look after Charcoal." Laurie was pleased for she was a willing witness. Besides, she would lead us to where Burrin was buried should Nipper decide to forget. So Yilboo came along to the evident relief of the other Mrs Charcoal. We were somewhat surprised at this lubra wishing to care for Charcoal after the vicious way she had given evidence against him. It was all to be explained later on.

We d better 'name' these women," suggested Laurie as we rode away, "otherwise personalities will grow confusing. We'll call Chalba 'Mrs Nipper,' Yilboo 'Mrs Charcoal,' and Yunga 'Mrs Oomagun.' "

"That will simplify matters. Why do they call Marmadu Donkey?"

Larry says because he's got a long rounded nose that reminds them of Fred Russ's donkey."

Young Dick joined the patrol as to the manner born. No doubt as to Dick's job in later life: astride the saddle before old Larry he took the lead as if all the bush were his.

Toby strode along magnificent in Larry's coat. Yesterday he had joined the patrol with nothing in the world but his spears, his happy laugh and his poddy little son. Now he wore a coat which Larry would never own again. Doubtless he would collect other possessions as we marched on.

Seeking the body of Burrin, mules and horses plodded cheerily along with only a' stray kick now and then at some disliked animal, a vicious twist of an ear threatening what the owner would do should it get a chance. Each animal battled on about its business, tail switching at an occasional fly or tickling vine, snatching a mouthful of grass while holding to the track marked by the animal before.

The secret service had learned that several witnesses of the Worachi murder case were in the locality, hunting. So that morning, while Jack Campbell was killing, old Larry had quietly circled the empty native camp and picked up the tracks leading into the bush. He had followed the tracks of these witnesses a mile. And now, well out of sight of the camp, we turned through the bush and cut those tracks, moving easily and swiftly despite the bush and logs and grass, following up these days-old tracks as surely and almost as swiftly as the men themselves had walked. And luck came. Davey rode well ahead, lest the hunters, returning, heard the patrol. In mid-afternoon Davey appeared suddenly, silently. A lone hunter was returning. The patrol halted and formed a spearhead from which Larry and Davey rode swiftly out, wide apart. The lone hunter came striding along, right into the trap. Before he could be warned by sign language Larry and Davey were upon him. Carrying shovel-bladed spears, a human hair belt the only shield to his nakedness, he stared at the patrol in voiceless surprise. He revealed that the men inquired about were hunting in a gorge thirty miles away.

Laurie camped. To have sought those witnesses over such rough country as they were in, encumbered now as we were with prisoners and sick, would have meant time and possibly failure. There was another way. Laurie made a bargain with the *munjon* hunter. A white-feller iron tomahawk and tobacco if he would guide Davey to the men!

He agreed with amazed incredulity, his hand twitching as he stared at the tomahawk as if it represented thousands of pounds. Davey stripped off with pleasure, adorned his body with his own tribal markings in ochres and pipe-clay, put totem feathers in his hair, chose a couple of spears and disappeared into the bush with the *munjon*.

A striking metamorphosis. In less than an hour, from a civilized, smartly clothed tracker, Davey was a naked, ochre-daubed savage. And his heart shone from his eyes.

The men he sought to make contact with would be wary. Should they see a clothed aboriginal coming towards them they would either fight or vanish. But now Davey was a *munjon,* his tribal and totem markings correct, he could make personal contact. I admired him. He was venturing alone into the enemies' camp thirty miles from the protection of the patrol. And not in disguise either. As a lone tracker among them he must fearlessly convince those witnesses, if he could, to accompany him to the patrol. If wanted men were there he would probably be called upon to fight or, worse still, be treacherously killed. His daring, his bushcraft, his knowledge of native intrigue and jealousy were his weapons and hope of success. We watched him go into No White-man's Land. Ahead of us now there were no white settlers.

We had pulled off the packs apparently by one of the far upper reaches of the Hann. Rustling with pandanus palms, lined with tall white paper-barks, the sunlit pools were now splashed with shadows, the western bank a pink meadow under thick-leaved wild flowers on which horses and mules dined luxuriously. This slightly broken tableland was strewn with clumps of wild fig and messmate peculiarly uniform in size, with here and there dark forests of cypress-pine. As we rode along week after week I used to think rather glumly of the axe of man someday ringing in this wilderness. The timber throughout though comparatively thick was rarely tall except for. the beautiful paper-bark and gums that line the rivers and lagoons, the Kimberley cypress, grey box, and coolabah. But man is merciless. I would hate to see that land again should ever the ring-barker's axe and the fire-stick ravish it. And surely never was there an object lesson of the worthlessness of it all. No excuse. In this land that has never known an axe there is grass everywhere, despite the timber. If ever man slays that timber Nemesis will fall upon him; for nature has built the country in such a way that swift soil erosion will follow the first blows of the axe.

14
CHARCOAL, MY FELLOW AUTHOR

PODDY Dick adopted the patrol, intent on enjoying the time of his life: gossiping as man to man with the prisoners, toddling across to the women to supervise their cooking, sparing a word now and then to his shy girl-friend, Mrs Oomagun's daughter. The girl clung by her mother as elusive as a young wildcat, the very opposite of toddler Dick. Whenever Larry approached us Dick would come running after like a fat pup following the cook. The old tracker could give him many a tit-bit from the white men's tucker. Dick was going to be a white man's blackfellow.

"Freddy out there!" nodded Larry. "Fighting Freddy!"

"Which way he go?" inquired Laurie.

"Not sure. They think he go same way other feller man."

Laurie looked concerned.

"Freddy is a fighter," he explained, "inclined to be a renegade, but there is nothing serious known against him yet. Still, this makes me somewhat uneasy. A few months ago Freddy nearly chopped a white man to pieces with a tomahawk. The man deserved it. However, he never complained, and as I happened to know the aboriginal was in the right I took no official notice of the action. Freddy took to the bush. And now, if he has joined the men Davey has gone to meet, I'm uneasy lest he tackle Davey. He might imagine the police want him.

"What Freddy do that time he camp longa Dave Rust's?" he inquired of Larry.

"He sit down long time, plenty days, too quiet altogether. All a time he look out young lubra. One night time come. Big storm come, plenty tunder, lightning, plenty rain. Freddy grab spears, grab young girl. He run away; people altogether afraid tunder-lightning. Morning time they follow. No good: rain wash out tracks." Oh," said Laurie, "if he was only stealing a lubra it's all right. He probably is hiding from vengeance, away out in the ranges. I hope so. I don't want Davey crawling back with a spear through his ribs Well, here comes Daddy Toby with the billy. Larry, you'd better get Dick something to eat—if he can hold any more!" And he prodded the toddler on his temptingly distended belly.

Dick's father, Toby, laughed with the hearty laugh that was to help the patrol over many a mile. Singing or laughing or lending a hand with the pack-animals was all the same to Toby. With his mind on white employment, he had for two years past encouraged his baby son's education in pidgin-English. The mother had died young; father and son had been inseparable ever since.

"These white-feller names as well as the aboriginal are confusing at times," I remarked.

"Yes, theirs is a limited repertoire. There are dozens of Tobys and Paddys and Big Paddys and Tommys and Dicks and Freddys. It is easy to get confused."

"There are not many Donkeys ?"

"No. This Marmadu who is accused of complicity in the killing of Worachi is about the only one I've heard of in these parts."

That night, and during succeeding nights, old Larry was very cautious with the prisoners. Under Laurie's eyes his last job was to examine each lock that locked the chain around each man's neck, and the lock that locked the ends of the chain around their camping tree. Between every two men was a length of chain sufficient to allow both to lie at ease and coil around their fires in comfort. Larry's last job before sleep was to examine this chain and make sure that none of it was or had been in the little fire that was always smouldering at the feet of or between every two men. Night after night Laurie would awake and listen for the soft tap-tap-tap that would betray the hammering of a stone upon a heated link.

Morning broke sweetly: the cooing of doves, the companionly screech of mountain parrots, the twittering of innumerable feathered gems among the gum-blossoms, the harsher music of others at the waterhole, made the morning glorious. The lubras rubbed sleepy eyes as they sat up to put the fires together; the lordly prisoners with hoarse grunts and yawns showed wonderful teeth while stretching their limbs to the renewed fires, not deigning to arise until the lubras brought their breakfast. Little Dick pulled Larry's hair, urging him arise and cook "tucker belonga me!"

The animals still stood in sleepy-eyed contentment up to their bellies in the pink flowers across the river.

We spent a quiet day, the prisoners and witnesses gossiping and eating, idly chipping flints for spearheads. Young Dick pottered about amongst the cooking-fires, his little girl-friend following his adventures with longing eyes as he waddled about throwing reed spears at dis¬dainful birds. He installed himself as Larry's assistant with the particular job of carrying Larry's tucker to him and helping him eat it. Old Larry was very fond of youngsters, petting them at every camp we came to. As morning wore on we noticed that Charcoal was holding the dusky little crowd enthralled. Squatting around him they hung on every word.

His harshly animated face told he was rehearsing some great story. With play of limbs and fists he emphasized sentences in a rapid flow of gutturals, his frowning brow and glaring eyes undergoing expressive change as ever and anon he would throw back his head and laugh until even the distant mules listened prick-eared. But again he would crouch tensely forward hissing sentences fairly vibrating with passion. At lunch-time we asked Larry what the "big talk" was all about.

"Charcoal make him big feller corroboree all about patrol," explained Larry. "Spear him Burrin. Make him play what time pleece catch him, take him longa Derby, longa jail, longa all about!"

So Charcoal was going to dramatize his adventures on return from jail! No doubt the release of the great drama would be looked forward to by the tribes from far and near. I wished I could have understood his language and listened-in to the technique of my fellow author. He was a widely renowned playwright too, an eminence to which I have not attained.

Larry was proud that he was to be featured in a great corroboree by the most popular corroboree-maker in the Kimberley Aboriginal-land.

Later in the day there was a changed atmosphere. We noticed Allboroo and Oombali hanging their heads at some laughing, guttural remark of Oomagun's; scowling uneasily too, at a malicious sneer from Charcoal. We wondered if they were being threatened, or if the bolder spirits were planning escape. Laurie was careful not to leave the rifles or tomahawk handy, and he had the lubras and young Dick under surveillance lest they secrete a tool for the prisoners. Such vigilance was a constant necessity. Stone-age man is utterly different to the animals although he leads such an animal life; he can reason and plan cunningly and at the right moment put his plan into action.

That evening Davey and the guide returned. They had travelled eighty-five miles and looked it. In the cold of the night before they had huddled under a rock for warmth, not daring to light a fire. The men they sought had gone, travelling back in the direction of Grace's Knob. Davey had followed their tracks until certain.

"I hate having to go back on my tracks," said Laurie. "But I'll have to later on. After we find Burrin's body I must return and try to locate Worachi's at Grace's Knob, and catch Donkey and Company as well. But I think I'll leave that job until towards the end of the trip. They will have settled down by then, and as the patrol will meanwhile be out of their country they will think we're on the homeward route. But I'll swing round on a wide circle and surprise them, if possible."

While Davey and the guide were ravenously eating we smoked and yarned.

"Your prisoners will have seen a lot of country by the time the patrol is ended."

"Yes. They will be heroes and great travellers when they return to their own country. Charcoal will have absorbed plenty of material for his big corroboree. Every action of yours is being noted for inclusion in that forthcoming production. Mine too. We would get a few shocks if we could only witness it. The best among them are extremely good at mimicking any little habit of a man. But we'll see our fun when the *munjons* among this crowd first see Derby. That township is going to be the wonder of their lives. And if they get sentenced to Broome jail, they'll be speechless when they step aboard ship. It will be a trip to Wonderland for them. No wonder they throw out their chests when they return."

"I suppose funny incidents happen sometimes."

"Well, last patrol I had a crowd of *munjons* on the chain when we hit the Kimberley Downs road. The trackers secured them around a tree while we boiled the billy. A motor-truck hummed along. They jumped up with eyes big as walnuts then howled like monkeys as they tried to swarm up into the branches. After the truck rushed past they clung there panting, staring after the dust. When we arrived at Farrington's near Derby another truck appeared towing a trailer. They couldn't keep their eyes off it; thought the trailer was a baby motor and asked whether the truck was its father or mother. At Jack Knopp's store a car was being filled with petrol, and they thought the machine was enjoying a drink. They wanted to know whether it ate grass or trees or bullocks.

"Once, from away south of the Fitzroy I brought a desert native in. He was a splendid horseman. At the police station an old bike caught his eye—fairly dazzled him. I explained it was a white man's 'horse machine,' pedalled it around the yard a few times then urged him to mount it. He grasped the handles in an iron grip, put one foot on the pedal 'stirrup' as he would mount an outlaw horse then leapt into the saddle. He came an awful crash. But he hung to the handle bars as he would to the reins of an outlaw horse, then burst out laughing. He climbed from under and mounted again. At each attempt he leapt quicker into the saddle to get seated be¬fore it could 'buck him off.'

"I offered to hold it for him. He mounted with a jump that all but pulled me over. I wheeled him around the yard until he grasped the idea then wheeled him out on to the road, got a run on and gave him a final push down slope. Away he careered with his knees gripping the framework, his feet pressed well down into the 'stirrups,' his face one big surprise. Swaying along to right and left he tugged desperately at the handle bars until he circled in a lovely wallop. He lay there panting, then nearly laughed the place down as he scrambled up to mount again. After that I couldn't get him off the old machine. He rode it to pieces. When he finished his time, I mended the machine and he pedalled it back to the desert."

"Our wild man Oomagun has a treat in store."

Laurie laughed.

"So have all of them except the sophisticated Nipper. In a blase fashion he's been telling them all about the wonders they'll see. They'll probably look forward to the idea until we get to within a hundred miles of Derby. And then with every step they'll be wishing they were taking three steps back."

"The drag of their own country calling them back?"

"Yes. The wild aboriginal loves his tribal country passionately."

We were away just after sunrise, the pack-animals so fat we had to lengthen the girths, Davey riding in the lead seeking a kangaroo, with Toby striding behind. Then Oomagun, Nipper, Charcoal, Oombali and Allboroo with the leper and sick woman following. Then the pack-animals, old Larry riding behind with young Dick happy on the saddle before him. Then Mrs Nipper, tall and sturdy and pleasant humoured, followed by the definite Mrs Charcoal, and Mrs Oomagun the morose one, with her stubborn little girl straddled around her neck. Laurie and I brought up the rear with the untamed bush all around, the range crests hazy, and in our ears the crackle of bracken rarely trodden by hoofs of horse or mule.

"The troops look well breaking camp," I remarked.

"Now that's an idea," exclaimed Laurie. "To save confusion we'll call them 'the troops.' The wives of the prisoners will be 'the shock troops.' Notice how they'll stand out in liveliness after we've gained more sick recruits... It will be an easier way of distinguishing between trackers, prisoners, witnesses, sick, and wives of prisoners. Not to mention acquisitions like Toby and Dick, and future possible guides and all the rest that come and go in the travelling of a long patrol." And the classification *did* avoid a momentary confusion as the patrol developed.

The women carried their men's weapons, with family belongings in grass dilly-bags; the men carried nothing, except a hunk of meat Laurie had ordered each to carry. Even though on the chain, the aboriginal keeps an unbreakable control over his women, should they be within sight. Mrs Nipper, throughout, proved the most willing.

Laurie had constantly to be on the look out lest the other women thrust more than her share upon her. Not to be outdone by Mrs Nipper, both Mrs Oomagun and Mrs Charcoal had commandeered a dress from lubras whose husbands were employed by Dave Rust. Mrs Charcoal's dress, a vivid scarlet, we immediately christened the Flame. But on the first day out from Rust's the shock troops decided to disdain the conventions; each took her dress off and never put it on again until we came within sight of a settler's home. The dresses impeded travel. The Amazons certainly looked more natural without them, swinging along in fine style with the upright, tireless walk of the aboriginal, alert as they travelled, all eyes and ears. As we climbed up to the flat top of a tableland the soil became sandy and poor, the vegetation thinning into smaller, scrubbier trees. Towards midday we were winding over acres of bare sandstone, huge blocks upright in grotesque shapes: ragged stone pillars, isolated cairns. Near the lines of the McCann Ranges the country was almost weird; we wound along miniature valleys walled with low lanes of rock frescoed into the strangest shapes, and. surmounted by peaky little hill-tops. Some walls broke in upon themselves admitting glimpses of tiny glens, and an occasional cave peeping from behind the trees. Sometimes we moved down a green avenue of spring-fed reeds sentinelled by pinnacles of rock, the animal's hoofs crackling upon the fallen leaves of hardy rock palms.

To the sharp crack of the rifle the prisoners exclaimed "Wah!" and pressed forward eagerly, the shock troops speeding ahead and soon shrilling back glad tidings. We halted by a fairy-like pool where the proud Davey stood beside a wopper 'roo. The troops got to work with surprising speed, chattering volubly as they scraped out a hole in the sand while the lubras lit a big fire. Nipper picked up a flint and with one glancing blow against a stone had a knife. Though the aboriginal is the most primitive of existing peoples he can pick up a stone, chip it, and immediately has a tool or knife. They filled the hole with coals, ripped the 'roo open and sought eagerly for fat, then threw the unskinned animal in the pit, heaped over it coals and ashes then sand on top. Within twenty minutes they were wolfing the steaming, practically raw meat. They could have devoured three other 'roos with ease.

15
BURRIN'S SPIRIT WALKS

CLIMBING up over a divide the patrol crossed several head-branches of the Drysdale, travelling among a tangle of ranges from which head numerous rivers. Extraordinarily rough and broken country with Mount Hann looming near. From this main watershed the Drysdale, Mitchell, Carson, and King Edward flow north; the Prince Regent, Glenelg, Sale, Moran, and Roe vanish west towards the Indian Ocean; the Isdell, Chamley, Adcock, and Hann disappear down the gorges south-west to the coast. The beginnings of all these rivers are mere tinkling streams rising from mountain spring or palm-clad glen. It is interesting to know a river: to see its birth from a trickling spring; to clamber down its growing course and hear the creeks gurgling in to swell it; to ride its twisting, falling, louder-growing length until down on the flat country it becomes a river. Interesting still to follow its meanderings and note its tributaries flowing in; and finally to gaze on the broad stream rolling to the sea.

Towards sundown we were clambering down a stony divide all quaint castles and baby gorges. The setting sun reflected on Mrs Charcoal's coppery skin as she marched confidently on. Horses and mules gripping for a footing on the bare surface raised a film of dust and this, drifting up amongst the toiling animals and naked, copper-black figures of the troops with their long weapons outlined above the horses' heads was startlingly reminiscent of an eastern band of spearmen.

That night's camp was beautiful under moonlight, the fire-lit trunks of white gums plainly scarred where stone axe and latterly iron had robbed the bark for coolamon or water bucket. The listening quietness, the fantastic silhouettes outlined against a starry sky, breathed of the primitive. Hard to remember that elsewhere in the world were cities and civilization. A mopoke croaked hoarsely, his mate hooted in distant answer. All around was that listening, faintly whispering breath of the bush holding court on a beautiful night. Old Larry, murmuring some age-old lullaby, was bending over the prisoners, making sure that the chain locks were secure. Charcoal joined in with the lullaby, holding his head aside docile as a lamb while Larry ran practised fingers around the chain. And then, the whites of his eyes gleaming, Charcoal looked up into Larry s face and talked and laughed.

Larry came stamping back to Laurie, his gnarled old face comically indignant. Charcoal with gusto had assured him that we would find the body of Burrin but we would never find the body of Worachi. Oomagun and Donkey and Big Paddy had killed him all right but his bones had since been carried away by his people to be "cried over." Nipper had grinned, Oomagun had grunted, Oombali had smiled, Allboroo had looked sly. But all had grinned and been pleased at the telling of this news.

"Oh well," said Laurie "they may enjoy their little joke, but I shall find where Worachi was buried all the game. He laughs best who laughs last, even in Aboriginal-land. I'll find Burrin's body too; Mrs Charcoal will see to that, should Nipper try any forgetful business. There's a mystery in her eagerness that everything should be proved against Charcoal. She's spurring Davey constantly, whispering him details every chance she gets, doing all she possibly can to leave Charcoal no loophole for escape."

"She cannot love hubby."

"Emphatically no. Probably she's got another lover out in the bush. But I suspect there is some deeper reason. I would not give much for her life when Charcoal returns to the bush."

Mrs Charcoal's feeling towards her husband appeared to be one of grim retaliation. It could not have been due to incompatability of age. Amongst wild aboriginals the old men by tribal right possess all the young girls; an old greybeard may own five, seven, or even more young wives while the young men may have none at all—or a few old ones. But in this case the prisoners were in the prime of life. They had taken their young wives by the law of might and held them so. There is always trouble among aboriginal tribes over woman-stealing, the young men urging the young women to run away from the old men. When it comes to a fight an old warrior will more often than not cripple a young one, and speedily. But the men we had were exceptional. Even little Nipper, small as he was, gloried in a number of kills to his credit. No old warrior, however skilful, cares to stand up face to face with men such as these, for he probably has to stand alone.

They would accept none of the old women for wives. Perhaps Charcoal had taken Mrs Charcoal from a husband she liked better. There could be a number of explanations.

As to the prisoners chuckling among themselves day by day that the constable would never find Worachi's bones, that was explained by their usual tribal customs.

When a man dies, the aboriginal in this district buries him among the rocks or up in a tree, according to that particular tribe's custom. Later, his near relatives make a pilgrimage, collect his bones and after a series of ceremonies and in the course of time carry them back to "his waters" — the river or waterhole by which he was born. The bones are "cried over" and finally buried there. The ceremonies and time-period all depend on the age and initiation degrees of the man, and his unit value to the tribe. The skeletons of some men, according to totem and custom, group, horde or tribe, locality of birth and degree in initiation, are finally laid out on ledges in sacred caves, probably encased in a roll of paper-bark red ochred.

In the small hours, I awakened to stare into Laurie's warning face A deathly silence, the tracery of leaves above distinct and moveless. Then softly, "tap-tap." Silence. "Tap-tap-tap." Silence. Slowly we sat up. The trackers were sleeping heavily. All was night shadows. Around the prisoners' tree was blackness, accentuated by the red glow of one dying fire. We jumped up and hurried across. But the women lay huddled around their own tree; deep breaths of sleep murmured in the darkness. The big body of Charcoal lay sprawled across the head and cicatrized shoulders of Oomagun. This looked suspicious. Laurie hastily kicked the coals together, threw on dry grass and called the trackers. The fires blazed up lighting the camp in high relief, the eyes of the huddled women gleaming. The chain was examined; it seemed perfect.

Systematically old Larry was rubbing it link by link. Suddenly he exclaimed. He. had rubbed dust and ashes from a link and it shone brightly, a brightness caused by steady blow following blow. Oomagun blinked; Charcoal stared interestedly; Nipper was all eyes; Oombali blinked uncomfortably. Allboroo was scratching his foot. The bright link was near Oomagun's neck just where it would be hardest to detect by day.

Each man was closely examined. The trackers ran expert fingers through the tangled hair lest a stolen file should have been secreted at Dave Rust's. They searched the human hair belts; carefully searched the earth where the prisoners had been lying; raked the ashes of the fires; dug into the ground where the bodies had been sprawling. But no file or ironwork or stone was found. It was a stone tapping the link resting upon another stone that we had heard. While Charcoal was doing the tapping the others, women and all, had been glaring across at us. They had seen our shadows rise and the stones had been thrown out into the darkness.

Laurie had them removed to another tree lest the stones be secreted amongst the grass. For the circle of men can draw the chain close to the tree then worm in against one another while stretching out in line. Thus the end man's body is some yards distant from the tree, his outstretched legs are farther; he actually reaches a surprising distance from the tree, and his monkey-like toes can scratch around and pick up anything within a wide circle, the circumference of which is yards out from the tree.

Constant water wears away a stone. Constant tapping night after night wears through an iron link immeasurably faster than that, especially if they rake a few coals from their fire, lay the link across it and shield the coals with their bodies while one man blows with his mouth as a bellows, occasionally adding a charcoal to replenish what is actually a forge. Thus, if the patrol officer relaxes vigilance for a single night they will, given opportunity and all else is favourable, cut through a chain in less than the night.

Modern man may forge links of steel but stone-age man can gnaw through fetters and laughingly glide away.

As the patrol advanced, particularly when more prisoners and sick were added, unceasing vigilance became necessary. The fire-arms were always secured lest one of the sick people, or perhaps little Dick or the little girl, should come snaking through the grass and take the tomahawk or a fire-arm or both to the prisoners. Their spears were easier handled. Laurie disliked disarming the sick; they clung miserably to their weapons as a woman might cling to her wedding-ring. The spears were lashed securely in bundles, after which they were always stowed between Laurie and me at night, with pack gear piled upon them in such a way as to make it impossible to snatch them. A stealthy attempt to remove a bundle would have awakened us immediately. The free people were the danger— the sick and witnesses and women urged by the prisoners. It was the patient awaiting some propitious occasion— an unguarded moment or a time of great physical weariness when a concerted attack upon the fire-arms might be made—that made us uneasy.

One night this was attempted. It was planned that the sick men were to crawl over and simultaneously seize the fire-arms and bash us with them while the women flung themselves upon the trackers. The attempt failed.

Next day we rode down a wild creek that by the map was one of the headwaters of the Prince Regent River. But for every range marked on the map we could see five others. We rode up a valley walled by red precipices on which clung grey-green trees, their gnarled branches defying space and wind. Up by the rim of the precipices, outlined by the blue sky, a black cockatoo flew heavily, occasionally voicing a harsh trumpet-like call that thrilled with its loneliness. A primitive setting this valley for the march of its wild sons: the sun kissing their muscled bodies, their upright walk and carriage unexcelled by any athletes in the world; their eyes roaming incessantly as they marched steadily on; their ears hearing things unnoticed by us. And behind them marched their wild wives: Oomagun's wife with her cub clinging to her shoulders and hair; Nipper's wife striding along like an Amazon in dull bronze; Charcoal's wife with a fiercely set expression treading cat-like steadily ahead to show us the body of the man her husband had helped slay; Chalba, now suddenly springing aside to chase a scuttling *bungarra*, unconcerned that soon again she would see the scene of the killing and gaze upon the body of her lover.

They were utterly unconscious of the tragedy of it all the tragedy of their self-practised fast declining birth-rate, of disease; the tragedy of intrigues and superstition and killings that is constantly depleting the little man-power they have left. All over Australia wherever a few aboriginals are collected together the same law applies: the hereditary lust to kill in accordance with tribal laws and superstition, or sheer lust killing whenever opportunity and inclination occur. So will pass out the last of the stone-age men. We halted to examine a great cave in a red cliff-face that towered six hundred feet. High up, it had been a lookout place of primitive man for centuries. Its walls were ornamented with crude ochred drawings of men and crocodiles and fishes, devils and birds and snakes. On the floor among broken spear-hafts were stone axe-heads still with the hafts bound on with resin and kangaroo sinew where they had recently been discarded for roughly fashioned axes of iron. By the ashes of fires were water coolamons beside heaps of chips of flint and quartzite where tomahawk and spear-head had been made. The grinding stones lay there, on which, and by continuous labour with the aid of sand and water and patience, had been ground to a blade edge odd chunks of iron that had been secured from station blacks working for far distant settlers.

Next morning early we cut the fresh tracks of a small hunting party. Though quite fresh, dingoes and wind sweeping the grass had quite obliterated the tracks to our eyes. But the trackers followed easily with only a glance now and then over the horses' necks. We heard chopping and came on the hunters unexpectedly, in a thicket of messmate and palm. They were cutting bark for water buckets. A wild little lo with emu plumes in their clay-daubed hair, human hair belts girdling their waists, they stared at the patrol in astonishment though answering the swift gutturals of Nipper and Charcoal. One young girl looked actually pretty in her wild amazement.

The bark water buckets of these tribes are very well made, and rarely seen elsewhere in Australia. Of woolly butt, but preferably of thick and pliable paper-bark, a circular piece is cut for the bottom, a longer piece is bent over into a cylinder and stitched strongly together with split cane, the holes being made by a bone awl. The seams are made watertight and strong with resin from trees. The rim is strengthened by resin and a stitching of cane. The handle may be of baobab-fibre string, cane, or human hair. Artists among them ochre the outside with paintings of the tracks of animals.

Nipper led us where we would never have ridden our-selves. A tortuous, winding climb into a bald land with vast patches of sun-baked stone, sandstone knobs and pates of what once were hills rising like gigantic an-beds. Clumps of stunted timber with dull grey leaves often prickled were draped with creepers in sombre flower. Drab patches of scrub were occasionally intersected by shallow waterholes fringed with intensely green water-grass and lined with white gums. The only bird life was an occasional brown bird, elusive and shy. On the bare rock patches the horses' hoofs rang like castanets. We expected to ride out on a precipice edge any moment. Occasionally there was a distant glimpse of the Synnott and Edkins Ranges under a brilliant sky. The guides twisted and turned all day, dodging the sharp rock patches and prickly bush, instinctively guided by the height and shape and colour of growths on the ground ahead. Thus the reason why in rough country an aboriginal track rarely runs straight ahead—the bare-footed man naturally picks the way easiest to his feet. Near sundown we reached the edge of the tableland which fell away in sloping terraces of rock. Away below was a dark line of river trees.

The mules and horses climbed down there just as intent on the job as the men, with necks outstretched examining the stepping-places from ledge down to ledge before trusting their weight upon it, walking farther along a ledge to seek a surer place when doubtful of the step before. The lop-eared rogues among the mules looked comically cunning when it came to caring for their own hoofs and skins.

The sun had set when we reached the river and camped exactly where the trouble had occurred twelve months before. Murder will out! That saying holds good even when the murder is committed out in the wilds by primitive man. This was an old hunting-camp; broken spear- hafts were lying about among old stone axe-heads and knives.

That night, the troops gossiped low toned and seriously, no laugh or joke or chant of song. Even Toby's rollicking laugh was missing and his good-humoured stories that always brought laughter. I thought they were planning on what they should say on the morrow. Not so. Even young Dick was quiet, and Larry and Davey. When Laurie asked them why, they replied in low tones that the spirit of Burrin was walking about.

And that was why Davey had not been able to shoot a kangaroo. The spirit of Burrin had walked before him and frightened the kangaroos away!

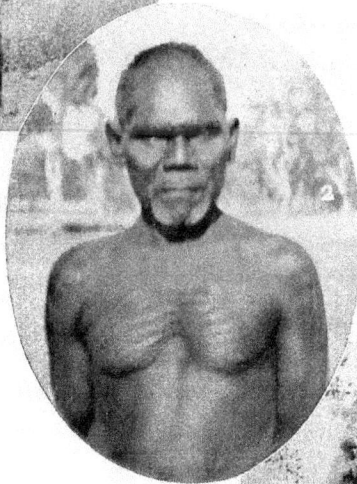

MEN OF CHAROO—BUT LEPERS

15
IN AGE-OLD COUNTRY

WE awoke at dawn. The trackers were crouched over their fire.

"Wha's matter?" inquired Laurie sleepily.

"Burrin!" mumbled Larry.

"What name?"

"Burrin try choke me last night, he nearly get me too! Steal my tobacco. Steal Davey's too."

"You've lost it," assured Laurie. "Look about!"

But nothing would convince them. Larry had awakened with phantom fingers at his throat.

"Put the billy on," ordered Laurie, "then look all about tracks. See if sick people stole your tobacco in the night."

They did so. Their faces plainly told they were going to find no tracks.

The morose trackers ate an uneasy breakfast. The troops ate silently, Charcoal with a sneering whisper at the white men's dumbness in not understanding spirit life.

After breakfast, Nipper supervised the pantomime that portrayed the last act in Burrin's life.

The natives sat in a semicircle around the fire, then the curtain rose. The man acting Burrin, as if sensing his time had come, sprang to his feet and raced away. Nipper leapt up imitating the throwing of a spear. As the man fell Charcoal rushed at him to strike him on the back. They acted the incident in detail, taking keen interest in explaining so that we might fully understand. Mrs Charcoal interrupted to add a detail apparently over-looked. Her eyes glared at Laurie's face, her ears caught every word. Charcoal sneered covertly, showing his teeth. Mrs Charcoal will not last long when Charcoal returns from jail. Throughout the proceedings Mrs Nipper acted her part well and was deeply interested though caring nothing as to the ultimate result. Mrs Oomagun was bored.

Then they guided us up among some sandstone ledges and pointed to a few loosely laid stones, a gnarled tree growing beside them. They pulled away the stones. Below was a natural grave, a gutter between solid rock. So effective, so simple, a troop could have ridden over the spot and not known. Toby bent down into the ledge and with Larry pulled away the rotted bark. The chocolate-yellow skeleton of Burrin grinned up. The tribesmen looked on, wondering at all this trouble over a dead man.

The lubras had squatted a little way off among the rocks except Mrs Charcoal who crept up and perched herself, a black Nemesis, upon a boulder from which she could stare down over the men's heads. It suddenly came out now that Burrin was her brother. He had been a kind brother, much kinder than Charcoal had been a husband. And she swore that Nipper and Charcoal had been seeking an excuse to kill him for a long time.

For all their inborn superstition, Larry and Toby handled that dead thing as if it was a box of nothings, scooping out the bones by hand. As they spread the thing out on the flat rock to make sure every bone was there the others looked on with interest—no sign of dread or horror. Charcoal's wife stared alternately at it and us. I wondered if a white girl could thus stare at the skeleton of a loved brother.

It was strange, standing there, to think that here where no white man that the patrol knew of had been before, some primitive men should stage a murder, and that twelve month later the White Law should reach out, catch the two killers, their wives and several witnesses, and actually locate the skeleton of the murdered man.

That skeleton had to be taken to Derby. And thus for the first time the killers were confounded. Larry raked it into a bag; Charcoal was ordered to carry it. He stared in consternation, then stared at Oomagun. Nipper stood speechless for once; the others gaped.

Sharply, Laurie ordered Charcoal to carry the bag. Reluctantly he obeyed. The patrol marched back towards camp.

To the aboriginal, to kill a man is one thing. To carry his bones is quite another, because the spirit is maliciously vengeful against the human who is carrying his bones away.

As we walked off, Larry and Toby were hurriedly rolling the stones back into the grave. This was in the hope of deceiving the spirits of Burrin's father and mother so that when they came they might still think the bones of their son were down below, otherwise they would join him in dogging the patrol and add their vengeful spite to his.

The spirit of the Australian aboriginal does not rest until his bones have been buried beside his waters.

We saddled up and marched away. Laurie was going to ride straight bush towards Walcott Inlet away across on the coast, his next call of inquiry. Donkey and the tribesmen at Grace's Knob who had helped Oomagun kill Worachi would now be expecting the return of the patrol. But the patrol would pay them a surprise visit on the return trip six weeks or more hence. To a joyous carolling of butcher-birds we rode up this branch of the Charnley, if Charnley it was. Still over wild country, the home of wild men once considerably more numerous than now. Continually we rode over old camps littered with fragments of stone weapons and tools, the rocks scored by the campfires of centuries. Occasionally a cave or deep, over-hanging ledge bore evidence of families and groups having used it as a wet season cave. Or it might be a sacred cave with primitive drawings and a musty skeleton here and there, bundles of bones, or a sun-dried child wrapped up in ochred fibres till it looked like a mummy package.

We camped early, curious as to a waterfall murmuring somewhere near by. Besides, Laurie wished to send Davey after a Too; he had not got one all day and the troops were ravenous for meat. This was Davey's country, too Quite near here he was born; he had been riding all day as if years were lifted from his age. He was continually pointing out to Larry pages in this history book of his tribe; every landmark being steeped deeply in memorable incident or m traditional lore. The contours of his tribal country is the aboriginal's everlasting history book But Davey did not get a Too. Instead, he returned to camp at sundown with a river crocodile. This was immediately thrown on the cooking-fire together with a few tree-climbing rats the women had caught in hollow trees. For the rest, Laurie fed the troops from the reserve stores in the pack-bags.

Gloom was in the air; poddy Dick was dumb. The troops crouched around very small fires; but ours lit up the white paper-barks and turned the messmate trunks into bronze. At the rustle of a bandicoot we noticed the upraised gleam of eyes around the fires. Mrs Oomagun's daughter crouched quiet as a little black mouse. Laurie called Larry and Davey.

"Why all man so quiet?" he asked.

"*Ogilla!* Debil-debil."

"Spirit man belonga bone?"

"Oo ai. He follow all a time. He here now! Last night Charcoal hear him cry for bone belonga him!"

Larry's voice hushed, his eyes rolled. Davey stood there, his eyes staring above parted lips that could not form the words to convince us of the spirit's presence. Old Larry had been with the police all his life, he was familiar with the life of white towns, had grown grey among the whites. But at one whispered touch of the supernatural he was right back in the primitive. Speaking faster in hoarse undertones he assured us the spirit had followed us—was here now, the spirits of the dead man's relatives too. That spirit would follow us all the way to Derby.

Davey then swore he had seen the spirit's track.

"Spirit no more makem track!" protested Laurie.

"Oo ai!" assured Davey earnestly, "all a same man!" In grim earnestness he explained that a spirit can make a track just like a man if it wishes to impress on men that it is taking a material interest in their doings.

Davey knew every track of man and woman in this country—it was his country. And the spirit track was the track of Burrin! He had hunted with Burrin; had roamed this very bush with him. He knew Burrin's track The crouching natives were listening intently. A mopoke croaked hoarsely; the eyes of an owl shone from a dead limb; the murmuring of the waterfall came plainly now.

"Suppose Jack take bones longa Syd-nee?" inquired Laurie.

Their eyes nearly leapt from their heads. Both gesticulated at once. Hoarsely they emphasized that the spirit would certainly follow me to Syd-nee. He would follow his bones everywhere.

While under this superstitious spell, they told us more of their spirit beliefs than a man could have learned in years amongst them. Ordinarily, old Larry would have laughed off any question, or given a misleading or non-committal reply, or simply expressed interest himself and asked a question in camouflage that the subject was new to him. Probably he would have laughed or shrugged contemptuous disbelief as sophisticated aboriginals generally do when questioned on their spiritual beliefs by white men. But for the time being these two were primitives in Stone-age Land with tongues loosened by the dread certainty of spirits actually present; and they could express their convictions in quite good English and translate their thoughts understandably.

Their beliefs were practically identical with aboriginal beliefs throughout the continent. The aboriginal is a confirmed spiritualist, and various beliefs of his of life after death seem reasonable. I am not alluding to the childish stories with which he will amuse any inquisitive white man, but to his deeper beliefs, those which fringe closely on his secret or sacred life. Although a spiritualist, his belief is tinctured with metempsychosis (the transmigration of souls) in that he believes, under certain circumstances and conditions, that the soul of a man can and does come back to earth and lives earth-life over again in a new baby body, or even as a bird or animal.

Next morning Laurie ordered Davey to take the rifle and keep walking until he did get a 'roo. Meanwhile we would find the waterfall. Davey called it Bulwallingarra, and casually mentioned that no white man had been here before.

However, we had travelled the continent too widely to believe that. An examination of the official map, though, showed that none of the few explorers' routes crossed this particular comer. Hann's 1898 track missed it as did Brockman's route in 1901; Bradshaw's route and Allan's were nowhere near, nor any track of Dr F. M. House. Crossland's expedition of 1905 did not touch this particular area nor did Price-Conigrave's 1912 expedition. Easton's Kimberley Exploration Expedition of 1921 crossed the Charnley farther towards the coast. No explorer, surveyor, forester, or police routes were marked as crossing this particular little area.

"I've done twenty thousand miles of patrolling in the Kimberleys," said Laurie poring over the map. "But this little corner is new to me. I know every man over the range, but I haven't heard one describe this particular spot. They are cattlemen and would certainly have followed up this river to find the extent of these well-grassed flats. They would have heard that waterfall away in there and would have turned off and surveyed it. A cattleman looks for water as surely as a prospector looks for gold. And there has not been a prospector in this country that I know of. If there had been he would have made for that waterfall, to test the river as a possible sluicing proposition. But prospectors are practically unknown over the range. I know all the half-dozen wandering dingo-poisoners intimately, but they have never mentioned this locality."

He studied the map musingly:

I had always thought the Leopold expedition of Pollett and McClay and Jones went straight through here in 1921 before McClay was drowned. Larry," he called, "which way you go with Constable Pollett?" '
Larry pointed away behind us:

"Cross river long way farther down. No white man been here before."

Davey was born in this area. The prisoners shook their heads when we asked them what white men had been here before. "It's just possible this little corner may have been missed," Laurie added. "Anyway, the possibility will make the walk still more interesting."

It did. There was no such thing as exploring about it of course. The last big exploring in Australia, except Donald Mackay's aerial explorations, was probably finished before I was born. But the probability of being the first to step upon even an acre of virgin soil always gives a little thrill. Larry was left in charge of the prisoners.

Blocked by a mass of trees and boulders we stepped from rock to rock up a low hill-side, and presently saw a long stretch of slippery rock gleaming under the sun, ribbons of water racing down it. A bee-eater in a shimmer of gold, green and bronze sped by, his two long tail-quills holding our interest as he sped above the rock that, like a slippery road one hundred yards wide, was a rapid and not a waterfall. It ran between black, pink, and grey walls ten feet high. At the head of this rapid was a large circular pool ringed with black rock as if cut by the chisels of pygmy giants. A sprinkle of sand was marked by tracks of freshwater crocodiles, the only sand along the whole quarter-mile length of glistening rock. Above this first pool gleamed a' further long slope over which water raced, then another walled pool, emerald clear, with fishes swimming in it. Above it was still another slope across the top of which ran a broad causeway of steel-hard rock. Ten feet below this the water came spurting out of a tunnel where the fury of countless wet seasons had torn away the softer rock. Beyond a further pool the long slope of smoothed rock rose rapidly to its summit silhouetted by a fringe of green pandanus palm. This was the lip of a low tableland. And here gleamed the top pool where, from around an island of rocks and palms, two green streams swept out on to the bare rock to join in a swift race down into the Chamley.

Turning around and looking down this we saw that the series of falls ran approximately from north-east to south-west. Down that quarter-mile slope the vertical fall was probably not much more than one hundred feet, its centre sparkling under a thin ribbon of water. But what a magnificent sight it must be in a heavy wet season with a raging fury of water tearing down there. We could see flood-marks twenty feet high. Such a volume would be overwhelming, roaring down that quarter-mile slope with its hundred-foot fall. This once great torrent was now withered and old. It had been a mighty stream in ages past when these hills were mountains. The dwarf trees on the summit, the prickly scrub, the weathered sandstones, the old-time plants like the tufts of coarse spinifex grasses and pandanus palms, were the grey hairs in this very, very old land.

17

CHAROO

DAVEY returned without a kangaroo, his face sullenly intimating that he was not going to get one. Burrin's spirit still stalked by his side, hunting the kangaroos away. We saddled up and rode on, climbing along the course of the main stream towards its head and leaving the murmuring water chute to our right. The river growth was almost a jungle flanked by the sere grey of forest hills.

Presently Davey began shooting up into the trees black with massed flying foxes. Their screeches heralded excited talk from the hurrying troops, for flying fox is a delicacy. The densely-foliaged trees hedged a sombre pool, deep and quiet. As the slain foxes dropped into the water the snouts of river crocodiles popped up and devoured them. Mrs Nipper plunged in with Toby diving at her heels, while the others kept lustily shouting and splashing. Swimming and twisting with not a second's pause or movement in the same place the swimmers threw out fox after fox, often from before the snapping snouts of the crocodiles. Laurie and I and the trackers blazed away, for the screeching foxes never entirely left the resting trees but clung to one another like bunches of grapes. Soon the little river crocodiles came too fiercely, forcing Chalba and Toby to leap up the bank as if devils were after them, An hour later, Laurie spied a crocodile while riding past a lily-fringed lagoon. The patrol halted, for this lagoon was shallow, its edges green with reeds. The pack-animals immediately turned aside to munch the grass. Each riding animal then gazed around, obviously inviting its riders to dismount and give it a chance.

The men in line stepped into the shallow end and com-menced cautiously wading up the lagoon, peering as they stepped, arms hanging loose like baboons ready to grab. Toby jumped in with a crocodile spear, Davey and Larry watched from opposite banks with rifles ready, Laurie sat his horse watching for the first sign of the crocodile. The women waded on the flanks of the men. Then the two children plunged in, all hands laughing and chiacking each other as to whose fingers or toes would feel the first bite. They had waded half-way up the pool when Oomagun yelled and plunged down his arm. But the crocodile shot away then twisted with a tail splash and slipped back between the men. They turned, eyes agleam, bending with finger-tips touching the water as they waded cautiously back. Then Toby jabbed with his spear, but the hide was too tough. There was a glimpse of yellow and black body, splash of tail, and the crocodile had wheeled and torpedoed back up the pool. They turned again. Then Mrs Charcoal dived down her arm and with a delighted yell held up a squirming tortoise. Once again Oomagun located the crocodile but failed to grab its tail as it slithered under a stone.

Laurie called warningly, as a wisp of yellow water-snake slithered into the water. It remained stationary on the surface, staring at the men in midstream. They yabbered excitedly and edged towards the bank. The snake charged straight at them, and those six strong men plunged madly for the bank. It was a surprisingly courageous snake and meant business as it sped straight out over the water. Men and snake reached the bank simultaneously; the snake slithered up the bank and disappeared. If the men had not splashed sideways out of its path it would have tackled the lot of them.

What a roar of laughter! The others out in the pool and the women and youngsters shrieked in delight. Unlike most water-snakes, this was of a deadly variety. If bitten by it a man would live only a few minutes. All returned for the crocodile, but it had seized its opportunity and hidden somewhere in the reeds. Practically crawling now, they felt their way along with arms under water, Oombali and Allboroo a bit starey-eyed at the chance of their hands being gripped by needle teeth. Oomagun and Charcoal were laughing in delight, the lubras as they came into deeper water splashing and diving, Mrs Oomagun' shrilling triumphantly as she too held aloft a tortoise. Then Nipper, who was ferreting under water like a woolly dog, suddenly yelled like a big man and jerked up a water-goanna, swinging it around his head until he could swing it against a tree. Water-goannas are quick at using their sharp teeth.

We camped soon afterwards by a palm-lined lagoon into which all hands hurried seeking water rats and tortoises and lily-seeds. Davey tried again until after sunset for a 'roo. He got one shot, missed, and returned glumly to camp. The troops shrugged. The spirit of Burrin was still following us, still hunting the 'roos away.

Next day we alternately crossed basalt flats and low sandstone ridges. Mrs Nipper dived into the grass the tops of which rustled ahead of her as she chased a frill-necked lizard. Catching its tail just as it leapt for a tree she bashed it against the tree and rejoined us, laughing. Toby laughed in sympathy; it had been some days since the patrol had heard his boisterous laugh and joke. Then Davey shot a 'roo, a wopper. Instant delight spread through the patrol — the hoodoo was off! Eyes gleamed, teeth flashed in hearty laughter to a triumphant hunting lilt from Toby, joined by the deep bass of .Charcoal and Oomagun. This was the boundary of Burrin's country. His spirit could not affect material things materially past here, though it could still follow us—anywhere.

Laurie halted and allowed the meat-hungry people to roast their 'roo. Young Dick wolfed that singed flesh as if he had not recently gorged a civilized breakfast from our pack-bags. Charcoal's and Oomagun's wonderful teeth crunched even the bones, cracking the larger ones for marrow. Their teeth seem made of living steel. A big 'roo among all those people was merely an appetiser.

Very soon we were ascending into harsher country following the windings of the trackers as they climbed little stony ridges each with its connecting saddle. The mules would clamber up from boulder to boulder, then methodically trudge across the saddle to climb down the opposite slope and out on to a miniature plain with its centre boggy and intensely green. Then as the country fell away another saddle would loom ahead as a bridge to higher ground and another tiny plain. As we climbed we caught glimpses across the scrub of hazy precipice rims forming the black lips of gorges. With nod or grunt or finger sign the women pointed out yam vines ever and anon. Strangely enough, the poorer sandstone country always grew the most native foods; the vine-tangled ravines were the homes of wallaby and possum and rat life, the poorer soil the innumerable vegetable foods. Apparently because the sandstone tablelands throughout the year oozed many scattered springs, whereas the well-grassed basaltic and plain country was dependent for water on sky, river or lagoon. Thus the sandstone country appeared actually to be a slowly oozing reservoir. If white population comes to that country, this fact will benefit the aboriginal, for the white man's stock will prefer the lower sweet grass country that grows the fewer native foods.

Laurie nodded towards Davey away in front.

Davey is eager as a schoolboy. He's in his own country now though nearing the sacred country, so old Larry tells me. Apparently some revered Mecca of the tribes. But notice how subdued the others are becoming. Their march is slowing down. They are tribally forbidden to tread on the ground ahead except at the sacred times of the initiation rites. Notice that warning glance from Charcoal to Oombali, and the alert fearfulness of the women: eyes glancing to right and left, stepping like cautious cats ready to dodge and run at a movement. All hands expect a shower of spears at any moment."

"The expectation has quietened the women anyway, and made them cling together."

Laurie laughed, leaning over his horse's neck as we scrambled up a steep bank.

"They're a quaint lot," he said. "Many a time while on patrol I've thought of Kipling's Julia O'Grady and the Colonel's lady. These aboriginal women are pure-bred sisters of Eve, just as modern in their tantrums and loves and jealousies and vanities as their white sisters. They are tiger-cats if you scratch the tigress in them but all honey if you butter the bread enough. They'll follow their buck through thick and thin and do anything for him. I've even known them die for him—when he was the right man of course. I sometimes wonder whether Life has really advanced as we believe. I don't mean man-made discoveries and improvements and inventions; but actual human life itself."

"I've wondered much as you do. It makes a man doubt the evolution theory, and wonder if there's not a lot in the Adam and Eve story after all."

"Yes, something like that. All sorts of other things fit in too. For instance, a few of these people's beliefs are our own old stories. How did these people get these same beliefs thousands of years before a white man ever saw this land? I've got a shock sometimes. Have been quite alone but for the trackers in a wild nigger camp when some incident has occurred that proved these people knew or believed something I thought was a cherished idea of our own civilization. It is only a sort of vague link here and there of course; still, it gives a man something to think about out here alone. But we'll have to get a move on or Davey will outdistance the patrol."

The file closed up—prisoners, sick, witnesses, women— all walking seriously ahead with no word spoken, the pack-animals trudging along occupied by the climb. Young Dick sat quietly on old Larry's horse, Laurie ordered Oomagun to carry his daughter and give Mrs Oomagun a rest. Then the trackers wheeled their horses and began climbing a precipitous spur that apparently led to a dead-end amongst scrub-covered bastions above. But it gradually broadened out into a scrub-covered plateau.

A surprise indeed; its presence would be quite unsuspected by a rider in the country below. It was an "old" looking plateau; old rocks, old trees, coarse tufty grass that might have been among the first species of grass to grow in the world. A blue sky above sunlit stillness. And by a hunched-up gargoyle in sandstone a beautiful rock python, coiled like a carving in copper and black. The natives edged away; it was a sacred snake; they forbore to glance at it. In any other locality they would have rushed it yelling and had it on the cooking-fires in no time.

Presently, we rode on to a placid creek that ran over bare rock with loamy banks hedged by cadjuput, gum, and pandanus palm. Rapidly the creek grew into almost the shallowest of rivers with miniature islets of palm. Long-beaked birds called piercingly; a spotted goanna rustled from under the nose of a loafing mule.

The trackers reined in and the cavalcade grouped around. Davey's eyes were shining, but apprehension clouded the faces of the others. Old Larry explained that this was Charoo, the sacred country belonging to the sacred tribe. This was the country where the laws were made. Davey became animated the more rapidly he talked. On this spot he had been initiated into warrior-hood; had learned the sacred secrets in accordance with his degrees attained; had taken part in big fights; had seen many things. Before the "big sick" came this had been the great meeting-place where at certain times of the year marched the men of Walcott Inlet to meet the men of the Isdell, of the Gibb and the Hann and the Upper Charnley. The Ngarinyin and tribes equally as far away marched here to fight and initiate their young men.

There was the sitting-stone upon which sat the Old Man of the victorious tribe while his warriors danced around him. Beyond, in a great circle, were other stones circling a flat amphitheatre of ground. Within that big circle sat the winning tribes after all fights were over. Well outside the circle sat those who had no present active interest. And in the bush behind, crouched the beaten people.

Davey was a different man, the stories he told would not have left his lips in other circumstances. He even explained the eating of the heart, kidneys, and liver of a slain enemy by the warriors of his tribe, but not the organs of any of their own men. Such a thing is not done. Occasionally a young plump lubra is taken into the bush, killed, cooked, and all of her eaten. This, however, is done only on a special occasion.

We followed the stream, clinging to its edges as the ground farther out developed into morass. Soon the going became rough, the horses clambering from rocky bar to bar. Stone heaps here and there marked symbolism and tradition; in some places stones were patterned over several acres of ground. But an atmosphere hovered over all betraying that these larger symbolic yards had not been used for some years—evidence that the people were dying out; that soon grass and shrub would obliterate these evidences of their age-old beliefs. The water broadened into big pools blue-white with water-lilies and margined with the intense green of water grass. Suddenly a long blue pool appeared lined with tall white trees, and beyond it acres of gleaming bare rock. Beyond these, again, the calm of other and larger pools. Queer shapes in jagged sandstone began to rise on either side.

We took the men of Charoo by complete surprise. They stared, seemingly incapable of movement. Here and there a half-poised spear trembled in nerveless hand; one old warrior frantically chewed his beard, his eyes like those of an animal paralysed with fear. All crouched in whatever attitude they were when we appeared among them. The women covered their faces with claw-like hands; children buried their heads under the mothers. The warriors were glaring at our horses, more than at us. When we dismounted I would not have been surprised had they dropped, for one legend of these people is that in the faraway ages half-man half-animal beings had come to their ancestors and told them the laws.

There were only some twenty-five of these prehistoric people; another twenty-five we met next day. Throughout the whole patrol they were the only people we met entirely in the stone age, though we met some hundreds who were just beginning to discard their stone weapons for rough hewn tools of iron. But these people carried nothing but stone axes, stone phallic knives, stone spear-heads, secret stones, magic stones, medicine stones; human hair belts around the waists of the men; the wildness of Eve in the eyes of the women. They were carrying their "spirit" bones too. The old witch-doctor wore an eagle's claw through his nose and a necklace of human knuckle-bones. At first glance they looked just like animal men and women and cubs—and smelt it too. They lived materially right down to nature, while living, too, day and night in a spirit world. Laurie battled hard to win their confidence. Their fears gradually became tinged with a frightened curiosity. But we would not have held them a moment had it not been for the reassuring presence of Davey. They had initiated him; had seen him fight; had known him obey the laws. Rapidly he told them his unbelievable experiences since they had seen him many moons ago, before the "white pleece" took him away to the land of the white men. They listened with wrapt interest, fearful of the horses and mules. Davey assured them we meant them no harm; that we were great curers of the sick; that we were only travelling through their country and soon would be far away.

He gained their partial confidence. Interest gleamed from eyes where fear had shone before, the women began peeping between their claw-like fingers.

At last Davey turned to us and explained that a little farther down the "river" was a waterfall where the laws were made.

"We'll see it," declared Laurie. "This is jolly interesting."

We had to leave the horses because a broad street of rock swept clean by the torrents of ages spread ahead, walled now by great sandstone boulders and clumps of grotesque rock left standing where water and weather had churned through a hill-top. Trenches black and cavernous had been cut through the solid rock by the boiling fury of water. On higher ground walled by rock were large cleared patches, the "sacred grounds." Here were held the Councils of the Old Men; here too the operations on initiates were performed. Davey pointed to a gnarled old chap whose withered chest was picturesque with the white down of the eagle, gummed on by human blood, and stone phallic knives in his belt of human hair. This old primitive had recently operated in such a ceremony. Numerous circles of stone were laid down, each some distance from the others, and all enclosed in a huge outer circle. Farther ahead, the hissing water vanished, the bare rock broadened where it was torn into thousands of shapes by waters gone. "Underneath us," explained Davey, and tapped the rock with his foot, "the water flows under the rock." A quaint looking primitive grinned and bent his ear to the rock. I took the hint and heard a low, subterranean murmur. Then we looked over the lip of a hundred-foot cliff straight out between the red walls of a gorge that came to the cliff like the outlet to an amphitheatre. The cliff had once been the lip of a waterfall. Below gleamed a green pool upon which the snouts of freshwater crocodiles floated motionless. Black boulders rimmed the pool. Looking down into that calm, mirror-like surface produced a strange effect; after a time the thing seemed to invite a man to leap out and over. I wondered if that had ever happened during the frenzy of superstitious rites that throughout ages had been enacted here. From a tunnel one hundred feet below, water gushed out among black rocks and frothed into the pool.

The mighty river that once had thundered out over the fall had cut its way through the range opposite whose bare red walls were now the gorge. It was nature's object lesson in geological time and the power of water.

"Well," said Laurie after a long pause, "I never knew of this before. We seem to be on some little plateau surrounded by valleys. Perhaps these Charoo people never leave the plateau, and the tribes who visit them are forbidden to mention the place because of its sacred associations. It all gives one rather a queer feeling."

Davey then interpreted while the Old Men of Charoo acted in an interesting pantomime. They explained that here had been made the laws of stone-age man. Here, when man was a lonesome thing terrified by convulsions of nature, chased by gigantic animals and monstrous birds and serpents, the first Old Men stood and held up supplicating arms to the skies.

When the sun-god rose in fiery dawn they chanted his coming through the spray-veiled mists and trembled to the strange voices that came in murmuring answer through the water thunder.

On moonlit nights they stood within the Magic Circle and gazed on the glory of the moon, and trembled to the answers that came in the swish of wings as bat-like birds sped by. Those were the days of the under-gods, half-man, half-spirit, that were sent from the World of Stars to teach laws to man upon the earth.

Man was taught how to make fire, then how to harden a pointed stick in the fire to make a spear as protection against enemies.

When man multiplied and had grown into tribes, these were taught their intricate marriage laws to prevent in-breeding among such small communities, and later their initiation rites; and eventually how to limit their members to the number that could be supported by the food produced on their tribal area.

So came all the laws to the men of Charoo, who in turn taught those laws at the meeting of the tribes in each great seasonal meeting.

Alas, the men of Charoo are doomed. For the "big sick" has come among them even though they do not know the white man.

18

DEAD MEN'S BONES

WE would have liked to roam indefinitely over Charoo. With those rugged old primitives squatting there, their eyes gleaming as in deep gutturals they unfolded to us their story of man and the stars and earth, of beasts and birds and fishes, of their tribal story commemorated in rock after rock, waterhole after waterhole, we felt queerly near the beginning of things. It was indeed conversing with men born at the dawn of time. But these are present days and in due time the patrol marched away from the past—and heard a hunting-cry, long-drawn-out and happy, ringing through the trees. Instantly the trackers turned the pack-animals and hurried them and the troops under a tree whose enormous branches drooped to the grass. There in that cloistered silence the bushland noises came to us, a faint whispering of breeze-kissed leaves, hum of insects, the conversational clucking of a bird. A little later, and again the long-drawn cry, closer this time.

The huntsmen were coming up in line behind us, each man well away from the huntsman on either hand, each keeping his position by occasional call one to another. Their flank men would walk swifter towards sunset while gradually turning inwards until a circle was formed.

Then the huntsmen would close in around the game. The centre of that circle would be the huntsmen's camp for the night.

Game does not fall effortlessly to the aboriginal spear. Three or four huntsmen can walk out and probably kill enough game for their needs for the day. But to feed a tribe is a very different matter. Thought and organization and the keenest bushcraft must be used in conjunction with untiring sinew and vigilant eye.

Coming towards us from away back a huntsman appeared above the grass, a wild man of the woods happy as a bird. Feathers were in his long hair which- was tied back from his corrugated forehead with a dyed band of animal fur; his coarse beard covered a square chin; his sinewy body was heavily cicatrized, bands of plaited grass around his limbs, a human hair belt girdled his waist. He strode forward utterly unconscious of our presence, swinging his wommera to cut off the heads of the grass, his spears grasped in one claw-like hand. A man of Charoo, smaller, leaner, less intelligent looking than the prisoners, he carried that primitive air of the utterly wild thing. I knew that the troops could actually smell him. From the huge tree the trackers were snaking out through the grass towards him. They rose at his very feet. He stood a living statute with leg outstretched, one arm half raised, a wonderful expression on his face. The trackers laughed into his eyes. He gasped, and shivered back into normal.

To Davey's questions he replied that his hunting party was very small, the horde was a "long, long way away." He volunteered the information that two of Nipper's tribesmen were awaiting them half a day away. The luck of the patrol! These two were witnesses mentioned by Charcoal's wife in the murder of her brother.

"I must make contact with them if I can," said Laurie, "and before this tribesman's hunting friends can warn them."

He offered to guide us. It was a hurried ride to beat the sunset. He stepped smartly with the horses at his heels, skirting sandstone rises with the horses' hoofs squelching into black mud, ringing on the stones. Again and again he dived straight up over the rocks where there was a hollow between two low outcrops. It looked a certainty for a broken leg, impossible to catch up with the hunters. When rounding these sandstone knobs we travelled quickly and softly, for then the morass mud drowned the noise of the hurrying hoofs. Keeping to the edges of these sandstone bluffs shielded us from sight and kept us up out of the little green bogs that were everywhere among the bluffs. By now the loaded pack-animals had sensed when quick movement was necessary; they kept the line in haste and without pause, putting their mind to it as if they were eager riding-horses pressed by eager riders. At three miles the trackers stood suddenly in their stirrups then bent over the saddles. Simultaneously the riding-horses were plunging past the patrol and past the guide and were at the gallop up a sandstone mound. I got a glimpse of a wild man leaping erect with spear poised, lubras crouching, dingo dogs loping for the rocks. Then several more men snatching at spears but hesitating, their eyes glaring as their chests were thrown back for the throw, the trackers shouting in dialect:

"Stop! We only want to talk."

Laurie wheeled from the fires shouting *"Cock-ai! Cock-ai!"* (Come here! Come here!) as a warrior leapt from rock to rock. I followed Laurie, the old grey plunging from rock to rock, and gained the marshy edge on the other side. Laurie's horse was disappearing around a sandstone ledge. We plunged around too and there was Laurie a hundred yards ahead at the heels of the flying man. The bog there ended in a waterhole right at the end of the ledge. In one startling moment horse and rider collided with the ledge, plunged sideways, and disappeared in the waterhole. The flying man stood poised in the act of running, his head turned over his shoulder, mouth open, eyes wild, a wonderful sight of petrified fear and astonishment as the struggling hoofs then head of horse then Laurie's head appeared above the water. Laurie gasped and shouted *"Cock-ai! Cock-ai!* I only want talk longa you, you blithering fool!" As the horse wallowed up Laurie stepped from its body on to the ledge and strode to the tribesman, staring him in the eye. The man never moved. If he could have come to life he might have speared Laurie then disappeared into the swamp with the greatest of ease. Only when Laurie touched his arm did his limbs relax; with a deep sigh he turned completely around, trembling. He threw his spears at the feet of Laurie.

"Pick them up," pointed Laurie reassuringly. "I don't mean you any harm, blow you."

Laurie's horse had galloped along that ledge until it suddenly narrowed to six inches. How man and horse had not broken their necks, let alone been drowned, beat me.

We scrambled back over the rise to the patrol. Davey was explaining to the people that we only wanted them to camp with us that night, then next day supply a guide to find the two wanted men.

We unsaddled while the shock troops hurried to make a fire and fill the billies, then selected a tree and bending got busy at pulling up the grass tussocks from around it preparatory to a comfortable camp. The prisoners, guf¬fawing and laughing at the munjons' expense, immediately started pulling and kicking out the grass tufts around their tree, each man making himself a comfortable place on which to sleep. Our new discoveries turned to their just-lit fires, the men squatting silently, the women not daring to look at us. Easy to understand these people's astonishment. That here in Charoo, their sacred country from time immemorial, the white man at last had set his foot. They stared at the mules and horses busily cropping the grass, stared at Mrs Nipper swinging the iron tomahawk, stared longingly at our knives. This was the extreme boundary of the Charoo country, Davey explained; the two witnesses in Burrin's murder were half a day's journey away.

The Charoo women carried long funnels of paper-bark slung in a band of paper-bark which hung over the shoulder like a belt, the women when walking resting the left forearm on the funnel and thus keeping it at balance. From her carrying funnel one of the women took out her day's collection of game: small possums with a little tail, the grey fur in places tipped with black; a small species of bandicoot too with even and barrel-like body, sharp-pointed nose and very short tail, thick, yellow-brown hair. The wild women cooked their quaint animals and lizards in a striking silence compared with the laughing gossip of the lubras with the patrol.

Suddenly, we all jumped to the crack of the rifle. In the gloaming Davey had shot a dingo. It had come for a drink at the lily pond, a beautiful animal with long, lithe body, hair of a wonderful golden shade, its head sharply defined but not peaky, ears pricked but not sharply so, the tail-tip bushy. He was as purely unadulterated as the Charoo primitives near by. And grimly tenacious of life. In no time Mrs Charcoal had the wild dog on a fire, turning it by its legs as the body frizzled and stiffened, rubbing off the burnt hair with a stick, her eyes seemingly not feeling the smoke nor her face the heat. In groups apart we sat or squatted around our separate trees, little Dick smoodging around Laurie while he was serving out the trackers' tucker. Night fell with all hands wolfing 'roo or lizard, bandicoot or wild dog; reaching out to the fire and tearing off a hunk of meat, chewing it where it was lightly burned, holding it to the coals while gossiping again. When the evening air currents gently wafted the smoke our way it brought plainly the strong animal smell of the people of Charoo.

After the meal a smoke.

"That beetle-browed Charcoal' is working mischief," said Laurie. Sharply he called to Larry to bring along the huntsman guide. The man's eyes were shifty; he mumbled in answer to Davey's questions. He contradicted what he had said before, said he only "thought" that two men of Burrin's tribe were camped half a day away. But presently admitted that Charcoal had threatened him and told him not to tell where the men were.

Next day Davey and Toby left camp to try and induce the two witnesses to come in. They had not got out of sight of camp when they ran into a hunter. He accompanied them back. A wild-looking specimen, his only clothing a striking girdle of long, fluffy tails of the pretty flying possum dangling from a human hair belt. His body ochre-painted was strikingly outlined with fluff of the wild kapok, his small hands grasped twelve-foot spears iron tipped. His big feet had the stubbed and broken toes that so often mar the hardest worked limbs of the aboriginal. His eyes were uneasy, his smile propitiatory. But this wild aboriginal had only a few weeks previously been wearing clothes, a civilized boy holding a responsible job at Walcott Inlet. Laurie recognized him as Gunner and began asking him about the Inlet. Obviously uneasy, he gained confidence and answered straightforwardly enough. Then went and sat with the prisoners, presently joining in their conversation.

"I think that chap was holding something back," said Laurie, "and yet he spoke honestly enough. All seems well at the Inlet and certain natives there who were fearful of their lives seem quite all right. But he was not telling everything. While you are taking photos, I'll take the opportunity to write up my patrol notes."

Several of the primitives passed the time away by flaking stone spearheads, fashioning them very much as glass ones are made nearer civilization. Only here they had no wire tools, they gouged the finer chips from the stone with spike-like tools of pointed kangaroo bone; *chumbee* they called these chipping-bones. It seems unbelievable that hard flint can be flaked or chipped by bone, but these primitives were managing it methodically. The only difference was that the work was harder and slower than that on glass. One old expert, forgetting all about the patrol, gradually became absorbed in his job. He bit his lips, staring down at the fashioning spearhead, levering with his body stiffened, eyes and mind and cunning hand concentrated on every chipping. He cut his finger on a splinter, absentmindedly wiped the blood off on his hair and bent again to the job. For the last chipping which makes the needle point and tiny serrated edges so true and delicate he used a smaller bone and with magic touch produced a truly exquisite thing. But he did not finish the job until sundown. Throughout the day several lubras were uneasily making string from human hair, working it just as they do animal fur, though the stiff hair was more troublesome than fur, which can be beaten into fluff. Most of them, however, sat quietly conversing, in sign language, unnoticeable to the inexperienced eye.

At sundown Davey and Toby returned with a little crowd of men and women, among whom was one of the witnesses. He quite willingly corroborated the account of the killing of Burrin.

It was an unusually silent meal that evening. Night came strangely quiet, the sky overcast; not a sound from the scattered little groups, not a real fire except our own blaze and a faint glow from the trackers' fire.

"A debil-debil night, the ogilla is here again," remarked Laurie.

"The atmosphere is ghostly enough anyway."

As if at sound of our voices Larry arose and walked towards us. He mumbled that a man wanted to sell me some bones.

"Bones!" I exclaimed.

"Yes. Spirit bones, charmed by big witch-doctor."

Laurie filled his pipe and lazily asked for particulars.

It appeared that wherever those bones went, the spirit of the man would follow, and if the possessor of the bones knew how to talk to the spirit the spirit would answer and tell him things.

"They must want to get rid of them for some very special reason," murmured Laurie, "yet dare not throw them away. If they can pass them on to you in accordance with tribal laws then all is well, and the spook's unwanted attention will follow you. They probably have experienced a run of exceptionally bad luck and lay the blame on the bones."

They were a knobby pair of human bones, yellow brown, polished by unknown years of handling. In the firelight they looked harder and older and more "animaly" even than the face of the crouching primitive who wished to get rid of them. To tell how those bones had been charmed and what were the inherent properties supposed to be in them would occupy too much space here.

The big-gun "doctor" who had charmed them had recently died and, from what these natives would explain, his spirit was following them and playing malicious tricks through other spirits' bones. As to why tribal law allowed them to sell such prized possessions, they would give no clear answer.

"You're buying a pig in a poke," said Laurie. "They're too jolly anxious to get rid of them for my liking."

Then Davey came up with a beetle-browed little primitive of almost negroid expression. He also wished to sell bones though not "spirit bones," and he also could get rid of them under the same law as the spirit bones. But there was a much clearer reason in this case. All the relatives of the dead man, those to whom the bones should have passed, had completely died out. The deceased was a Cape Voltaire native, speared on the coast. These two arm-bones had been passed from tribe to tribe, but now they learned that the "big sick" had carried off the last relative to whom the bones should be given. The responsibility of the carrier was thus ended.

The bones were done up very neatly in a cylindrical paper-bark package, bound tightly and painted with red ochre.

With a curiosity for detail that I have always felt in strange things or places or people I asked the dead man's country and name.

"Winidot," replied Davey.

"By Jove!" Laurie sat up, quite interested at this material statement. "That's Winidot, the murdered native who figured in the case I told you of where his killers escaped from around that tree during my last patrol. This is a coincidence."

"Remarkable I think. Winidot was speared north of here in wild country, and yet in a place like this twelve months later the dead man's bones should be brought before you."

"Yes. Just as well a man is not superstitious or he might imagine Winidot was crying out for vengeance."

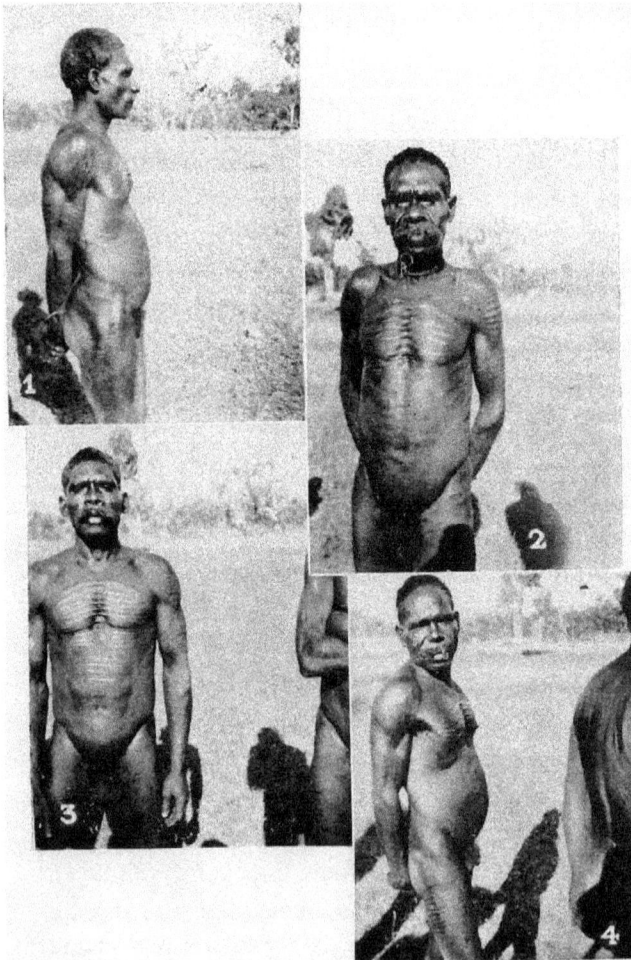

1. MARMADU (DONKEY)   3. MARMADU'S MATE
2. DUNGART   4. ARDGAT (GEORGE)

19
THE WITCH-DOCTOR'S CURSE

OLD LARRY explained that among these tribes a dead man's bones are carried by his nearest relatives for several years and then in a sacred place, are sung over by the tribe. They are then hidden in secret caves—all except the arm-bones. These must be carried about until that generation of relatives die out, when the arm-bones are deposited with the rest of the skeleton in the cave. Every year a pilgrimage is made to these secret caves, the bones are carefully examined to see that the white ants are not eating them, then all the skeletons are sung over.

The old tracker paused, his eyes gleaming as he murmured that those forearm bones of Winidot had been charmed; had already been sung over by the noted witch-doctor Wantadedgo and that now the spirit will follow me to Syd-nee. Warming to his subject as the trackers crouched closer to the fire he explained the burial customs, the vengeance feuds and laws regulating the vendettas of tribes within a great radius around. He explained that the doctor who had charmed my spirit bones was a great witch-doctor whose speciality was in killing men by malign influences from a distance. The mystic influences allegedly set working are too long and complicated to explain here, but the material operation is that the doctor would catch a certain species of lizard under particular circumstances at a particular time. He would croon over it the name of the man while gently rattling his "devil bones," thus calling up the evil spirit that follows these particular charmed bones. It is this spirit that really encompasses the death of the distant man. The doctor eventually digs a hole by a flat stone and holds the lizard in while he rolls a red-hot stone upon it, crooning that as this lizard dies so will the man die; he will "burn up inside." He then smothers the spot with sand. As the days go by he waters the spot while crooning instructions to the waiting vengeance spirit below. Then, when the summer heat comes and the waters dry up, the malign spirit is liberated to do its work, sickness strikes the man, and he dies.

Old Larry was in deadly earnest, his low husky voice had been listened to in utter silence by the people crouched near by.

Devil bones were terrible things, whispered Larry. Crouching there, staring up at us, this old tracker was baring his unchanged, primitive heart, trying to convince the two white men. Hoarsely he mentioned name after name of aboriginals known to Laurie who had died in the Derby native hospital. Those particular men had been "sung," he swore; no white doctor living could have cured them. A white doctor can cure most sicknesses, but never a sickness that has been sung. "White man no can understand," insisted Larry. "Black man know true!"

Then he drew attention to bush natives whom Laurie knew had been sung and died—a Big Paddy in particular. And now, he whispered feverishly, "Harry, him die soon! Arm belonga him drop off up near Vansittart Bay."

Laurie was staring at Larry.

I asked if there were any really "big" doctors in the country around. Larry frowned down at the coals, then called softly for Toby who came with little Dick clinging to his shoulders. They whispered a while, then hissed out into the night for Davey. All three started an urgent, whispered conversation.

Little Dick began to whimper. Toby walked away. Davey followed. Then old Larry walked away too, after lamely whispering, "Any dishes to wash up?"

We were left in a deathly silence.

"Now this is extraordinary," said Laurie presently. "First Winidot's bones to turn up here and to me, then I get news of Big Paddy and Tracker Harry. They were both with me on the Winidot patrol. Big Paddy was one of the finest trackers I ever had. Intelligent, over six feet tall and as strong as a horse; a cheerful man, willing and agreeable. During that long chase after the killers of Winidot he and Harry rode up to one of the largest native camps I have ever seen. Hundreds , of natives were yelling and brandishing spears from the rocks. Only one man stood firm; an old monkey of a witch-doctor crouched there cursing the trackers as I rode up. They sat their horses and stared at him; you could hear his screeches ringing all down the gorge. Well, he cursed Big Paddy and Harry to die.

"A few days later Big Paddy 'became sick.' There was nothing the matter with him, just mental fear and inborn superstition. He became worse. Ashamed of himself, he tried to carry on so that I would not know. At last he mumbled that a stone had got into his foot, that it was working up his leg, that when it entered his body it would touch his heart and kill him. I tried hard to break the man's conviction. It was useless. We managed ' to get him to Walcott Inlet—and buried him there. A young man, what we call 'civilized' and one of the strongest and finest physical specimens of aboriginal manhood I have ever seen. I've told you the rest about our catching the murderers and their eventful escape. When we returned to Derby Harry deserted, the first tracker in the history of the Kimberley police to desert at Derby. The witch-doctor's curse was preying on his mind of course. And now Gunner tells Larry that Harry is dying by inches, his arm has dropped off. Leprosy I suppose. But it must have become uncannily virulent in his case. And now you have bought the forearm bones of Winidot. I wonder how many have already died over the spearing of Winidot."

"It seems, or anyway it feels, natural enough that in surroundings like these their minds should be strongly influenced by primitive superstitions."

"Yes. I wonder who really started them off in the first place? Who were really their first men? Who gave them their first ideas ? I wonder what it was that started our minds working on other things. If we hadn't taken a different mental track we might still be as they are."

"They've been nomads since the dawn of human history, never agriculturists. All their time has been occupied in hunting. They have never sought to make two blades of grass grow where one grew before. If they had they would have won the leisure to think and do other things as we have done."

"Oh, well, all the bones and spooks in these ranges won't trouble my sleep," said Laurie as he yawned and stretched down between his blankets. "Good night. If the spirits come for their bones just speak to 'em quietly and tell 'em not to disturb me."

Next morning, while the billies were boiling, the primitives timidly approached with message-sticks.

"This one war one!" explained Davey significantly. "Make fight talk, Ngarinyin say make war if altogether Chamley men don't altogether watch out."

Sounds important," said Laurie. "International complications."

Davey translated this threat of war. It was from the Ngarinyin tribe at Walcott Inlet and its translation in English was: "You men of the Upper Calder, Charnley, and Isdell tribes have committed numerous murders against us, the Ngarinyin. You have killed our hunters right up at the head of the Three Rivers; have even come low down to the Ngarinyin and killed them at the Lower Crossings. Now don't dare come lower down than the middle of the Three Rivers. If you do, we warriors of the Ngarinyin have sworn to kill you, to chase until we catch and kill you."

Deep-cut lines in the stick represented individual men particularly warned, joined by another line representing individual Ngarinyin warriors who had vowed to take their lives.

One of the tribesmen particularly warned was Charcoal.

I took the stick across to the prisoners and had it re-translated there. Charcoal was very pleased, his deep-lined face fairly beamed when his own mark was pointed out to him. That mark represented his death sentence in time to come. But what did Charcoal care! They had to kill him first!

I bought this impressive reading message-stick. "Threats of war" souvenirs are uncommon in Australia.

Then Charcoal, squatting there with his big chest thrown out, looked up and smiled. He had waited his moment until all hands were intently listening.

Davey translated. In slow deep voice Charcoal told how the warriors of the Oonyaryin, of the Upper Charnley, of the Gibb River and others had accepted the gauntlet and forwarded their "Declaration of War" to the Big Ngarinyin.

I wanted that Declaration of War. I told Davey to remember the name of the warrior who had carried it to the Ngarinyin and as soon as we reached Walcott Inlet to try and secure it. I promised him a new pipe and Capstan tobacco in Derby, and five sticks of tobacco and a pocket-knife for the man who now had the stick. As a precaution, I noted down from Charcoal the "wording" on the stick so as to compare it with the translation at Walcott Inlet. Charcoal was proud of the "Declaration." As tribal author he had suggested the wording to the Council of the Old Men. In the course of time I did secure this stick and the translation tallied exactly with Charcoal's memory.

Laurie called Davey to give a hand with the horses. Fortune smiled on the prisoners. The very next stick gave details of the killing of Worachi by Oomagun's people. Nipper eagerly volunteered to decipher it. Oomagun smiled broadly; he was now to have his turn in the headlines.

The markings on this stick told that Whisky (I use their white-feller names where they have one, as the aboriginal name may be confusing) advised the conspirators to leave the man alone. But Donkey (a powerful man) insisted that Worachi was very strong and he was going to kill him. . (The killer believes that he absorbs some of the strength and cunning of the slain man, should he eat portions of his kidney fat.) Jack, for the same reason that moved Donkey, also wished to kill Worachi. But

George prevented him at the critical moment. Three men, Moby, Womerun and Ardgat warned the now hunted Worachi that the killers were close on his heels, and advised him to hide in Parrywarri Creek. He did so. Eventually, reconciliation took place and Worachi returned to camp. Later, he was treacherously slain, just as told by Oombali and the witnesses. Grace's Knob, and the place where Worachi was killed, were marked on the stick.

The reverse side of the stick told that the slayers and their associates (Oomagun, Donkey, Marmadu, Dungat and Oombali) were now threatened by Worachi's tribal relations, who threatened to come from their camp at Turkey Creek (East Kimberley) and attack them. The marks of these coming avengers, the locality where Jack first attempted to kill Worachi, and other localities were also given. Yet another stick, an old message this, gave details of two previous killings by Oomagun of a man and a woman, in which killings Big Paddy, Duncan and Donkey were implicated. Unfortunately the animals were packed and the troops were moving off before I could jot down all the markings on this stick. It was a slow job, to draw the stick on paper, get the certain interpretation of each mark, and jot it down mark after mark.

But it was an interesting job; these sticks and others we had seen and were to see had been passed from horde to horde, tribe to tribe. They were the newspapers of the wild. Each one that was not merely a play-about stick or an ordinary message was an aboriginal "true life thriller." An occasional one was easy ho decipher, granted a knowledge of the aboriginal and of his methods of drawing, painting, and signs. They were really "short-hand pictographs." A few lines and dots would faithfully represent an entire hunting story translatable in accurate detail. Vertical or slanting notches for instance told whether the individual men portrayed were camped, walking or running. Tiny dots which were its tracks even told whether a dog was with the man or party. The circle within the circle was reference to the origin of life. A few apparently meaningless dots, lines, notches, circles, zigzags, would tell a story to the aboriginal just as we would read a newspaper story. (These story sticks were for all to decipher, as apart from the memorized stick whose message was in confidential form.) Then there was the totem message-stick, the message in which could only be decoded by men of the same totem. Probably we would have learned a great deal more of the aboriginal if only long ago we had studied his message-sticks sympathetically.

As the patrol rode away, the primitives gave us a silent farewell. Several days later in rough country we were twisting and turning in a long climb down. Mrs Charcoal suddenly crouched, then lay down, bent up with pain; it-was evident she would not move for hours. We were in an awkward position, zigzagging down the side of a gorge upon which no animal dared turn around. The woman moaned that some time ago Charcoal had given her a more than usually brutal thrashing, hammering her across the stomach with a fighting-stick until she was unconscious. Little wonder she was pleased at seeing him in the hands of the "white pleece." We left Toby with her to bring her along on a horse; we could do nothing until we got to level country. While scrambling down I did a fool thing for which I might have been sorry all my life. Mrs Oomagun was carrying her big daughter, and I dismounted, calling out to her to put the child on the horse. Willingly she did so, but the child stubbornly resented it. I lifted the obstinate kid into the saddle, made sure she had a good grip, then led the horse. The girl let out an awful yell, the horse plunged forward, and the youngster's head struck me on the back. I just managed to catch her arm as she pitched head-first for the rocks. As it was, the skin was scratched on her scalp.

If the kid had cracked her skull it might have proved dashed awkward for me.

That night we camped by the Calder River, its wide, boulder-strewn bed witness to the tearing floods that roar down there in the wet season. Davey set Mrs Nipper to washing his clothes.

"Why old Larry's sarcastic glance?"

"The superiority of the married male who owns a good-looking wife," answered Laurie. "We'll be at Walcott Inlet tomorrow and Davey will cut a dash among the young lubras. Larry can't be tempted, but you'll see him washing his clothes too before the trip is finished."

Next day, over basalt hills well grassed under bundle bundle, we drew gradually nearer the impressive Harding Range; big grassy hills with a tableland perched upon a rampart of cliffs.

Riding down the valley of the Calder the country opened out, the ranges spreading to right and left with fertile flats in between. Then appeared the red-painted buildings of Munja, the Walcott Inlet Government Aboriginal Station, with a big lagoon from which came faintly the call of wildfowl, a level patch intensely green under cultivation (a surprise in the wilderness), a large native camp. Dogs barked; white men, a white woman, and several children stared.

22
WALCOTT INLET

So we were welcomed to Munja, Walcott Inlet, Julabarra of the natives. A business-like air pervaded this small outpost, an impression of human endeavour battling cheerily against nature. Vegetables, bananas, passion fruit, pineapples, Austral berries, mangoes, African beans, in abundance, were evidence of the first round having been won. Mr Reid expected us: his natives had kept him informed of the wandering patrol. He and Laurie were soon discussing the events of the last twelve months; I was more interested in how life dealt with this white woman, all alone out here. Mrs Reid was a quiet, pleasant looking woman, with an unobtrusive air of capability that was confirmed by her surroundings. A woman must be very strong willed, or else love the environment, to be content in the rugged isolation here.

"A quiet life, a quiet home and a happy one," she explained with a smile.

The children were bright and healthy. The only worry was that, should sickness come, there would be no hope of a doctor. All communication was to Derby south by sea; and that only by the Port George Mission lugger every month or so during the dry season—weather permitting. Until Mrs Merry came, Mrs Reid had seen only one woman visitor in two years, the wife of the Port George missionary when she went south for a holiday. But now Merry lived over the Harding Range only forty miles away. Mrs Merry was expected from the south at any time with her first baby. Imagine what that meant! The two Reid children were the only white children in the Nor'-west Kimberley. And now had come this new baby!

Here was the Reid cot on the veranda. Reid and Merry were going to convert it into a sedan cot. Ngarinyin warriors would come from Merry's, and this wild bodyguard would carry the baby pioneer to his home over the range.

There were no other neighbours inland until one reached the East Kimberley, towards the Northern Territory. Farther up the coast there were Mrs Love and Mrs Macdougal, wives of the Port George the Fourth missionaries. And far north of them were several sisters at the lonely Drysdale Mission. No others.

But there was plenty to do. Apart from the interest in the household and her husband's work, there were the native women. Their babies and sicknesses and constant intrigues and jealousies kept her busy with a helping hand. Then there was that red-letter day, the arrival of the mail from Broome by the mission lugger, or from Derby by the packhorse mailman to Mount Hart, one hundred and thirty miles away over the range. From Mount Hart this mail was brought by native rider to the Inlet. Reading the mails and books comprised the family's sole recreation. Mrs Thompson at Kimberley Downs station sent her books by this roundabout way. The two women were firm friends, though they had never met.

Disappointment was in store for Toby.

"By Jove, Laurie," said Reid, "I'm glad you brought that Toby along. Can you let me have him? He is a good stockboy and knows my country. I'm very short of horsemen."

"Of course. He is only travelling with us; he gives a hand with the packs. He wants to go to Derby."

"Well, I can make good use of him here for a month or so."

"You can have him."

But Toby's good-humoured face clouded when Laurie asked him would he work for Mr Reid.

"Why you no want work?" inquired Laurie.

"Work all right," answered Toby glumly. "Black boy here no good. Too much trouble over lubra. All a time fight."

Toby was unusual amongst aboriginals in that apparently the feminine interest did not appeal.

"Mr Reid very busy," explained Laurie. "You work for him a while, then when he finish you come longa Derby and I'll see if I can get you a job."

Unwillingly Toby agreed. He mumbled darkly that it was a cruel thing to leave a man all alone to the tender mercies of the Inlet womenfolk. Reid, quiet and thoughtful, was a typical bushman, tall and spare and brown. His job was to try to teach the aboriginals to do something for themselves; to prepare for them a place in the scheme of things should ever white settlement come to these parts. Cattle were bred here by the Western Australian Government exclusively for the natives. Apparently the natives took no particular interest in the beasts, except to eat them. Reid was very keen on teaching them agriculture. He had a fair acreage under cultivation; the millet broom looked well, but his pet crop was peanuts; he was now harvesting the surprising crop of just over a ton of nuts to the acre. He considered he had solved the white-ant problem by repeated ploughing. The pest is so bad in the Kimberleys that the ants eat the living young plants. Continued ploughing, however, breaks their tunnels, smothers them, breaks up their runs, and they leave. After the third year, the damage done by the ants was trivial. If the industry gets a hold, Reid will have been the pioneer over the range. It was he who had urged Dave Rust to try a crop and suggested the idea to Merry. Reid dreamed of making the station self-supporting. Generally, there were two hundred natives on the place. Others arrived in nomadic gatherings. In the course of years he had counted seven hundred different people around the Inlet at the one time. Now he was hard put to hold a hundred regulars, they were so afraid of the "big sick" and the rumour that the white men were going to send all the sick ones away from their own country.

Scotty Salmon and young Ron strolled along for a yarn. Scotty was Dave Rust's mate, and was anxious to know how Dave was progressing on the new place at Mount Elizabeth. Scotty's face lit up at the news we were able to give him. We assured him we hoped the new place would grow into a great station carrying a mighty herd.

"So do I," agreed Scotty enthusiastically. "But Dave and I saw lots of those hopes busted when we tried to make a station out of Karunjie in the East Kimberley. You never know your luck though in these parts. Anyway, I'd rather be swinging to the end of a cow's tail out here than twanging a harp in heaven."

Scotty was a little chap in a "Jackie Howe" singlet with a shock of loose hair, somewhat prominent nose and eyes, and still with a Scottish twang. Able to see the humorous side even of misfortune, he was full of beans and as tough as the hills. He had stopped a revolver bullet through the throat and "watched myself spitting blood out of two holes—me mouth and where the bullet went in, and felt it bubbling where it came out at the back." His own iron will and an Afghan camelman had saved liim, far from other help. Then, with blood still oozing from the wound, he had mounted his famous white camel, the Kimberley Prince, and ridden yet farther into the wilds, either to die or recover. Like the stricken blacks, he sought the immemorial hills. But that is another story; and being a true one, under the circumstances it might need careful handling.

As a boy Scotty had taken "a fireman's ticket" to see the world; had slaved in the stokehold in rival races be¬tween great liners; had seen the world by water and a lot of it by land; had sailed all the seas and twelve hun¬dred miles up the Amazon as well as up other great rivers. He was very proud that he had been noted as one of "the banjo fiddlers," who accompanied the "firemen's chorus" with shovels on the boilers. He had been fireman on the Lusitania and got a big thrill out of it.

"Every day was great," he assured us; "every day I said to myself .'even my little strength is helping to push this big along.'" He had been a stoker on the Carmania, and could still read enthralled of its victorious encounter with the Cap Trafalgar.

Ron was a quiet lad who had taken a fancy to the country. As soon as he had gained enough experience he was determined to take up land and carve out a home of his own.

We stayed some days at Walcott Inlet. Several of the mules were sore-footed; Mrs Charcoal was still ill and could barely travel; Laurie had work to do. And proof was soon evident that he needed to be a Sherlock Holmes. Apparently all was well with native life; everyone was happy. Still, Laurie sensed an undercurrent of fear. There were natives here who wished to seek protection but dared not. Besides, he wished to find an old man and woman. He sent the trackers out to seek them—and they returned with two skeletons. The cat was out of the bag. The prisoners then decided to develop sickness. Taking advantage of Mr Reid's sick parade, Laurie doctored the sick ones. Charcoal and Oomagun grimaced disgustedly; Nipper spat violently. He was advised to take another dose but earnestly declared: "Me feelem better."

"Another little dose won't do you any harm," soothed Laurie as he measured out the awful looking stuff. "One more dose and you feelem better altogether!"

"Me feelem better altogether arright now!" assured Nipper desperately as he.waved the glass aside: 'Me altogether good man now; pinish medicine altogether." Oombali and Allboroo assured Laurie that they had never felt better in their lives. Mrs Nipper and Mrs Oomagun, who had anxiously watched the results of the physicking, declared that they felt in the pink. Little Dick had waddled up in eager anticipation but Charcoal's disgusted grimaces sent him running with Laurie in pursuit. A line-up of the boss boys was ordered. Laurie's confidence was not increased when he saw that the two chief boys were Doolarri and Bundamarri (otherwise Leggings and Paddy) who had been with young Fred Easton when he was taken by a crocodile whilst crossing the Inlet. Among various whites in the Kimberleys there is a lurking doubt as to whether the death of the young white man had been satisfactorily explained.

The natives swore that those two skeletons were of old people who died naturally. But one skull showed evidence of a severe blow. Mr Reid believed they had died of old age. He had found them away out in the bush, an old blind man being led around by an old lubra. They were reluctant to stay with the natives at the Inlet so he took them to the Banana Springs a couple of miles from the house. A fighting man, one Gunner, was looking after this particular garden. Two other half-blind old people were quartered there too, receiving rations from the station. At about the time that "native wireless" first brought the news that a police patrol was coming Gunner had come into the station for his supply of rations, and taken them away. Shortly afterwards, Pindart and Mungulla, two lubras, visited the old people, found two bodies and buried them, but could not find any other people. They returned to the Inlet, saying not a word to Authority. Then Mr Reid heard a rumour that Gunner had gone bush. Surprised, he immediately thought of the four old people, and went out to the Springs. No sign of them. After much cooeeing and searching, they heard a faint answer and found two of the old people hidden in a dense clump of grass. They explained that the other two people had died, that Gunner had gone away, and that they had been afraid and hidden. Mr Reid had brought these old people back to the Inlet; Laurie sent the trackers to fetch them quickly before they could be spirited away.

Suspicion pointed to Gunner. He was the hunter we bad met back near the Charoo country. Laurie had been right when he sensed that this man knew something about
Walcott Inlet.

Gunner was a trusted man, the "Guardian of the Springs"; a fighter, not afraid to camp alone at the Springs. He had led the fighters of his tribe against the fighters of the Upper Charnley and Prince Regent. Brave and notoriously quick with his fighting weapons, he could hardly have been taken by surprise, and hardly probable that he had been forced to help or look quietly on at the killing of the two old people. There was no known reason, tribal or otherwise, why he should kill them himself. And yet he had fled

"Do you believe he did it?" I asked when Laurie walked thought-thoughtfully away.   .

"No. I was certain something was in the wind when we met him near Charoo, but I don't think he did it. I believe he knew all about it though. He was afraid to drop a hint, and would be afraid now if he were here. That points' to something exceptionally strong in native vendetta. I've an idea the little outlaw band that runs between Mount Hart and the coast did the job. Gunner would be helpless against them. It looks just like their work, sudden and wanton killing; and fear of their vengeance is so great that even tribal fears and jealousy and intrigue daren't betray them. However, I'm going to get to the bottom of it." You amuse yourself for a few days. I'll be plenty busy. Here comes Larry; we'll see what the two old lubras say about it."

The tracker approached very slowly with the two old lubras. One was blind, the other nearly so. They seemed pathetically glad to be in the hands of the "white pleece." The one who could see a little seemed to think she could not be blamed now if she talked, now that she was actually standing before a white policeman. She mumbled that Willie, Jimmie, and Dickie's band had sneaked on them at early morning time. The first they knew was the thud, thud, of the fighting-sticks on the heads of the two old people. She had just time to recognize Jimmie leaping towards her when she was struck across the neck, but her mate had not had time to recognize the voices before she was struck too. They both collapsed shamming death. They lay thus for many hours, then crawled away into the thick grass, fearing every moment that Willie's band would return and find them and finish off the work. They were satisfied to lie there and slowly starve to death, rather than venture out. When Mr Reid found them they told him that the two old people had "died." They daren't tell otherwise.

Immediately Leggings and Paddy sensed that the truth was out they hurried to tell themselves. But the police now knew what every man and woman in camp had known all along. When asked why they had not spoken, they replied that they looked on the deaths of two old people as of no importance. When asked why they had denied all knowledge of the fact they merely shrugged, or gazed across at the hills.

From start to finish it was a knotty little problem for Laurie. He had to find out about it first, then solve it, then catch the outlaws if possible. He had to pierce the veil that shielded the action in one hundred aboriginal minds, then quickly assemble the facts by his aboriginal knowledge, aided by a wide local geography and knowledge of hard-doer outside blacks and of their country.

In addition, he had to foresee the actions of many as point by point he solved the case. The police officer on patrol has an interesting job, but he must have gained a wide and practical experience of the aboriginal, be blessed with bush-mastery of a high order, have initiative, and the aptitude to retain a quick grasp of locality in an imperfectly mapped country.

There still was an atmosphere of tracks being covered up; even our own prisoners appeared to be in the conspiracy. Laurie sent Larry for Mungulla and Pindart, the two lubras who had gone out to the Banana Springs and hidden away and buried the bodies before Mr Reid could arrive. But the lubras had gone. Laurie ordered Davey immediately to circle the camp, pick up their tracks and follow them until he found them. If they had separated then bring in the one he caught first. Larry was to get busy on secret service work.

Walcott Inlet is a pretty place, the Harding Range to the right hemming it as half of a far-flung horseshoe down the centre of which the Calder runs into the Inlet. This "horseshoe" enclosed the widest flats and best alluvial agricultural country we had yet seen. The left of the horseshoe is the wildness of the Isdell and Charnley ranges, the great gash of the Charnley Gorge being plainly visible. The cliffs there run up to six hundred feet high. Some great ledges and caves form the art galleries of stone-age man. In those deep gorges where they approach the coast the native hide-outs are well nigh inaccessible. From the sea, the Inlet is narrow like a river running between cliffs; then it broadens to three miles wide only to narrow again in its forty-mile course inland, through picturesque country along the boomerang formed by the Artesian Range. Like a shallow river with muddy banks, it passes Munja homestead forty miles inland, until four miles farther on it ends where the Calder River flows into it. At the house, even at high tide, fresh water can be dipped from the Inlet, because the salt water forcing its way up the Inlet pushes the river water to the banks. The supply lugger at ordinary water can anchor within nine miles of the house. But on one day before full moon until five days after, and for a similar period at new moon, the lugger, like a pretty toy ship, comes sailing placidly on the tide right to the house.

When the Calder is in flood it comes roaring down carrying big trees to toss them into the Inlet whose oncoming tide furiously meets the flood-water, spins the trees like ninepins, and sweeps them back to the river from whence they came. From the distant sea that wall of foam comes atop of steadily advancing, swiftly rising water to resistlessly meet and force its way against the beaten hiss of the river stream. Hundreds of birds hover over the advancing foam, sweeping down on fish that come swimming up with the tide. Pelicans come gliding just behind the foamy wall. Occasionally when one experiences trouble in swallowing a big fish it carries the wriggling thing in its bill to the quieter water by the bank and there swallows its meal in peace.

Up with the tide too comes an occasional crocodile, snout awash in the swiftly moving water. One afternoon an aboriginal's dog on the opposite bank sniffed the air and smelt that a beast had been killed across at the station,

He leapt in to swim across. Presently a crocodile rose and moved leisurely out from the house bank. The dog turned and swam frantically back. When it was almost at the bank the crocodile swirled forward. As the dog was struggling up the bank the crocodile reached out a forepaw and clawed it under. Reid waited until the crocodile rose again, then shot it between the eyes. It raced to the centre of the channel rearing half out of the water, its thick forepaws clawing the air, its tail thrashing the water. But its day was done. It measured eighteen feet. A nuggety fifteen-footer with a tremendous barrel was shot; its upper forearm measured one inch more than the chest measurement of a four-years-old child.

When the tide is out the Inlet is a deep channel gleaming black under the sun. Except for the thread of river- water it is mud over sand, a clinging, sucking mud that in certain areas engulfs unwary horses and cattle, then squeezes their ribs with slow, awful pressure.

Returning from an inspection of the aboriginal art-galleries on the big sandstone ledges in the ranges, Toby and I wandered round the "lake," a marsh noisy with bird life, teeming with fish—a sportsman's and naturalist s paradise.

"Look aht! Cheeky feller!" warned Toby suddenly.

A stumpy reddish-brown snake, strikingly marked with thick black rings encircling its body every two inches apart, swayed a vindictive head almost at our horses hoofs.

"S'posem he bite man, he die quick," said Toby as the horses plunged away.

Half a dozen varieties of the wild plum gave an inkling of the aboriginals' knowledge of botany; a knowledge that sometimes enables him to foretell a season. This same knowledge of botany coupled with a knowledge of the movements of travelling bird life may suggest the clue by which certain old rain-makers at times foretell rain and floods. Mr Reid had been very anxious as to the coming "wet," but the aboriginals confidently foretold a big one.

"How you know him plenty wet ?"

"Plum-tree he plenty flower — altogether flower! He only

flower that way when big wet come."

The wet season just over did prove exceptionally heavy.

Incidentally the pear-tree (chestnut it is sometimes called) exudes a transparent gum strong as gum arabic. The aboriginals eat it, besides making it into a practically colourless liquid. It is very adhesive and has been used in that way for years past at the station. If gum arabic is commercially valuable, this wild gum at Walcott Inlet might well be utilized commercially.

There were three "characters" of dogs at the Inlet, Cobber, Jet and Lassie. Reid had trained these dogs to look after Mrs Reid and the youngsters during his absences. Full well those dogs understood their job. Lassie would sleep on the back steps, Jet on the front, Cobber in the yard midway between the steps and the gate. No native dared approach anywhere near after sundown. Sometimes Mrs Reid would take the youngsters for a walk to the lagoon where the bush birds and wild ducks and pygmy geese were always a sight worth seeing. Old Cobber would go too and warn off any native who dared venture near the pram. But the dogs took their duties too—enthusiastically shall we say? At meal-times, the natives would walk from their camp to the kitchen for rations. Cobber would hide under a corner of the store while Jet and Lassie formed an ambush near the kitchen. As the natives walked away with their rations the two dogs would spring out and menacingly demand a titbit. Whether they received blackmail or not the result was the same, for when the natives were returning past the store old Cobber would bound out with a roar and some startled lubra was certain to drop her tucker. Old Hancock, the greybeard, would invariably come limping along last, forgetting the robbers' lair until Cobber with a nasty growl was sniffing at his heels. The greybeard would wheel around, walk backwards, call "Good doggie" in soothing blackfellow gutturals, nervously throw Cobber a crust of damper—then turn and hurry on. But Cobber would come again and again, and each time the old man would turn and throw the dog a crust. By the time he reached camp he would have bribed Cobber with half his meal.

The game became so heart-rending at last that one day old Hancock stood helplessly and bawled pathetically for "Missus!" Only then was the full extent of the dogs' bushranging discovered. Reid was experiencing quite a task in breaking the well-fed dogs of this habit. Not that they wanted the few crusts they blackmailed; it was sheer animal enjoyment in the knowledge that they had the whip-hand over the natives.

21
HOME IN THE WILDERNESS

MEANWHILE, a well-organized conspiracy of silence was being maintained in regard to the native murder. Laurie had not experienced such complete unanimity before or such definite precaution. Probably other killings had taken place, and the tribesmen were apprehensive lest the complete solving of this one should lead to the discovery of others.

After a rapid chase, Davey returned with the lubra Mungulla. Her mate Pindart had disappeared towards Bundagin, the native name for Fred Merry's.

Mungulla uneasily corroborated the story of the killing. She had helped bury the bodies. She added that Gunner had "gone bush" just before the killings.

Through Nipper and Davey I sought the "Declaration of War," the message-stick sent by the Upper Charnley men to the Ngarinyin. Fortunately it was still lying about the camp. There were seven main points and it was translated thus:

1. To the people of the Oonyaryin and Ngarinyin at the white-fella house at Walcott Inlet
2. Ladmurra's fighting men are ready
3. Ungandongery's (Charcoal's) spearmen are ready
4. The men of the Gibb River are ready
5. The men of Youngindah are ready
6. We will come down the Isdell and meet you where the paper-bark creek meets with the river
7- We will return to the Gibb River and fight.

The stick gave the precise directions as to where the enemy allies were to congregate. Each enemy warrior particularly challenged was marked on the stick. Directions were given for the enemy to march upstream to the meeting-place. After confirmation of hostilities and a preliminary skirmish, both sides were to march to the Gibb River for the big fight.

So the roaming patrol had frustrated a promising war. It must have been aggravating, especially to the principals: Nipper, collecting his spearmen en route to the Gibb River assembling grounds when the patrol caught him; Charcoal, away across at Mount

Elizabeth mashalling his warriors to march to the Gibb River and meet his Youngindah allies. With these feverish movements of fighting men over the country a wandering patrol must have assumed very little importance until it captured the "generals" and stopped the war.

"We will ride to-morrow," said Laurie one evening. "Right. Have you solved the killing?"

Yes. That outlaw band did it beyond doubt—just ordinary blood lust."

"Are you going to arrest them?"

"No. It would require a special patrol to catch them. They've vanished in the most inaccessible country in the Kimberleys, and they know it like a book. They know the police too, worse luck. I nearly had them once, closed on them, but just didn't have that last moment necessary to rush and grab. They were away like wild goats and went the faster when I shouted I'd shoot. They knew perfectly well I was aiming at their feet. Since then they've boasted to station-boys that even if the police can surround them they'll only shoot to frighten them.

No, it will need a patrol equipped with no other object in view, to arrest them. I'm encumbered by prisoners and sick and will soon have more. My job, now, will take me up the coast north to Port George Mission. Then I'll turn in a half-circle back to Grace's Knob and try to catch the Worachi murder men. If we run across that little outlaw band while doubling back it will be just one of those lucky things that sometimes happen."

Next morning, to the glum farewells of Toby and Dick, the patrol rode away in fine trim, humans and animals freshened by the spell. Mrs Nipper and Mrs Charcoal swung along in great style, singing some haunting native chant. When out of sight of the Walcott homestead Mrs Charcoal divested herself of the Flame, the others following her example with laughing relief. Even Mrs Oomagun had mislaid her scowl for the time being. Nipper was as lively as a tom-tit; Charcoal and Oomagun strode along in animated talk carrying their bags of bones. We had three skeletons now, but the last two did not seem to matter so very much; they belonged to "another country." Burrin's skeleton too seemed to lose its phantom properties the farther we travelled from his country. We wondered if the spirits would return when we doubled back and traversed that area again.

We were climbing grassy basalt hills, under the shadow of the Harding Range. The prolific bird life around the Inlet was thinning out but grey rosellas and zebras and painted finches made the bush merry, while as we climbed into the sandstones the pretty spinifex pigeon tripped along ahead. Above, a black cockatoo wheeled in heavy flight, his harsh lonely cry ringing out far above.

Very soon Baby Merry would be climbing this same trail, a baby pioneer to his pioneer's home. He would ride over the mountains in his little sedan cot, his baby eyes gazing at the ochred backs of his savage bodyguard; at vistas of mountains and valleys and tree-lined torrents; he would wonder at forests of giant grasses rising to either side; would see sunlight kissing the cliffs and vast miles of tree-tops; would watch an army of grasstops rippling prettily under the breeze. He would hear the gurgling of creeks as bare black feet splashed across, and listen to the laughing gutturals of the Ngarinyin, and the dingo's mournful howl in the chill of evening. His wondering eyes would watch the great shadows falling from the range, and see the campfire dancing on the white paper-barks. His lullaby would be the crooning of stone-age songs, the whispering of the night.

Fitting lullaby indeed for the son of a pioneer in the last pioneer's land.

When we camped at Brockman's Creek, Davey set Mrs Charcoal to washing his clothes. He was very particular about a large, spotted blue handkerchief that adorned his dandy neck. Nodding towards him, I said:

"I suppose that means we meet people tomorrow."

"Yes," answered Laurie, "he leads a butterfly life. No sooner farewells one crowd of ladies than he has his clothes washed to meet another."

"Oh, well, he didn't enjoy much social life at the Inlet."

"No, I kept him busy. Still, I have my suspicions."

Towards sunset next afternoon the patrol suddenly quickened its pace, a sign that we were approaching a camp. Larry and Davey cantered ahead. Almost immediately we rounded a tiny hill, turned sharply to the left, and rode past a long rocky mound covered with gunyahs from which rose coils of blue smoke. Natives stood staring, ubras leapt into the gunyahs with youngsters running at their heels, dogs barked but were snarled into silence. Before us stood tall white paper-barks of the Sale River, beautiful yellow gums amongst them. Between the trees on the opposite bank glowed the grey bark roofs of low buildings tinged pink under the rays o the setting sun. We rode down into tall green grasses then splashed across the gurgling river. The little buildings we had seen were fronted by green rows of sweetpotatoes and pineapple. Ten acres of peanuts stood out vividly green, and across the flat, just visible, was a small mob of sheep. All this represented the work of one mans hands. From the homestead dogs came snarling; natives drawing a crowd of rations stared towards us; the mules hurried to group around Laurie's horse cheerfully aware that another long stage was done. A white man came striding out:

"Hullo, Laurie!"

"Hullo, Fred! How's things?"

"Not bad. Glad you came. I'm just about perishing or a. talk. And I'm a bit uneasy about this 'big sick' question. But introduce me to your friend."

" 'Jack' Idriess," waved Laurie. "Fred Merry "

"Glad to meet you," said Merry as he shook hands and rather hard. "Doctor, I believe?"

"Laurie laughed at his obvious disappointment.

"My mistake," explained Merry. "Smoke-talk! The natives signalled that the patrol was coming with a 'big feller doctor' to cure what they call the 'big sick.'"

"I'm afraid I'm only a wanderer, Mr Merry."

"Welcome just the same," he said heartily. "Hop off and let the boys take your horses."

"I suppose Pindart has gone?" said Laurie as we dismounted.

"Yes. She took to the hills with a leper. From the smoke-talks I really thought you must have been bringing out the native Leprosy .Commission that I've heard vague rumours of."

A little over medium height, broad shouldered, alert with a cheery smile. Such is Merry. He must have an iron will to have withstood the terrible loneliness from the day he rode here until he carved out his home and married.

"Joe!" he roared. "Call the boys and give a hand with these packs. Quick feller now."

"They'll look after the animals," he said as a quiet, Indian type of half-caste came with half a dozen stock-boys. "Pick out a place for your 'guests' while I hurry the kitchen wenches. Sling your swags inside and by then I'll have dinner ready. The sooner it's over the sooner we can talk."

The prisoners, with swift glances at the homestea blacks, were fixed up comfortably; the sick and the women chose their camping-places, gossiping low toned. The sun sank in cool twilight. Mule-bells tinkled. From the bush blacks' camp across the river a long-drawn cry shrieked into conversation or message. From the homestead blacks, a cry arose in answer. After a wash, healthily tired and hungry, we strolled into Merry's home.

He was hungrier for news than we were for food. News of Derby and the outside world, and of the settlers over the range.

Not until we got up from table did Laurie get a chance to slyly remark: "I believe we may congratulate you on an addition to the population of these parts."

Merry laughed boyishly.

"Yes, he'll be in full possession in a fortnight, in this very room. Mrs Merry didn't want to go away but I stood on my dignity and insisted. It was the first real row we had and I won. She wanted to compromise then and go to Walcott Inlet. But I wouldn't stand for that either! Mrs Reid would have looked after her like a mother, but what if anything had happened! Impossible to get a doctor you know. What good would all this have been to me if I'd lost her! A man can easily get another selection but a wife and kid who suit is a different matter. So I made up my mind she might as well go right to her people in Victoria and make a real holiday of it. And when I pointed out she could fly from Broome and have an aeroplane ride, she began to see sense in it. But she no sooner got there than she wanted to come back again, fancy riding in a plane three thousand miles and seeing Perth and Adelaide and Melbourne and being in a hurry to return to this! Just listen!"

Before we could get a word in edgeways he had produced a well-thumbed letter and was reading extracts."Bring me back home. I long for the smell of the bush. I miss the bleat of the sheep in the evening and the corroboree songs at moonrise."

Laurie and Fred, being married, seemed to have some bond m common. I glanced around at the iron and bark walls decorated with spears and ochred totem-sticks, at the bare floor of hard earth, at the hurricane lamp dimly glowing upon rough, bush-made furniture. The cleanliness, the stern simplicity of everything in this big living-room, was fitting ornament. No room for anything but the most useful articles in an area where transport is a terrific problem. But it was easy to imagine it home, a palace in the wilderness where all was sternly primitive.

22
LIFE IN PIONEER LAND

"THERE'S fierce competition among the house lubras as to who is to be nursemaid," laughed Merry. "My wife and the lubras were playmates when she was a girl at Port George. She brought her favourites along here when we married. When I told them a white piccaninny was coming, skin and hair were flying within minutes; each was certain she was better qualified to nurse a white piccaniny than the other hussies. They've never seen a white baby. The daily argument intrigued my old nigger, George. He came along and said: 'Hey boss! these gins no good! *They* no more savvy white missus piccanin! Me savvy. Last time me longa Roeboume jail me look after white missus piccanin proper feller!' But I thought there might be trouble with the missus if I engaged a one-time murderer as nursemaid. Old One-Eye had overheard George's application, so next day he shuffled up and said, 'Boss! that feller George dam humbug! Him no savvy look after white missus piccanin. Me savvy plenty.' He waved a-skinny arm towards four murderous-looking black kids quarrelling in the dust. 'Family belong me!' he announced proudly. 'Me look after white-feller piccanin.'

"There's a little gang of youngsters from the bush natives' camp across the river," said Merry to me. The wife and I call them the 'Kelly Gang.' You wouldn't find a more promising crowd of future bushrangers anywhere in the continent. All day long they're spearing goannas, frogs, lizards, birds and fowls when they're not swimming in the river and trying to hold the little girls heads under water. They're always stealing eggs, watermelons, peanuts, and every bit of iron or wire they can lay hand or toe to. When I'm working in the shed they often turn up and become greatly interested and ask most intelligent questions; and all the time they are collecting nails between their toes. It's astonishing the number of nails they can carry away like that. And every nail is worth money out here. We've had to warn them right away from the house, but must still keep constant watch against their raids from the river. To put us off the scent half of them keep splashing and yelling in the river while the others spy out the land. If we are busy in the shed they're in the house or outbuildings. Those kids are sophisticated monkeys and, in general, play merry hell all day long. They've picked up pidgin- English from the few old regulars I keep about the place and speak it much better than the old hands themselves. I told the Kelly Gang one day about the white-feller piccanin.

"'Him walk?' the leader demanded.

"'Not yet. Close up.'

"'We teach him!' they volunteered and brandished reed spears. *We teach him spear him lizard, spear him dog, spear him 'roo, bimeby teach him spear him man'. We teach him wommera, corroboree, totem, teach him track, teach him fight, teach him allasame warrior!'

"So I wrote the wife telling her that as the Kelly Gang have volunteered to tutor the coming Merry, his education may be regarded as assured."

Laurie laughed:

"I can see all sorts of complications a year or two from now. The youngster will pick up the abo language faster than his own."

Yes," said Merry grimly, "the swear words first of all. And as the mother speaks native fluently there'll be some battles royal with the growing Kelly Gang."

In the small hours of the morning we turned into bunk. Then Merry voiced his worry.

"This leprosy, Laurie! I never troubled about it when I was in the bush on my own. It didn't seem to be of this virulent type. But now with a wife and youngster it has me all upset. Is it contagious?"

Laurie explained the leprosy question at length, and then asked if it had broken out here.

"Yes. It's among them. I know of two bad cases at least that are camped separately out in the hills. There's quite a ring of campers all around the place and I suspect them all of the 'big sick.' They knew you were coming and took to the bush. They are convinced that if you take them to Derby they will die there, and they would rather die out in the hills. I'm really worried. I've had seventy of them down with influenza; it would have been a wipe out if I hadn't had plenty of influenza mixture. I've worked a miracle: only lost one patient—an old man. They've got him up in a tree now with half a ring of stones around him. The rest will be completed when he dries up a bit, for old Wantadedgo the witch-doctor has found a 'black spot' in the small of the corpse's back. Wantadedgo reckons there is a poison stone in there, an he hints that he knows the man who charmed it in. So the corpse awaits vengeance until the doctor makes his autopsy. Then there'll be another case for you, Laurie.

"There's so many that a dozen patrols travelling all the year round couldn't keep touch with them. But," he added grimly and reached for his boots, "I'll fix Wantadedgo. Which camp is he in — the bush camp?"

"Do you want him?" asked Merry and leaned up in his bunk.

"Yes I do He was responsible for the killing of Winidot at Cape Voltaire. I'll stop him from killing this new victim anyway."   .

"Too late!" said Merry and lay back in his bunk. "He's gone."

"Oh!"

"Yes. Got word of your coming by the usual means and just vanished. You won't get him."

"One of these days I'll catch him. That old devil is responsible for other killings.

"   Well," resumed Merry, "I got the whole crowd of these influenza people on their feet, all except the most important man of all — barring Willie. He is away at the Inlet now, with loading. Willie is the king of this crowd and staunch to me. The sick man has a lot of influence which is very important to me as he is a good worker and satisfied and friendly to Willie. Together they hold the crowd to me against the influence of the wild *munjons*. And now this man is just about on his last legs. He was the first man but one down and he is the last to get up, except the old corpse. A big, powerful fellow, strong as a bull. But I can't cure him; and yet I've cured sixty-eight."

"I'll have a look at him in the morning," promised Laurie. But there's little hope of me succeeding if you have failed, after the years of experience you've had in doctoring them."

"You might know of something I don't that may turn the tide. It's a stitch in time saves nine, Laurie. There's going to be a big job for you if he passes out."

"Why, particularly?"

"Because he is a 'big man.' Your old friend Wantadedgo is already muttering vengeance. He says the Walcott Inlet men have sung him, and this tribe will meet the Walcott men and fight when the big walk-about comes, after the peanut season. Old Wantadedgo reckons he can hammer the Walcott men; there are sub-branches of the Ngarinyin away out in the hills he can influence. He'll try and drag in a few of the Worara and Wonambun men too."

"Oh, well," said Laurie, "I can't help it. They are wiping themselves out in just the same way all over the bush."

Next morning Laurie held sick parade. There were only a few sick among them. Then came the job of trying to induce the runaway lepers and Pindart and several others that Laurie wanted to come in from the hills.

"I can't stay more than a few days," he said to Merry. Can I have the loan of a couple of good boys who know the country and the hide-outs?"

"Yes. Take Joe; he can pick his own mates."

Half-caste Joe is a quiet, slim Indian type, holding his job and his destiny too among the bush blacks by means of quiet thinking. Joe has lived among whites for years yet is heart and soul an aboriginal. Fully initiated too. His wife is a bright little lubra. Having the sense to live a little above yet with the blacks, Joe is studiously loyal to the whites. Destiny has placed Joe in an awkward position.

In a soft, quiet voice Joe told us of several other lepers in the hills, bad cases. They only came down to the homestead occasionally on the off chance of cadging a little tobacco from the regulars. He volunteered to go out with several boys and try to induce the lepers to come in. "How did the influenza come here?" asked Laurie.

"A boy brought it from Port George. He had a message-stick."

"Then why do they talk of fighting the Walcott Inlet people."

"I don't know. Perhaps because the 'doctor' doesn't like the Walcott Inlet 'doctor'."

"What will happen if the sick man dies?"

"They will put up the stones. When the wind blows it will show on the stones the men who killed him. But the Old Men who see won't say a word."

"What then?"

"Nothing. The doctor will kill a lizard. Then he will sing the *ungulla*, the 'poison stick.' Then he will go alone to the 'sacred hill' where the 'watcher' minds the 'sacred phlora' sticks. When he comes back he will sing the men who charmed the dead man."

"What then?"

"When walk-about time comes they will go all together to Walcott Inlet. Walcott boys will go walk-about, and old Yobudda, the rain-maker, will go with them. One day they will take the sung men on a kangaroo hunt, and kill them."

"Then there'll be a fight?"

"Yes."

"Very well. You tell them that I know all about it, and that if there are any killings, the next time I come I'll take all the killers, and the doctor too, to Derby jail."

"Yes."

"Davey!"

"Yes, boss."

"You take tucker for three days. Take good boy too. Get on the tracks of Pindart. Bring her in, and the leper who is with her."

"Yes, boss."

A sudden, long-drawn howl curdled out from across the river. A human dingo might have made such an awful sound. Merry threw out helpless hands. "He's gone!" he said. "The death-wail. I've been listening for that all the morning. There you are, Laurie, you'll, have a fresh case soon!"

Violent crying broke out, wailing of lubras. The house lubras ran from the homestead straight towards the river; hunters from the homestead camp strolled more leisurely down, carrying wommera and spear. The wailing increased from the opposite bank.

"Shall we look at the sheep?" suggested Merry. "There'll be nothing doing today."

We strolled across the cultivated patch where bags and big-pronged forks were scattered, dropped by the natives who had been digging the peanut plants when the death-wail curdled out. Merry pointed to a patch that showed signs of a struggle: "I had a bit of a scrap here two days ago. One of my boys had been nursing a grudge for weeks and he tried to jab a fork into my back. But I had been expecting something to happen."

"How did you fare?" I asked.

"Oh, we wrestled for a bit, then I managed to wrench the fork away. I thumped him then. He battled gamely. Couldn't fight, but he was good at all-in wrestling—legs, arms, claws and teeth. He forced me to beat him to his knees before he gave in."

"What did the others do?"

"They just looked on. If he'd got me down they'd have rushed in to the kill. Instead, he got the father of a hiding. So they went on with their work when it was all over."

"And the boy?" asked Laurie.

"He's all right; was working cheerfully next day. Don't say anything to him, Laurie. According to their lights it was a fair fight and all is over now. I'm only too pleased he got it off his chest; I was waiting for it a long time. It's a bit nervy out here, all alone among a hundred of them, when you know that one man backed up by his mates has got it in for you."

We came to the sheep in a lawn-like paddock fenced with brushwood, low rocky hills behind.

"There are just sufficient sheep in there to keep the grass eaten down. See the grass around the fence? It is four feet high. That lawn in there is the same grass only the sheep keep it mowed. This grass never grows high enough to produce the grass seed that old hands say will prove fatal to the introduction of sheep over the range. This is only an experimental flock, just to prove it really is possible to breed sheep here."

"How about dingoes?" inquired Laurie.

"Troublesome, but poison-bait keeps them down. Perhaps there never will be sheep in large mobs in this country; it is too hilly and rough, with the grasses untried. Still, who knows! There are countless small valleys between the hills where a small flock could be run to help the settler. When I came here on my old horses I had never grown a cabbage in my life. Didn't know how to handle a plough. Knew nothing about sheep. Was a cattleman pure and simple. And you see what I've done in five years. Why shouldn't others do the same and better? There's country enough for thousands so far as that goes. Of course, every man must learn the little differences in local conditions: the species of plants to put in; and the type of sheep and rams for the country.

"A man must he prepared to ride the country, find his own land, then squat down and put up a hut. That means shepherding the sheep for a start, building a brush fence until he can afford wire, and so on. One ton of wire costs £25 to land here. When a few wild nigs come in he must 'educate' the most intelligent looking; they will come in handy. When he finds a likely looking black- soil flat he should dig and find if the soil goes down eighteen inches or eighteen feet. I've proved that, here anyway, there is no difficulty with grass seed so long as I shear in March before the grass seeds fall. The wool has a tendency to grow fine and tender, but this can be remedied by utilizing big-framed rams. The sheep grow used to the country and soon learn to clamber up both the basalt and sandstone hills. The sandstone tabletops sometimes are ten to twenty miles wide with 'spinifex' water even up on the flat tops. So you see the carrying capacity of the country grows. There are some valleys that are good for breeding but not for fattening, and vice versa. The blowflies come in March, but if a man shears then the flies don't bother much. The flies strike young lambs, but then the lambing could be regulated.

"There are lots of local problems the answers to which a newcomer would have to learn for himself. He would have to find and make his own tracks, of course, because there are none here. He must learn that the basalt country if burned late does not shoot so readily, but that the sandstone country gets a shoot on quickly, because of springs and soakage. Bullocks in October and November will grow fat if they poke in under the sandstone while those on richer basalt are poor. Bullocks are afraid of the sandstones. They like to poke out on the basalts where they can see all around them—and have a chance to escape the blacks' spears. Creeks and rivers in the lower country, in certain areas, could be easily fenced to hold say five thousand sheep. Away back on the Moran and Roe considerably larger areas could be fenced. I'm convinced, provided a man was prepared to be lonely and willing to learn, that this country could be quickly developed to carry a few thousand homes anyway."

"What of transport?"

"That is the real problem, the killer of development. I solved it personally by buying three mangy old camels from a dingo-stiffener. This is not camel-country but they have worked the miracle for me. I've got more now. They pack my peanuts to Walcott and the lugger takes them to Broome whence they are shipped to Freamantle, only about another thousand miles away."

The Patrol boils the billy.

23

"WHO WILLED THE WARRIOR TO DIE?"

IT was a plucky experiment, to risk bringing sheep into this Country. And droving them there was a little epic in the present-day annals of pioneering. Bob Thompson brought them from Noonkanbah station on the Fitzroy River, West Kimberley. With his cunning dogs he and four aboriginals drove the eight hundred and fifty head over the great range and the many ranges between, finding his own route, carrying the sheep across the Isdell. The job took three months, the aboriginals shepherding the little mob when Thompson had to poke away ahead and find a route over some particularly tricky stage. The ewes lambed on the way. Bob allowed the lambs to find their feet, then pushed slowly on again. All told, he lost only fifty.

During the next few days Merry and Laurie were busy, so I just prowled about. Old George, one of Merry's regulars, hoping for tobacco, volunteered as guide. But his little wife, Rosie, demurred. Jealous as a wildcat, she was positive that if I gave George tobacco he would sneak away and share it with some other damsel. She told him so in a voice that shrilled while her eyes fairly jumped in her head.

Rosie, then a demure little thing of sixteen, had originally appeared at the homestead with two other young lubras, in charge of an old man of eighty. She was a *munjon*, as wild as the hills, ready to run at a shadow. Old George urgently wanted a wife, so Merry, as a reward for valour, "bought" the *munjon* girl from the ancient and christened her Rosie. Tribal etiquette being favourable, the marriage was satisfactorily completed, and wild and woolly Rosie was given a blanket and told she was civilized. With bowed head she left the wild bush camp and came across the river to the homestead camp. Meekly she followed George and threw her blanket down beside his.

For a time, the gunyah showed every prospect of blossoming into a happy home. But Rosie's primitive upbringing spoiled the idyll. One bright morning she was climbing a tree for nuts. A young lubra, glancing up from beneath, giggled and passed a rude remark.

Rosie slid straight down and leapt at the cheeky one. Skin and hair flew while they screeched and kicked and scratched. Rosie won by biting her antagonist's ear.

Old George was delighted; a proud man indeed—until his turn came. She had her claws in his hair and her teeth in his ear before he could snatch a fighting-stick.

Hence, I was wary of encouraging old George lest his excitable bride bring trouble to all.

Caution was justified, for during the following days George's domestic troubles loomed thunderous: glum looks from Rosie in the homestead kitchen; a strained expression on old George's face as he pottered around the yard. Then one morning early he came agitatedly up to the homestead.

"Hey, boss! This *munjon* gin belonga me won't wash does belonga me."

"Why won't she?"

"She too sulky feller! All a time growl, growl, growl!"

As domestic trouble among his henchmen was not conducive to happy working Merry treated Rosie to a little lecture on wifely duties. She listened in a sullen silence —until George crept back home at sundown.

"You 'summons' me!" she shrieked in native, "you take our troubles before a white man! You spineless son of a black snake! You haven't the guts to tackle me, a weak woman! You! the sooner you are off the earth the sweeter everything will smell!" She worked up to it in fine style tiptoeing round him like a cat with arched back, her eyes blazing, fingers clenched, body trembling until with a final passionate scream she flew at him. From the mix up down there in the dust came an anguished yell as George broke away leaving her a fistful of beard. Panting, thoroughly aroused now, she chased him to Merry, with blazing eyes shrieking accusations against him. When Merry quietened her it appeared that the real cause of the trouble was that old George had given the weekly supply of beef-bones away to "Some other thing!" and for "a week" they had not had a "bite to eat."

Old George had to do penance for that little lapse. George shivered all that bitterly cold night on a bag outside the gunyah, while Rosie slept inside with the entrance hole blocked up with a sheet of bark.

Old George had to eat more dust before Rosie would take him back again.

"You've been working well lately, George," said Merry to the miserable man several mornings later, "I'll have to get you another young wife."

"No fear, boss!" exclaimed the startled George.

"Rosie one too much!"

A night came, ominously quiet. The spasmodic wailing across the river had ceased; little flares of light peeped among the trees over there; larger fires from before the huts of the homestead blacks.

"I don't like it," said Merry. "It's too unusual. Perhaps the wailing has ceased because the police are here, but I don't think so. I'm worried about what will happen when Big Willie returns from the Inlet."

"He is a steady boy," reassured Laurie.

"Yes, and with influence luckily. He orders all the corroborees; keeps the bucks in order; quietens the whole camp when trouble breaks out at night, and keeps a strong hand on the nomads who come in from the hills when the peanut season is on. There are better fighters in camp; but he's got a solid little crowd behind him, and the individual fire-eaters know they'd be mobbed if they started trouble. Still, that man who died is important; he was forty years old, and at that age a man is an asset of great value to a tribe. This particular man, too, was a fully initiated warrior, and had a good deal of authority. I admit I'm worried. There's no telling what those Old Men will work the young fellows up to while Willie is away. And Wantadedgo is sure to be in touch with them."

"They won't start anything while the patrol is here."

"No. And if you will only return this way from Port George Willie will be back by then."

"I'll return this way if I can."

"Good. I wish you could clean out the lepers, too, Laurie. If that disease spreads there'll be few of these natives left in another ten years or so."

"I'll do my best," promised Laurie. "But what chance has one patrol of cleaning up scores of thousands of square miles of country? And I've got my own particular job to do as well."

A warning smoke had gone up to the lepers in the hills. The tribesmen had denied that the "big sick" was amongst them, yet we knew that messengers had gone out to every hidden native; knew there was a close espionage on all our movements.

Meanwhile under their trees near the house each group of the troops was comfortably settled, enjoying the spell while with expressionless face, or scowl, or sly sarcastic laugh noting the strange blacks who ever and anon passed by. Feeling comfortably safe under police protection; quite aware of all that was going on; knowing more, probably, than we knew. Proud men too. Charcoal threw out his chest to the scowling glances as certain natives walked past. For he and Oomagun were "bad" men. Charcoal was more of a wanderer than Oomagun and was particularly well known among the Ngarinyin and Wonambun. Oombali was obviously uneasy whenever a group of munjons appeared. Allboroo seemed concerned in another way; we found later that tribesmen in passing were sign-signalling to him. The coast near here was his country.

The shock troops, with Mrs Charcoal in the Flame and the others variously attired, were thoroughly enjoying themselves though not venturing near the tribal lubras.

An aboriginal woman's dress is a simple affair. If a *munjon* she wears nothing, and looks well in it. If civilized, her dress material comes from a bolt of dungaree. The height of the lubra is roughly measured, then with shears a doubled length is cut out of the dungaree (generally three yards). Sew the sides together. Put a tin plate under the top end, then cut around it. This is the neck. Then cut a piece out of both top corners. These are the arm-holes and the dress is made, and is the model. But if the gin cuts into the waist and tucks it, it is a "creation." If she sews a piece of red calico around the bottom and armholes and neck, it is a "limousine."

One day while walking among the hills I suddenly heard a chopping. Curiosity may get a man into trouble, but it teaches him things. Over rocks and among shrubby timber I climbed down on to a little flat between two low hills. In the centre of the flat, tribesmen were erecting a sort of shed. They kept on working. They might not have done so but for the puzzling white handkerchief on my hat. This being the "big doctor" travelling with a police patrol ensured a box-seat in a ceremony I might not have been allowed to witness otherwise. I sat down quietly fifty yards away. The framework was of strong white gum forks, three to one end, two to the other, each fork about nine feet above the ground. Poles connected the forks. On these poles were laid cross-poles, very much as in a bushman's bough and sapling kitchen. Underneath the erection and for a radius of sixty feet around it every blade of grass had been pulled, leaving a bare, red floor. Bearded tribesmen were cutting slender timber on the rocky hill close by; others were carrying it down to the building. They worked seriously, each man to his job. No women were present. Two men were carrying from the creek selected flat sandstones like small slabs; most were about two feet long, eight inches broad, and up to three inches thick. These were being laid evidently as the beginning of a circle that would enclose the cleared space and the erection. An old witch-doctor was squatting some yards from the circle, with an assistant six feet behind him. They looked like two black crows, their eyes unblinkingly staring towards the stones. The old doctor had a red and white ochre band around the head and a broad white bar across his forehead that gave a queer effect to his wrinkled eyes. His skinny limbs were heavily cicatrized. A long moustache and beard com¬pleted the adornment. Presently he got up and walked to the first stone, squatted, and began rubbing it with the flat of his hand, mumbling. Patiently he rubbed red ochre over it, his lips moving as he charmed this stone to take its place in some drama. Evidently, this was to be the burial platform of the dead warrior, and here was the witch-doctor making all ready to ascertain by divination the person responsible, by malign influence, for the warrior's death. Now there came a low hum of voices from lubras hidden amongst bushes. The doctor squatted, motionless. The assistant got up and walking to the creek knelt as if to drink. He returned with his cheeks bulging, knelt, and squirted water all over the stone. The stone turned a bright red; he rubbed it with the palm of his hand till it became a rich dull red all over. Stone after stone (each one of which repre¬ented a man) was treated in the same way. And among those stones were one or two that would ultimately be stained by a man's death warrant. The tribesmen that these stones represented had been selected by the Council of Old Men as being probable enemies of the dead man and may have caused his death.

Some of these fateful stones they ochred white, according to the tribe or horde the suspected man represented, and to his initiation or totemic degrees. Size and position counted too, varying with the man's degrees and the geographical position and importance of his tribe. Each worker was deeply in earnest, each careful to the smallest detail. New men came along with white bars painted across their foreheads. These laid seven poles across each end of the framework, leaving a gap in the centre; then they laid more poles at right angles to the first, always working from the sides towards the centre. A centre stick completed the work and made a platform.

A sudden wild call and all, including doctor and assistant, were on their feet. A guttural discussion broke out.

After a while, the doctors returned to their work; the others hurried away fan-wise soon to return loaded with freshly cut gum-leaves.

They dropped these and returned for more, four men remaining to complete the frame-work. During this particular work the old doctor crouched upright to superintend the laying of each stick. Down the centre, apparently where the body would lie, a row of smaller sticks about four feet long were placed with an especially thick one two feet in length where his head would probably lie. There was much discussion, and many directions given to the man on top, as to the exact placing of these sticks; for the warrior in his last rest must lie in the exact geographical position. Then came an especially long and strong stick for the opposite end. To help place this a second man climbed up. Then the leaves were handed up, the two doctors now squatting on the ground and directing.

The leaves were spread thickly but carefully, for this last touch to the warrior's couch appeared important indeed. When finished to every one's satisfaction, one man solemnly stretched out on that bed of leaves. He tested it, buried himself in the leaves, the while staring up at the sky. And there planing in great circles was an eagle. And already on gaunt trees on the nearby hill-sides crows were collecting, karking companionably, patiently waiting. They dared not come near yet.

Below the platform men stared up, awaiting the verdict of the man lying on top. They advised him to try a slightly different position. He did so, squirming himself down into place. In rapid grunts they voiced final approval, and the man climbed down.

All was now ready for the sleeper. Without a word the bearers hurried away. Only the old doctor, his assistant, and I remained.

THE SILENT WITNESSES

24
LIFE IN ABORIGINAL-LAND

THE old doctor and his assistant, methodically working, had now most of the painted stones erected in a ring around the cleared patch. The doctor crooned as with a deliberate, mesmeric movement he rubbed his hand over the smooth face of each. I wondered if any of his forbears thousands of years ago, perhaps in ancient Egypt, had done the same thing.

Distantly, a wailing of women's voices as if something dear had been lost. Then silence. Shortly afterwards a black group appeared, bearing the body of a man. Lubras followed, carrying his sheets of tea-tree sleeping-bark. The body was put down and an old man climbed on to the leafy platform. The lubras disappeared. The old man carefully spread the sleeper's bark on the depression made in the leaves, and then perforated the bark with a pointed stick. Meanwhile the bearers folded the dead man's hands naturally across his body and then tied his thumbs together with hibiscus-bark string. The old doctor, now carrying his weapons, walked fifty yards away then turned and stood facing the burial platform directly in line with the spot where the sleeper's head would lie. He placed his spears on the ground beside him, but still grasped the wommera. Sternly, he voiced an order. The dead man was lifted to men standing on the platform. Every move was now made in response to deliberate instructions. The sleeper was laid on the hark, then swathed in bark sheets and covered with armfuls of fresh green leaves. All was done thoroughly and so that the waiting crows should be disappointed. The doctor mumbled to his assistant, who went and spoke to the toilers. One of them came to me and insinuated with a smile:

"We go dinner-time!"

I took the hint. They had been very decent. Whatever secret rite was to be performed now was not the business even of a "big doctor" who had come to cure the "big sick."

When returning to the homestead I passed the *munjons'* camp. Not a soul was to be seen, not even a dog. Then from the other side of the rocks a young lubra came swiftly. Her chocolate body gleamed in the sun; matted hair hung down over her forehead; she stepped with the aboriginal's noiseless action that can become speed on the instant. Suddenly she poised, her black eyes dilating, teeth gleaming, then wheeled and leapt and vanished. An opportunity missed for a striking snap-shot of Eve.

Next day curiosity took me to the burial platform. I was the only visitor, apparently the only living soul near it. The warrior was compactly encased with green saplings upon which were still green leaves. All the "divining" stones were erected, twenty-two altogether; eighteen of them were white, four red, and all were securely embedded in the ground. At the eastern side of the ring, with their backs exactly to the risen sun, were three stones planted two feet behind the others: one very small, one larger, and a large square one—all white. The smallest of all the stones in the circle were red, and the painted surface of each squarely faced towards the man.

The warrior lay with his head pointing north of east. Easier to realize now how a drip of fat might mark any stone. Already that had begun. The ground directly below the body was moist; flies hummed there. An occasional drip was coming from the perforations made in the bark sheet yesterday. I looked around. The place was the dead centre of a tiny valley between two low spurs of hills and enclosed at one end. When wind comes, it sighs over a ridge-top into the valley where the low spurs turn it in practically any direction. Hence, any current of air may, when a drop is falling, carry it towards any stone. It may not splash a stone, or reach one; it may be carried over the top, or fall between two stones. The body is so encased by saplings, bark and leaves that each drop must come through one of those perforated holes—and fall straight down if there is no current, or take its equal chance of being blown anywhere if there is one. The man on whose stone the first drop fell would be "unlucky." Sooner or later that would happen, and the man represented by that stone would die.

Musing on the grim chances of primitive life, I wandered over bare rock hillocks where queerly shaped rocks appeared naturally stacked among the short, scrubby trees and tufted grass. These indicate where the storm-waters swirl in the "wet." I climbed a gentle rise of shining, flint-hard rock washed bare for hundreds of yards. The sides of this great bare patch were lined with tufted spinifex. Upon the rock itself were rows of table-topped sandstones the size of corn-sacks, placed as if for giants to sit in council. Along the lower slope, in groups, lay long stones roughly resembling ancient Egyptian sarcophagi.

Everywhere on the bare rocks were little flat chipping- stones and piles of chips where primitive man had been chipping stone axes and spearheads for centuries. Spinifex pigeons, quaintly pretty with their topknots, ran ahead across the hare rock. In the whispering silence came a sudden, distinct "tap, tap, tap, tap." I looked around expecting to see a native chipping a spearhead. Couldn't see him. I sauntered along, and bent down to examine some bright-red chips of stone. "Tap, tap, tap, tap," sharper and clearer. But silence when I stood up. Presently I tried a ruse, bent down as if to examine something. "Tap, tap"—it stopped the moment I wheeled around. So the game went on. Possibly this was taboo ground and this mysterious tapping the method to frighten the trespasser.

Davey returned to the homestead with a big, powerful native and his lubra. He was a bad leper case. Just above his eyes the forehead was swollen into ridges. All down his back were the ominous lumps. He gazed at Laurie from dog-like eyes. His arms hung limp, bereft of the twitching strength to hurl a spear. The poor brute's shoulders were bowed a little. Obviously, he could not understand. His dull eyes should have been alight with fire and life; his powerful form should have been bounding over the hills spear in hand. I could imagine how his voice would ring when excited in the chase. And now he was only a big man slowly petrifying away. He had crept into the hills when the patrol came. Now he gazed at Laurie, his swollen face pathetically suggestive of a stony hope. Mutely, he showed Laurie yet another disease, the disease that is hideously worse than leprosy. Truly, this poor wretch had been doubly accursed.

The trackers also had Pindart, the woman witness who had helped bury the old man and woman murdered near Walcott Inlet. Her ribs spoke eloquently of travelling far and fast with but few halts to dig food. She glared at Laurie, her hair a mass of clay balls. But now she was caught she was wearily glad. She was quite willing to describe what she knew of the killing.

The trackers had induced another leper to join them, but he had become frightened and slipped away in the night. Both trackers had covered nearly seventy miles on foot.

"Put the Big Leper with the other lepers," ordered Laurie, "and Pindart with the witnesses. Then get yourselves a good meal. Tell one of the witnesses to go to the kitchen where one of Mr Merry's boys will give him food for the leper and Pindart."

As they walked away Merry said desperately:

"I wish I knew a cure for leprosy."

"All the world wishes that," answered Laurie.

The trackers enjoyed but scant rest. It was learned that two lubras we were unaware of had taken to the hills when the patrol came. V.D. was immediately suspected.

"Clean up the whole place if you can while you're here, Laurie," said Merry. "You won't be here again for another twelve months. When you go, these lepers and venereals will come creeping back, and will infect the others. I can't cope with diseases like those. Besides, I've got the wife to think of now — and a baby."

So Larry and Davey after a few hours' rest circled the native camp, picked out those old tracks from all the others, old and new, and away they went The half-caste Joe and his mate had not returned. Evidently Joe's chase was a stern one.

The prisoners were enjoying a fine time; gossiping, sleeping, eating, all day long in a comfortable possy under a shady tree near the house. The lubras had taken possession of one tree, the prisoners of another, the sick of a third. From around the prisoners' tree all grass had been cleared; there was no chance of a friend throwing them a file that would lie in the grass until after dark.

"Did I ever tell you about how they solved the problem of the tobacco?" asked Merry. "It was stick tobacco in a padlocked, steel-lined chest, that took two men to comfortably lift it. I was away from the homestead for three weeks. The abos couldn't break the steel bands nor open the lock, and did not think of an axe to chop it But they did think to shake it. The lid did not fit tightly, so they took it in turns to shake the heavy box until dust of tobacco began dribbling out through the crack. When I returned, all the sticks of tobacco were worn very small, and the square ones had rounded sides and ends. And the abos' faces were innocent as babies."

Though very few of the Ngarinyin or Wonambun desired conversation with Charcoal or Oomagun, a home-stead black would occasionally carry on a shouted conversation at a distance; the native can do that without effort. But the conversation was really for Allboroo.

The sick were too miserable to take much interest in anything. Every day, Laurie insisted on all hands bathing in the river. The he-men prisoners guffawed, but had to obey. The sick, who needed a bath most, objected strongly, The witnesses took it as a nuisance to be done with as quickly as possible. The women enjoyed it. They could shriek and laugh and attract the attention of the he-men in the bush camp and yet know the patrol was handy should anything untoward threaten. After each daily bath, Laurie did the best he could with the medicines and ointments at his command; Mr Reid had given him a fresh supply. Laurie had to stand by and see that men and women actually used each medicine as ordered. It was not a nice task, but it certainly gave the patients some ease.

The people here were of the Big Ngarinyin tribe, with a sprinkling of *munjons* from the headwaters of the Moran, Roe and Drysdale. These wild looking fellows were off-shoots of the Ngarinyin but not quite of them. They informed Larry that we certainly were going to meet trouble in catching Donkey. It was Donkey who had helped Oomagun to kill Worachi at Grace's Knob. Oomagun and Charcoal were bad men, but Donkey was worse. He was a notorious native killer, besides being a trouble maker and cattle spearer. He always camped alone, and at a spot overlooking a maze of rocks or a waterhole into which he could dive at the breath of alarm. Though he had been sighted in a raid—even his woman caught while they were sleeping side by side—Donkey had never been caught. He swore he never would.

As the Ngarinyin were pleased the patrol had caught Charcoal and Oomagun, their pleased cocksureness that we would never catch Donkey, who had fought their men as bitterly as the other two, seemed rather strange. But it was merely one of those queer phases of native mentality. While he was a free man, he was a personality, a bad man to be feared and admired. When he was caught this personality would slip from him, until he was free again. Like sickness. A sickness belongs to the person sick; it is part of him; it has nothing whatever to do with any other person. That explains why you may see a squatting group passing a plug of tobacco from mouth to mouth although several of that group are slavering from influenza; why you may see a healthy man unconcernedly sleep beside a diseased woman; why children play in the ashes where diseased people have just been sitting; and why when chubby hands go to young eyes to brush away a fly, no hand is raised to stop them. The aboriginal will not understand that there is such a thing as contagion. Any disease to man or woman is merely personal to the victim; it cannot harm any one else.

This "personality trait" in the aboriginals is one of the confusing things about them that has caused many a white man to believe they have no mentality at all. Other phases of it have deceived learned men who have studied them.

25
THE HERMIT IN THE WILDERNESS

ONE beautiful morning the patrol saddled up to ride a further stage north. Half-caste Joe had not returned with his lepers.

A rough track stretched vaguely ahead. Merry's horses had made it on his first trip to Port George the Fourth a few years before. On subsequent trips to visit the one and only girl, those patient hoofs had marked the track each time a little plainer. Judging from our map, this partial track must be very near Brockman's long-overgrown exploring route of 1901. Though difficult indeed for the white man to follow, the track was plain to the trackers' eyes. All hands, and the animals, were invigor-ated by the spell. For miles the track crossed a series of small divides between tiny sandstone hill-tops, scrub covered : a gradual drop to another gradual climb; the grass poor and tufty except along the tiny creeks. Then down a little valley like a street of grass walled by rock thirty feet high that gradually fell away to meet the sandstone crests again. Wandering down among a maze of hill-tops we came to the Glenelg. A roaring river this in the "wet." Now a shallow stream breaking into long deep water- holes densely fringed with palms, beautiful paper-barks, and stately gums. Horses and mules splashed into the stream. The crossing was difficult. Ahead, was an intensely green island winding like a green snake over rich black loam. Between us and it tore a narrow millstream almost as green as the island grass. A rocky ledge led to the island. It was amusing to watch the mules and horses cautiously negotiating that slippery causeway; to be swept off meant an icy ducking in deep water. Old Kate nearly got it. She was too careful and one foot slipped; with a desperate grunt she recovered and stood there hunched up gazing around, her eyes glaring, one big ear twitching. I'm positive she was swearing. Once on the island, we had to manhandle the animals away from the lucerne-like grass, for there was another causeway to cross, washed by another millstream. After that, it was a grand ride down the river.

Towards sundown we gradually steered off the river, the country opening out into almost a plain of good grass. Laurie was pushing on rapidly, horses and mules putting their best into it, sensing that camp was some distance ahead and it was a case of beating the sun. Presently we entered a hidden pass, its quartzite walls like ancient castles with shrubs growing in the cracks. Then to the right another wall appeared but this in parts had collapsed as if some ancient bombardment had brought the old masonry crashing down. The hoofs of the pack-animals sounded like rustling velvet amongst the long, soft grass. Down the centre of this lovely glen ran a line of tall paper-barks above a whispering creek. This place might have been at the end of the world.

The sun went down. Hurrying in the sudden coolness we crossed the creek, climbed a rocky hillock and down into a little valley hemmed by low ridges. Soon, just visible, appeared the grey bark of a hut. The mules broke into a jog trot; a dog barked vigorously; a small figure emerged from the hut; black figures rose behind him in the gloaming.

Bob Thompson was so surprised that he could only shake hands and laugh. In three years his white visitors had been Laurie (twice on patrol), Mr Love (from the Port George Mission), Jack Wilson (the Little Iron Man), and Phil Ryan who rode from Walcott to Port George to catch the lugger.

Laurie smiled:

"You are not seeing ghosts."

Bob, with his eyes on me, laughed, "I thought I was for a moment."

Laurie nodded:

"'Jack' Idriess. Seeing the country."

"I wish others would come and see it," said Bob as we shook hands. "I wouldn't have to talk to my dog so often then. I've schooled him so that he knows the alphabet and can spell cat. Not that he's ever seen one. But chuck off your saddles, Laurie. I'm real delighted What has happened to the niggers though? They didn't send up a smoke; no talk of any sort that you were coming."

"I'm not looking for any of them in particular," answered Laurie as we dismounted. "Otherwise they'd have warned you."

"They might have," growled Bob, "and they mightn't. They're queer customers. The more you know of them the less you know. I hope you understand what I mean. I'm out of practice in talking, except to the dog. But let the boys look after your packs. Hey, Cockeye!" he yelled, "put on 'nother feller billy—quick feller now!" From the galley an old one-eyed lubra, wide-awake of countenance, lackadaisically rose to obey the order.

"Excuse my clothes," apologized Bob, "but the white ants have burgled my wardrobe. The only things they haven't eaten are the button-holes."

"I told you I'd come along some day and find you in a loin cloth and tomahawk!" sympathized Laurie.

"And it might come to that. Any man who lives in this country just to feed blacks might come to anything. But have a wash and come on out to the galley. That old heathen should have boiled the billy by then. I suppose you're hungry."

"My belly says my throat is cut!" agreed Laurie decidedly.

"Good-oh. I've killed a goat, so you can get some of that into you. Kimberley mutton isn't half bad—Hullo!"

We listened to the long-drawn howl of a dingo. As the cry went wavering away it was taken up by another, then quicker by another, then the pack were in full howl.

"The death-wail!" exclaimed Bob. "What nigger has died?"

"A boy at Fred Merry's," answered Laurie.

"So that's it!" said Bob with relief. "Your boys must have just told them."

"Yours are late receiving the news," I remarked.

"Yes. They're a queer crowd. Sometimes they get news quicker than a white man could send it. At other times it just comes dribbling along. The dead boy must have been a relation of some of my boys. My boys are mostly Wonambun; but there are a few Ngarinyin and Worara amongst them."

Out behind the galley-fire were shadow figures of tall, bearded men with clay-daubed hair drawn into a blunt upward pointing cone behind. They vanished towards the creek whence the death-wail again howled.

Hungrily, by firelight, we set to with damper and cold goat washed down by hot tea. That followed by damper and jam is a meal for the gods after a long day's ride among the Kimberley hills.

Why should a white man hide himself away out here? Directly to the north were no whites right to the coast. To the east, no whites until well into the East Kimberley. Some men love the farthest wilds, and that is reason enough.

"Did you require much capital to start out here, Bob?" I inquired.

"Just on one hundred pounds, a couple of pack-mules, a saddle, a few old bags and a bit of wire, a case of nigger twist tobacco, an axe—and a rifle thrown in. With the clothes I stood up in, and the old dog for a mate. What more does a man want to start a selection! And now I've got the mules and saddle and rifle and dog, but nothing else. The niggers have got everything, including three years' work chucked in. I work for them."

"I wonder you don't go crazy, living out here alone," said Laurie.

"I don't go crazy, because I haven't the brains. No man with brains could stand this life and remain sane!"

With a satisfied frown Bob felt for his pipe. Laurie offered his pouch.

"Thanks. It's a change from nigger twist. A man eats like a nigger, smokes like a nigger, and if he stays bush long enough he thinks like a nigger. But, you know, this country will come on some day, when we're pushing up the daisies. There'll only be a settler here and there, the country is too rough, but it'll hold far more than are here now. I've got a thousand acres, and all I pay is one pound a year rent. The government lets a man have land cheap enough if he'll only take it up. I must keep five acres under cultivation, then at the end of five years I get it freehold. And it's been fairly easy, to make it pay to cultivate, since Reid had that peanut brain-wave. It's a crop I can sell even if I am at the end of the world. So long as I watch out that the niggers don't eat all the nuts I'll have a few bags to sell at the end of the season."

"Transport?" I inquired.

"Oh, Fred Merry lends me his camels. On them I pack the nuts to Merry's, then to Walcott Inlet where they catch the Mission lugger for Broome, where they are trans-shipped to Fremantle. Of course, it's not all done in a day and there are not many nuts, because the blasted niggers eat 'em nearly all. I've got to feed and keep all labour; and all they want to grow is enough to feed themselves. They can't for the life of them see that I want something out of it too. And they wouldn't even plant what they do if I didn't bribe them with tobacco. Tobacco is money out here; without it no nigger would work in the Kimberleys."

"How about expansion in the future, supposing you get on your feet?"

"Easy. Nature has provided, so long as man does the work. I could take up more land if I wished. As it is I could easily feed two thousand sheep around the hut. The cattlemen away back towards the Big Range swore that it would be impossible to keep sheep over the range. But I brought that little mob of Merry's all the way fro Noonkanbah in the West Kimberley. Brought them over the range and hardly lost one. And they've survived and grown fat. I could keep a larger mob here; they only want a bit of looking after. I don't say that this area of the Kimberleys is sheep country, not by any means. But I'm sure that settlers scattered here and there in little valleys could keep a mob sufficient to make a living—with the help of a few acres of cultivation anyway. See my vegetables in my garden and banana patch tomorrow. Constant cultivation would beat the white ants. And if a mob of settlers only got together there are harbours along the coast waiting to be turned into ports."

"You've got no cattle?"

"No. I've not graduated to the squatter stage yet, I'm not close enough to a cattleman to pinch any. Goats are milk, beef and mutton to the settler pioneering in this nor'-west. I've got one hundred and fifty goats and keep an old gin to shepherd them by day and drive them into a brush yard at night against the dingoes. I've got to keep another old gin to squat in the peanut patch all day and keep the goats out. What with feeding goats to feed the niggers and feeding niggers to keep the goats from feeding on,the peanuts a man is just about ruined."

"Trials of a pioneer," chuckled Laurie.

"Trials!" grunted Bob. "To manage my mob I've got to have more eyes than a fly and more arms than a centipede. These Wonambun bareskins may be stone-age innocents, but they're tricky as monkeys. It's them who have the brains. When the Worara come along and the mobs mix I've got to be everywhere at once without sleeping at night. But you ought to have seen me when I was breaking in the donks and the nigs to the plough! I had a gin leading the donks; her yelling and tugging and trying to lead them while her buck was yelling behind trying to drive them. The more they yelled and screeched the more the cockatoos screeched. There was me coming yelling behind, trying to drive the gin and the donks and the buck while battling to guide the plough. We found all the stumps in the Kimberleys and every stone in northern Australia. Those donks were reared and branded in the backyard of Hades; but long before the first day was over I knew I was the prize donk of the lot. The gin was playing up, the buck was playing up, the donks were playing up, and I was as hoarse as a crow. The cockatoos in the trees stretched from here to the Glenelg, all with their crests raised and screeching themselves hoarse. All the niggers in the country were squatting around, just as if I'd put on a show for their benefit. They laughed in the shade while I sweated out in the sun. That was the last straw. I dropped the plough handles and took to them, but they beat me easily; I sooled the dog on them, but they only climbed trees and laughed from there. If ever I hated the human race and donkeys it was at the end of that day. When I staggered to the hut my backbones were cracking like nigger minstrels' bones."

"How has it all worked out?"

"Very well. I had to find the place, then start to work it, build the hut, clear and grub the ground, train the teams, the donkey-team and the nigger teams—not to mention myself, and not to mention teaching the most intelligent niggers English for a start. I should have been a schoolmaster and a dictator and a philanthropist rolled into one. I'd never handled a plough in my life and all I knew about cabbages was that you eat 'em. But I took one hundred pounds' worth of peanuts off a little plot of ground that first year. It doesn't sound much; but you think of all the transportation and costs and nearly two thousand miles to market and no banks to get overdrafts from—think of little things like that and all the rest of it and you'll admit the effort was not too bad at all."

"Surprisingly good."

"I made more money than that. I had to keep going; had to keep the tucker-bags filled somehow. When the crop was planted I saddled up the two old mules and scoured the country after dog scalps, worth then two pounds a scalp. Those dingo scalps helped a lot; they've helped more than one settler in the Kimberleys. But I daren't stay away long; I knew that as soon as the vines grew nuts the niggers would raid them."

"The hut is well built."

"Not bad. I built it with an axe and a bit of wire." "How have you managed alone here with the natives?"

"Oh, luckily for me Laurie came along with a patrol and promised he'd visit me once every twelve months. So the bucks knew if they knocked me on the head it would be found out sooner or later. Some of them wanted to give it a go all the same. But the mob was sensible; they argued that I was a fool who was going to grow them things to eat, and if they killed me they wouldn't get any tobacco anyway. So things have gone all right with a little watchfulness and the help of old Cockeye here and her buck. They camp just there, right close to the hut, and have been real faithful these last two years. I think a real lot of those two old niggers, and the old dog here." Almost adoringly Bob gazed down at the dog lying at his feet. I wondered how many times he must have lain awake in that hut, listening for a warning cry from his two faithful natives; above all, listening for the warning growl of the dog.

26
TRIALS OF A PIONEER

NEXT morning breakfast-time was a busy time for Bob; he had to feed his henchmen and start them at work. Twenty-five hairy-looking chaps, but amiable, squatted on their haunches near the galley discussing in laughing gutturals Laurie and me. I wondered if they were comparing me with their own old Bummungerrie, the old doctor, whose unblinking eyes were taking us in so unwaveringly. The ancient goatherd let the goats out of the yard and away they hurried for breakfast—towards the peanut patch.

"Drive 'em away there, you old bag of bones!" yelled Bob. "What do you think I'm feeding you for, you imp of mischief. D'you take me for th' goat?"

With shrill imprecations and much running on skinny legs the old lubra headed her cunning charges for the hills. Bob, hurrying back and forth from the kitchen to the galley, kicked at a rooster that leapt and squawked, knocking a spoon from his hand. The dog immediately tackled the rooster.

"What with niggers and fowls and goats," growled Bob, "life in this country isn't worth living. Look at them! Twenty-five grown men squatting there all with their mouths wide open; hungry gins with *their* mouths open; two hundred goats and a mob of fowls! And one little white man has got to feed the lot! And he must be nursemaid to the peanuts; water the bananas and hand-feed the garden; not to mention doctoring the mules when a snake bites 'em, see the dingoes don't get the goats, and watch the blooming donks don't clear out. And so I ought to. I'm the biggest donk of the lot!"

"You are," laughed Laurie as he filled his pipe, "and if you don't hurry there'll be no breakfast left."

At last Bob sat down to a well-earned breakfast and with his first mouthful said:

"Well, Laurie, what's your programme to-day?" "Saddle up and ride straight for Port George."

"Oh, no you're not," Bob frowned; then with decided finality: "I'm developing serious illness and it's your duty to sit by me and see a lonely settler through. Hang it all, you can't treat me like that. You're my one regular visitor. You come once a year; the missionary has only visited me once in three years. I might be with the angels before he comes again!

The Little Iron Man mightn't come this way again for another three to five years. And there's no one else. Here you've come and brought a stranger that it's a treat to talk to and you want to ride straight away. Be human!"

"But everything is all right here, and I'll be calling back this way," persisted Laurie.

"   Everything is not all right. I've just thought of two or three—I think four—serious complaints I want you to investigate. Anyway you haven't run the rule over the niggers yet."

"There's only twenty-five or thirty of them present. I'll examine them in less than an hour."

"No you won't," assured Bob. "I've got an idea there's serious illness among those niggers; there's something serious about to break out, something contagious."

Laurie smiled:

"You didn't mention it last night."

"I was a bit too worried."

"What are the symptoms?" asked Laurie gravely.

"Ah-er, they don't sleep too well of nights; they complain of internal pains, and they seem to have a sort of sleeping sickness."

"If they don't sleep too well of nights, when do they sleep with this sleeping sickness?"

"Well—er, I hadn't thought of that," admitted Bob. "But seriously, Laurie, there's something wrong with 'em."

"I'll line them up when you've finished breakfast," promised Laurie, "and have a look at them."

"Good!" Bob chewed thoughtfully.

Seen in daylight, Bob's hut was squeezed into the tiniest of valleys. Fronting it, low rocky hills pushed a tiny creek almost to the front door of the hut. One hundred yards behind was an abrupt ridge like a rocky wall thirty feet high. And from away behind there a light gust of wind brought a distant cry.

"Hullo!" exclaimed Bob. "They're up to some devilry; they always are."

"What's the matter?" asked Laurie lazily.

"They spy on me from that ridge," nodded Bob. "They can look right down on the hut from there. Any strange nigs arriving, always spy that way first. My own beauties do it too. Frequently I leave them at work down in the cultivation while I do some work here. As soon as my back's turned they send a man in a half-circle to come up behind on the ridge, and there lie down and watch me. When I leave again for the cultivation he yells that cry o f theirs and they're all working when I come along."

Shortly after breakfast, Bob lined up the natives. Laurie took them over for medical inspection. Bob winked and beckoned. We walked away, and when out of ear-shot he said:

"I've put that little lot up to something. They will keep him occupied for an hour anyway. Come and I'll show you the plantation."

"But Laurie will be wanting to saddle up."

"Of course he will, but he won't go without you. Good heavens! I only see a white man once in twelve months. Surely you're not going to turn me down!"

I laughed:

"Right-oh, so long as you shoulder the responsibility." "I'll shoulder anything," said Bob cheerfully. "I haven't got much breadth of shoulder, but I've got a wonderful breadth of cheek." Suddenly he ran forward shouting: "You low-down thieving old trollop! I'll wring your scraggly neck into sticking plaster, you miserable old shag!"

From a lean-to of bark an old lubra hurriedly emerged. She cast one glance towards the tiny cultivation then hobbled screaming towards it, waving a stick. A hundred goats were enjoying a breakfast of peanuts.

"All she's got to do is to lie down in the shade all day long," moaned Bob. "All she's got to do is to get up off her hams if the goats do come into the nuts. But she's too damned lazy to do even that."

"Didn't I see an old shepherd lubra take the goats away an hour ago?"

"She's sleeping off breakfast out in the hills somewhere," exclaimed Bob angrily. "She's let her dog mind the goats and the dog has probably invited a couple of dogs from the niggers' camp, and by now they'll be worrying a goat for their breakfast."

"Well, you know, Bob, it's you pioneers carry the country's burden," I sympathized.

"Carry my purple grandmother! We're the goats; that's what we are! Just look!" He pointed as we walked across the cultivation. "See the vines trampled down where that old she-cat actually lets the goats camp day after day. Look at these vines here! dragged all over the place by the hoofs of the goats! And I feed that old girl and prevent her tribesmen from knocking her on the head because tribal custom declares she's useless. It's me ought to be knocked on the head!"

Bob was quietly proud of his little domain. He had a right to be. It was late midday before we turned back towards the hut. Laurie had had the dinner ready long since. He smiled as we approached.

"You're late."

"Great Scott!" exclaimed Bob amazedly. "I had no idea it was as late as this."

"You timed it well," said Laurie, smiling again. "It is too late to start out this afternoon."

"Now you're talking," said Bob almost gratefully. "Did you find any sickness amongst the niggers?"

"Only what you tried to put into their minds."

"Now that's relieved my mind quite a lot. I thought there was something serious the matter with them,"

As we started eating, a string of natives came up from the creek loaded with peanut vines, the roots thickly clustered with nuts.

"Put them there," pointed Bob. "No, not there," he roared. "Put them there, away from that dog, you stupid owls! Can't you see the fowls will get them ? Stack them over there!"

Ten minutes later, when Bob returned to the galley from giving his henchmen their dinner, he discovered they had stacked the vines all around one of their own dogs who was gorging on the nuts. Howls from the dog quickly developed into a dog-fight as Bob's dog joined in. Amused by several other minor interruptions we finished lunch then out came the pipes. But Bob was going to make certain he would have company for the night. Hurriedly he gave his boys orders for the afternoon's work then turned to me.

"Come and have a look at the Cha-nake stone."

"What is that?"

"Oh, it's some sort of sacred stone. It's only up on the ridge there, not ten minutes' walk. You're interested in their stones and cave paintings and all that sort of thing aren't you ?"

"Yes."

"Well, there's a prize stone up there on the ridge not two hundred yards from the house. It's the big-gun stone in these parts for hundreds of miles around. Every nigger from anywhere at all has got a free pass to visit this stone whenever he wishes. No nigger dare spear him providing he is coming to 'talk' to Cha-nake."

"What is the meaning of the name?"

"I don't know rightly. They've got two names for it but Cha-nake is the one I remember best. Hi!" he called to the old native, "what name that stone Cha-nake?"

"Ungoodju!" mumbled the old man and reverently bowed his head.

"Come on. Coming Laurie?

"No. I don't suppose I'll see you again until sun¬down."

"We'll be back in no time," called Bob cheerily as we walked away. "I don't think," he added softly.

I laughed.

"That boy is likely to saddle up and ride away in the middle of the afternoon if I give him a chance," explained Bob. "But I'm giving him no chance. I want someone to talk to this evening."

"You've been talking ever since last night," I pointed out.

"Why, I haven't got a word in edgeways," expostulated Bob reproachfully. "I haven't started yet. There's a thousand and one things I want to talk about; I've got a whole twelve months to make up."

WONAMBUN MEN, WHO MAKE LIFE INTERESTING FOR BOB THOMPSON

27
THE UNGOODJU STONE

THE rock wall behind the hut hemmed in the valley for miles, and though only thirty feet high commanded a surprising view. From the hut the valley hardly appeared to be of ten acres but from the wall looking down the valley it gradually spread out. In the distance were two little plains like green lawns among the trees. At its lower end the valley was apparently four miles wide, running towards the Prince Regent River only a few miles distant. It was a fertile valley, but up here on the ridge amongst great blocks of quartzite and sandstone the country was harsh with stunted grey trees and prickly shrubs. The Ungoodju or Cha-nake stone, four feet high and one foot thick, somewhat like an eye-tooth in shape, stood upright a few yards away amongst spinifex and tufts of coarse grass. It was firmly embedded in the ground, supported by five stones around its base.

"I've not taken much notice of it," answered Bob to my inquiries. "I don't bother about these things. I was looking for strayed goats when I found it. I used to notice the niggers' heads from the hut as they walked towards the stone, but never bothered. The Cha-nake stone is, apparently, connected with the python cult. The python is a sacred snake; the aboriginal legend is that their ancestors were shown the way here by a giant python ages and ages ago. That particular python was a spirit man that had to turn into a python before it could make itself visible to men. If you want to get at the truth of the belief, or as near the truth as a nigger will tell you, ask my old nigger all the questions you like tonight. He'll spill the beans so far as his creed allows him; he'd do just about anything for me."

On examining the stone closely I felt somewhat sceptical about Bob's python-cult theory; it appeared more likely to represent some phallic cult. Probably the two combined. We had our own serpent in our own Garden of Eden and there is a strangely haunting resemblance between this stone-age Cha-nake symbolism and that of the Garden of Eden story.

Late that afternoon Bob got the Wonambun men to treat us to the Eju Dance. With the dancers dressed up in feathers and ochres it had in it something from the very heart of the primitive. Far into the night the *kylies* kept sharply rattling in waves of metallic sound, the voices carrying far in bursts of song that ceased with startling abruptness. From deathly silence a warrior would lead again, the others roaring in with throaty chorus, the *kylies* sharply timing the perfect rhythm of savagely stamping feet.

Next morning we started on a rough ride, grass ten feet high in places, the rider ahead scarcely visible as each animal pushed on with its nose to the tail of the other. The boy in the lead had a chokingly rough job, for he had to force a path for the rest. Among the basalt hills the animals stumbled over the stones; loose basalt is much harder to travel over than sandstone. We were glad when we got into a valley in the shadow of the Macdonald Range. Mount Trevor (a hill, not a mountain) stood out abruptly. Pointing to its top, Laurie said:

"Brockman the surveyor built a cairn up there in 1901. This was his farthest point north. The natives tell the usual tale of a spirit living up there."

Across countless dry creeks we pushed along the wall of the range and camped thankfully at sundown; a lonely camp made more lonely still when a dingo howled mournfully among the rocks.

After breakfast we moved off into a lovely morning. The ravines and escarpments of the range were still in deep black shadow; the trees motionless; everything appeared to be quietly dreaming while half awake, an impression the early morning bush so often gave throughout that patrol. Where the Macdonalds dwindled lower and lower we rode right into them through a narrow gap, where a creek was still carving its way out. Above the palms and paper-barks that fringed it, overhanging rocks loomed from the gap walls above. Then came the white of quartz reefs. The old prospecting instinct awoke at sight of copper stains. Rocks overgrown with grass, looked very much like old graves. We wondered if they could actually be graves of the ill-fated Camden Harbour Expedition of 1864. That expedition with four thousand cattle in three shiploads landed on the nearby coast. A brave adventure in those far off days. Lack of knowledge of local conditions, with the great distance from civilization, foredoomed the expedition to the disaster foretold by the sailors when the *Calliance* struck a reef and the captain lost his life. In twelve months the cattle were dead, the settlers had gone, and the bush was fast going back to its present wildness, interrupted only by the eventual establishment of Port George the Fourth Mission Station. Soon we saw the glint of its roofs among the trees of Kunmunja Creek. A dozen or so iron buildings with a few acres of cultivation near by banana and papaw trees, and a fine vegetable garden. Natives were working about; black youngsters playing and howling. A rocky hill rose abruptly behind the Mission; indeed, hills were everywhere. At first sight it was difficult to tell where the Mission would find enough level ground to experiment in cultivation on any considerable scale.

Mr and Mrs Macdougal welcomed us hospitably. The world is a small place. Mrs Macdougal was a girl teacher I had met years ago three thousand miles east at Thursday Island. The missionary was the Rev. J. R. B. Love, now absent on holiday south.

Laurie had to make inquiries here about a native seaman who had disappeared from the Mission lugger. I put in time prowling over the maze of hills towards Brunswick Bay and Camden Harbour. A few miles south is where Kingsford Smith came down, right among a sea of peaks. Up on those wind-swept peaks I wondered if the ghosts of the Camden Harbour adventurers saw the strange machine-bird that so miraculously escaped utter disaster in a wilderness that claimed the bones of some of them.

Camden Harbour is one of the wildest harbours on the Australian coast; King George the Fourth Harbour is walled by cliffs four hundred feet high. There is no open plain country for quite a distance inland, and then only in comparatively small areas.

Still, in these modern days pioneers (quite unsung) attempt settlement with the smallest of resources. I had met the Haldanes away south in Broome—a big family. They and Brown and another friend named Cloverley, then in Wyndham, decided to take up land far up along the coast. Their vessel was a tiny boat in which I would hardly have cared to have crossed a boisterous river- mouth. Yet with a bit of tucker and a few tools and a boat-load of hope they took to sea. Mrs Haldane had an awful trip. They ran into storms, and drifted at the mercy of currents along that wild and inhospitable coast. But they got there. The men, to keep the pot boiling while their first crop grew, roamed the bush dingo-hunting. Cloverley walked overland from distant Wyndham, the port for the East Kimberley. *En route*, he went down with fever. His two faithful aboriginals carried him the last sixty miles to Port George Mission—a super-human task.

Unfortunately, the bush beat this little pioneering attempt. But the principals, driven back to Broome, were determined to give it another go when they got a few more tools and a bit more tucker together. Several similar attempts have also failed; Merry, Thompson, Russ, and a few others have succeeded.

Macdougal, about six feet three of busy missionary, was a lucky man; he and his little dark-haired wife were engaged in a life work that they loved.

Soon after leaving Port George the Fourth the patrol turned on its long ride back. The coastline farther north is one of the wildest and most picturesque stretches in Australia, but the only settlement there is the little Spanish mission called Drysdale. Near here the German aviators Hans Bertram and Klausman a few years ago met hardship and adventure followed by a very close escape from death. Farther east along the coast to the Forrest River Mission near Wyndham there is no white settler. All the wild "Corner" inland is the country of the blacks.

When we returned to Marie Springs Bob Thompson was lively as a cricket.

" Off saddle and enjoy a billy of tea," he invited. "Make yourselves comfortable for the day. I'm going back to Fred Merry's with you, so you can't leave me. You've made me dissatisfied."

"I don't see your mules packed ready to move off!" said Laurie.

"No. And you won't until afternoon, because they've cleared out to the Prince Regent; the nigger is on their tracks now. Come on Laurie, tell the boys to sling off those packs, another day's wait won't hurt you. Here Mary," he yelled, "you take 'em white men's clothes, wash 'em longa creek."

That's hospitality out there. Laurie dismounted, not too willingly.

"If you're not ready to move off sharp at sunrise tomorrow morning, I'm waiting no longer, Bob. I'm on patrol, and I've got to keep moving."

"I'll be up before the birds," chirped Bob. "I must set these fellows of mine a task for the few days I'll be away; dish 'em out tucker, make arrangements for the donks and the mules and fowls and goats, lock up, and attend to a few things like that."

Mary came striding out of the hut.

"Chope!" she demanded. "Me wantem chope!"

"Strike me pink! You'll want lavender water next, but you won't get it. Can't you wash the blooming clothes with water and sand?"

Grumbling, he entered the hut to fossick out a lump of camp-made soap.   .

A miserable looking blackfellow's dog stood erect, its ears pricked, wagging its wretched tail.

"Him know father coming," nodded the old lubra. And sure enough three huntsmen came striding along. The dog ran to the foremost, licking his feet and fawning upon him. The man bent down and kissed the dog before striding on to the camp. The second man did the same, and the third.

"They kiss their dogs," growled Bob, "but I've never yet seen one of them kiss his wife. Not that they're missing anything."

A NOR'-WEST KIMBERLEY GORGE

28

THE ESCAPE OF ALLBOROO

I CLIMBED the ridge to farewell Ungoodju, the Cha-nake stone, and was fortunate. A band of warriors in single file were coming towards their Mecca: their oiled bodies gleaming, brave in ochred bars and down of wild goose plumage, their hair coned behind their heads, brilliant in parrot feathers. Each warrior was in deadly earnest. When near the stone they halted and laid down their weapons. Then the leader, a stalwart savage, slowly approached, reverently raising his hand. Gently he touched the stone, stood with bowed head, and laid bare his heart as his forefathers had done since the dawn of time. Then walked slowly backwards to his friends. Each man in turn came forward, made his obeisance, and whispered his prayer. Then, picking up their spears they wheeled around and walked straight back towards their own wild fastnesses, turning their heads neither to right nor left, ignoring and ignored by the Wonambun men down at the creek.

According to Bob's own henchman, the stone represented something that was the source, or close to the source of life. But with the aboriginal you can never be certain. He will never give full details of anything that bears upon his inner life. A white man could live among them for years and yet be unaware of the fact that they had a "secret life." There are phases of the aboriginal mentality which must remain a closed book to us.

"I wonder why the aboriginal figures in the cave paintings are drawn with no mouths," I remarked that evening.

"God knows," replied Bob. "But if you'd only stay a week I'd show you some proper paintings, nigger paintings with dresses on."

Laurie laughed:

"It would take a more convincing tale than that to keep us here a week."

"But it's true, Laurie," protested Bob. "They're not dresses exactly, and yet they are dresses. Some remind me of Scotchmen's kilts. They're painted red and blue and yellow. One picture looks like a Red Indian with a grass skirt. The paintings are in a cave about forty miles from here, and the going is rough."

"How did you find them?"

"By accident. I was out dogging and poisoned a dingo. Next morning my nigger tracked him to a cave where he'd crawled to die. The walls of the cave were covered with these drawings. I've never seen nigger drawings like them anywhere else before. I don't think the niggers could really have done them—not our niggers anyway. And yet there was nobody but niggers in the country until the white man came."

This tallied strangely with Sir George Grey's description of paintings found during his expedition of 1837. He landed at Hanover Bay, and discovered the Prince Regent and Glenelg rivers. But a nasty spear-wound and the wet season forced him to sail away after only a few weeks in this particular area. He discovered and made colour sketches of figures drawn on cave walls that could hardly have been the work of aboriginals. These mouthless figures wore a sort of armless shirt; one was clothed in a long pink "dress"; some were adorned with strange headdresses of blue and red. From the heads of most painted rays resembling the rays of the sun formed a nimbus. He found, too, a well-shaped head carved in rock, its edges rounded by time. It is unlikely that the tools of the aboriginal could have carved that head.

Those paintings remain a double mystery: what strange race left them there we cannot even surmise; and they have never been rediscovered, so far as I am aware. This latter fact is easily understood. It is seldom that a white man goes through this country, and when he does he endeavours to dodge the rocky valleys where the native hide-outs are.

Reluctantly, we had to forgo seeing Bob's mysterious art gallery; Laurie had his job to do and the patrol must push on. Next day as we rode south to Merry's, a puff of smoke arose from a hill.

"Smoke-talk," said Bob, "a spinifex puff too. Fred will know we are coming."

Miles ahead on a hill-top an answering puff arose. Merry would know within an hour that we had left Thompson's. We arrived at Merry's late that evening.

"I've got a big dinner all ready," said Merry enthusiastically. "Let the boys unsaddle while we go inside and get it into us." Which we did.

"Half-caste Joe has returned, I see," remarked Laurie.

"Yes, two days after you left, and without the lepers. His approach was smoke-signalled, the leper collected his mates and they took to the rocks, camping in caves up in the heads of gorges. Joe's boys managed to follow their tracks; had to walk, too rough to ride. Joe tracked them right to Walcott Inlet. When near the coast one old man knocked up; they had then been travelling for three days without tucker. But the others beat Joe to the Inlet— got there while the tide was out. The tracks went straight on over the mud, but the tide, coming in, beat Joe. So he turned back."

Merry and Thompson were happy, for Willie had returned from the Inlet—with mail! Merry's peanut crop had been sold for more than he anticipated, and a larger cheque than expected had come for Bob. Above all was a letter from the wife for Merry. She would be home very soon, happy and contented with an earthen floor, bare iron walls, a bark roof—and her loved ones. The cool night air brought in through the open doors the stamp of dancing feet.

Merry turned on the gramophone, defying strong opposition from across the creek, a crescendo chorus at the end of every chant followed by ringing laughter from the lubras. The native music merged better with the night and the ghostly paper-barks than did the operatic star on the gramophone.

A shadow appeared at the door—half-caste Joe.

"Oh," said Merry, "they've decided who killed the warrior. The stones have been 'watered,' the grease drops have splashed two stones. So there will soon be another job for you, Laurie."

"It's tribal," he replied.

"Where are the two men who are supposed to have killed that man?" asked Merry.

Joe pointed over the hills where stars shone from the north-east.

"Oh, well . .

In the morning, one of our "guests" had vanished. Allboroo the cunning, he of the Malay features. The handcuff lock that locked the chain around his neck had been craftily picked, a job of which a first-class cracksman might well have been proud. Larry and Davey looked morosely solemn as they ran their fingers through the prisoners' hair.

Nipper was staring expectantly, Oombali apprehensively. Then Larry with an exclamation drew a piece of wire from Charcoal's tangled locks. Davey found another piece twisted deep within the shaggy hair of Oomagun. Laurie looked grim. The prisoners' hair except Nipper's was cut off, lest this happen again. The prisoners submitted without moving a muscle of weather-beaten faces. But what a transformation when their tangled locks fell to the ground. The first wild man to cut off his hair must have taken a long step towards civilization. All the same, my wild man Oomagun seemed to have lost something.

That handcuff lock had been opened with surprising cleverness; few white men, indeed, working under similar difficulties, could have done it. It was a screw-in lock, the key of which has a thread that screws into the cuff and screws down a pin that fastens the cuff. The pin that fastens the cuff. The key must then be taken out by unscrewing. To open the lock the key must be screwed right in and pulled hard thus pulling the pin back against a strong spring. The Police Department responsible for official locks are no bunglers. It would seem utterly impossible that primitive men could accomplish the job of opening such a lock without a key, a lock that has held countless expert criminals certain captive.

"How on earth did they manage it?" I asked.

"You could hardly believe it even if I showed you the tools," replied Laurie. "That piece of wire from Charcoal's hair was one tool, but the other is missing."

"Ha-Ha!" grunted Larry triumphantly. He had Nipper's head wedged between his knees, and from among those ash-daubed locks drew forth a short string of hair. Smart eyes, that could discover that hair-string amongst that tangled mop of clay and ash-daubed hair!

"There is the other tool!" said Laurie. "Examine it."

I did so, while Nipper's head was being shorn. The "tool" was eighteen inches long, a very strong string of many strands of human hair twisted as finely as the strongest modern fishing-line, but possessing too a creepy resilience that squirmed under the warmth of finger pressure.

"Now examine the wire."

The thin wire was only three inches long, one end had been fined out to needle thinness; but the sharp point was burred, yet so finely that one had to feel rather than see to detect it. The other thin point was faintly hooked.

"Imagine their patience and labour in fashioning that!" exclaimed Laurie. "And between two hard little stones that the lubras must have carried by day in their dilly-bags. They'd throw the stones to the prisoners each night. They would be working even before we went to sleep. While sitting under their tree gossiping and laughing one man would be grinding and rasping the wire between the stones, Using fine sand brought by the shock troops from the creek, and water from their billy-can. It wouldn't take much talk to drown the slight purring noise; and all the time they would be watching us. As to the hair, it is from Mrs Charcoal's, Mrs Oomagun's, and Mrs Nipper's heads. For the rest: cunning and patience and ingenuity they had, and opportunity came."

"How did they apply their ingenuity?"

"By working that hair right down into the lock between the screw and the cylinder, apparently an impossible job. But you see how this hair thread actually moves when you press and twist it; warm it up a bit by rubbing it between the palms of the hands and it becomes alive in a way, as if it absorbs electricity or something. . That's the secret of the thing getting down between the screw and the cylinder —it worms its way in. And it is the secret too of the seemingly impossible job; for not only has it to worm down between the tight and ungiving walls of the cylinder and screw, but it has to worm down in the grooves of the screw, around and around as it follows the grooves down. That hair thread almost has to be alive to do that. They start the thread by finger manipulation helped by the tiny point and burr edge of this fine wire. Once started, the rest is easier, given patience and a fine sense of touch. Gentle pressure is kept on the thread by the right hand while the left manipulates the lock, shaking and squeezing it gently, tapping it on the thigh. Those movements cause vibration and keep the hair thread moving, and it moves down and down and around and around the grooves in the screw.

"You can imagine its grip when it is wound like that right away down into the lock. When that is accomplished they just twist the outer end of the string around fingers and wrist and with a slow strong pull while holding the lock a certain way, at last unlock it."

"Impossible!"

"I told you you wouldn't believe it!"

Old Larry explained how, when each morning he had unlocked the handcuff that joined the ends of the chain around the tree, the prisoners must carefully have noted the depth and shape of the screw. They would note the action of his left hand as he held the lock, the movement of his right wrist too when, having inserted the key, he had to both turn and pull it in a certain way. They had watched this operation every morning for six weeks. They must have discussed the depth of key, the shape of screw and how it fitted into the cylinder—every action of screw and lock in minutest detail each day as they walked along; they must have planned for the length, strength, and thickness of the hair strand, and the shape of the tiny pin-point tool edges.

Then, explained Larry, every hair that went into the hair strand was chosen for shape or curl so that the completed strand would naturally, with warmth and movement, twist one way and that way would be down around the threads of the screw. Once the point of the strand was started it was, in a manner of speaking, comparatively simple. But it meant the possession of an uncanny feeling of touch, a finely tuned ear, and inexhaustible patience. It seems a sheer impossibility, but it was a fact.

Allboroo had not been able to release himself as the lock was around his neck, but the others had managed it while he lay there quietly. Why they had not unlocked the cuff that connected the chain around the tree and then all quietly walked into the bush and, at leisure, cut themselves free is a puzzle of aboriginal mentality. Though wonderfully adept in natural ways, and showing keen thought when inclination and circumstance force him, the aboriginal seems to utterly lack that urge to carry on to a bigger and better conclusion.

1. WONAMBUN MEN
2. THE TRACKERS LOANED THEM PANTS
3. HE BELIEVED THE CAMERA WAS AN EVIL EYE

29
ON THE MARCH AGAIN

SAYING farewell to Merry and Thompson the patrol marched again, definitely now on the homeward journey. The troops in fine fettle, reinforced unfortunately by other sick ones. The food-supply would be a problem. But why should the troops worry? Well fed, they cared not for the morrow, nor the day after. Charcoal and Oomagun and Oombali and Nipper striding along behind the pack-animals with their heads in the air, chests out, talking volubly as their eyes roamed to right and left, absorbed in the story of the bush, their bush. Behind them walked the Big Leper, a pathetic figure. He was going away, going to the white man's country, a land of terrors to him. Behind him walked his wife: she too had leprosy but not yet so badly as he.

"I doubt if we'll get him to Derby," said Laurie;

"What hope has he if you do get him to Derby?"

"What, indeed. The poor wretch might just as well leave his bones in his own country, he'd be much happier. But if I leave him here he might spread the disease to others, as he has already to his wife."

"Did you notice sickness away back there ?"

"Yes, here and there. But I can't take them all; I could not possibly feed them. Besides, I've got my own job to do. With this crowd hampering our movements, if I catch Donkey I'll think my luck wonderful."

"You are after him now?"

"Yes. We'll make a deviation straight back to Grace's Knob. We won't call in at the Inlet. No whites now until we get to the Knob."

"What about Allboroo ?"

"I'll pick him up on some future patrol if he is wanted. Luckily, he was not so important a prisoner as Charcoal, Oomagun or Nipper. If they had escaped at Merry's the tribesmen would have been after them immediately, glad of the chance to even up old scores. With Allboroo it was different; his tribe is over on the coast and he's in a safe hide-out by now. His escape actually helps me; every aboriginal within two hundred miles will think I'm trailing Allboroo hot and strong. That little mistake will help me take Donkey and Company by surprise. Instead of me travelling west as they will fondly imagine, I'll be travelling south-east. Davey!" he called. "Take the rifle and ride ahead and shoot as many kangaroos as you can. Get plenty of meat for the prisoners and sick people."

And Davey rode away on the work he loved.

"Old Larry is actually singing," I remarked.

"Yes, he commences to carol when on the homeward track. He is always glad to start out on patrol, but gladder still when we begin to return. His wonderings about his little wife Nancy burn brighter day by day. Nancy is an attractive little thing in the way of lubras but her tongue is knife-edged. The memory of it wears off somewhat after Larry has been on patrol two or three months. Then he begins to imagine her awaiting his loving return. Then he wonders if she is awaiting his return. When Nancy caught his eye she was young and flighty, and sniffed at Larry's attentions. But Larry is a tracker and a man to be reckoned with. He got his chance when Nancy's father Duncan was arrested for spearing young Clabby on Kimberley Downs station. Duncan was brought to Derby and while there came to an arrangement with Larry that he should have Nancy. Fortunately there were no tribal barriers I don't quite know what the bargain was, but doubtless an official in Larry's position could help a gentleman in Duncan's situation.

"Duncan kept his word when he came out of jail: did even better, for he settled in Derby and has since looked after Nancy while Larry is away on patrol. Looking after her means giving her a thrashing each time she encourages some aspiring Romeo. She does plenty of encouraging, and the Romeos would like to respond but are not keen, for old man Duncan is a killer; and as he is minding the police tracker's wife, the combination has awed all but the bravest. No buck has yet been so game as to actually run away with Nancy. Apart from the fear of Duncan, Larry has threatened he will follow and kill both the runaways should such a calamity occur. And he is quite entitled to do so tribally."

"Davey is not tribally married?"

Laurie laughed.

"No. His future wife will have some heart burnings in managing that Romeo. So far, he has been somewhat unfortunate: two of his adventures are now in the Derby Lazarette. He went to a lot of trouble over each of those young lubras, had to fight for each, but unfortunately they developed leprosy."

"His experiences do not seem to have dimmed his ardour."

"That lad is a trier," replied Laurie with a laugh. "But he is a good tracker and I don't want to lose him. On his third attempt he might catch leprosy himself."

That night was bitterly cold. The aboriginal can stand heat and rain, but the cold stiffens him. At sunrise dismal grunts and groans came from around the tree where the sick and older lubras camped. One by one they crawled from the ashes, stretching on their hands and knees to get the kinks out of their necks; stretching arms and legs, thumping bare backs, kicking the stiffness out of skinny limbs: a very different picture to that of the strong man or young lubra striding along on a warm day. The shivering sick and old got no sympathy from the prisoners and shock troops. This was where the law of the wilds that the fittest should survive comes in. The ladies Nipper, Oomagun and Charcoal, already warmed at a blazing fire, laughed as at a great joke when the poor old things thumped their bodies in grotesque efforts to coax the blood warm through their veins. The husky prisoners guffawed until Laurie made them walk to the ice-cold creek and bring up water and heat it so that the sick could wash and anoint their sores.

The following day we reached the Chamley, dropping down into the gorge from a picturesque tableland. It was thrilling to feel how the animals negotiated that steep descent; one slip and man or horse would have gone rolling and crashing to the bottom. When we scrambled down it was to ride between lines of black cliffs walling the river, the sky above appeared wispy blue and white from wind-torn clouds. Where mighty waters through the ages had pierced the solid hills the river-bed was acres of rock churned into grotesque shapes. These gorges are cut by the river right through to the coast.

Several days later we rode through good country with an eager patrol. For here was an unoccupied area where clean-skins had made their home. Voluble was the excitement when Davey spied the first mob. We tried to cut off a few of the wild beasts, but they beat us into the scrub. All hands now had eyes, ears, and noses alert for signs of anything to eat. Suddenly the lubras stampeded into the grass; some energetic rooting, then Mrs Oomagun jumped up, swung a goanna by the tail and bashed it on the ground. The prisoners from the moving patrol shouted over their shoulders to inquire whether the *bungarra* was fat. Then Mrs Charcoal ran ahead, her marvellous eyes following the flight of a native bee as she dodged bushes, vines, stones, and logs with effortless instinct. Away ahead the bee disappeared in the branches of a tall tree. With her tomahawk handle gripped between her teeth, the woman clasped the tree with arms outstretched and doubled up her body as she planted her feet flat upon the trunk. Then she simply walked up the trunk with a wonderful swaying motion, slithering her hands higher each time she swayed to a graceful step higher. High up on a limb she clung with one hand and her feet while with knuckles she rapped the limb. She soon found the hollow where the nest was; then, with her ear pressed to the tree, rapped again to catch the murmur of the bees inside. Still clinging, with sharp, expert blows she tomahawked into the hollow, exactly at the spot where the sugar-bag was.

Dropping the tomahawk, with bees all around her and with her eyes screwed up while snorting the bees from her nostrils, she pulled out the comb piece by piece and dropped it into a dilly-bag fastened to her neck by a forehead band. Then she slid straight down the tree. It was all done so quickly that the old loiterers at the tail-end of the patrol had not long trudged past her when she was running to catch up. I marvelled at these people chopping into millions of trees probably through-out millions of years, with stone tomahawks. No wonder that they will walk great distances, will do anything, to reach station blacks and trade with them for a piece of old iron. To the wild aboriginal one six-inch piece of iron is worth immeasurably more than a ton of gold. Gold to the actual wild man is worthless, but an iron tomahawk saves incalculable labour.

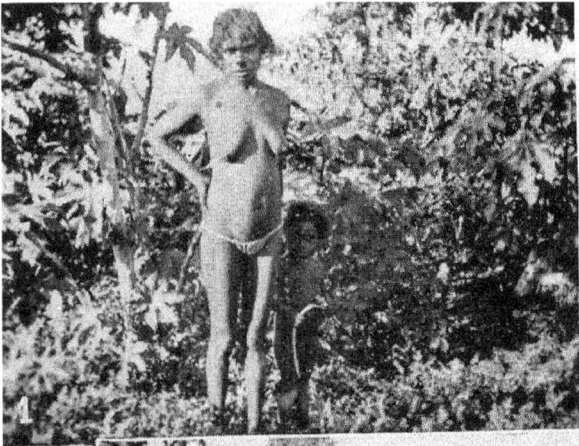

30

A FEAST FOR THE TROOPS

NEXT morning we rode out into level country luxuriously grassed. Laurie ordered Davey and Larry to ride well ahead lest wild cattle scent the patrol. Several hours later all listened to quick rifle-shots.

"I hope they've got a beast," said Laurie. "We'll have tight belts and hungry bellies to-night if they haven't."

The troops hurried on. Ten minutes later Davey came riding back, one glance at his face and the troops laughed in delight. All hands strode out at a great pace, the mules, sensing an early camp, almost jogging along. Even the Big Leper, falling farther behind every day, came stumbling along at his sore best.

Near a heavily-timbered creek Larry stood by a fine fat clean-skin. We unpacked quickly and all hands crowded around the beast. A group of meat-hungry primitives gloating around their prey is a sight indeed. Larry was master of ceremonies. Wielding a butcher's knife and tomahawk he handed another knife to Nipper while the other prisoners held out the legs of the beast, helping to skin it and roll it over. Each man knew just when and how to lend a helping paw. Evidently this was not the first beast they had hacked apart. The women squatted behind the men, their eyes gloating. Grunts of approval came when the rich creamy fat showed out; hands pawed in to rip out fat as the beast was opened up. Every man wolfed the raw stuff, laughing at its sweetness, while throwing handfuls over their shoulders to the snatching women behind. Quickly the beast was cut up and all were loaded. Only portion of the hide, the horns, and the contents of the paunch were left; every other scrap was carried to the camping-trees. Laurie ordered three big lots of meat to be put aside, the troops could gorge themselves on the remainder. Fires were quickly lit and the more easily cooked meat was soon sizzling on the coals, to be snapped away and eaten while fresh pieces were given a brief turn. Loud talk and laughter punctuated the sucking noises of squatting groups busily eating . . . eating . . . eating. Laurie allowed them to gorge; they would carry the food better that way.

This particular area was a native paradise; no white man owns it; no mission. Luxuriantly watered and grassed, there abundance of animal, vegetable, and fish food. The natives can raid the wild cattle to their hearts' content. It is a favourite meeting-place in the wet season; the tribesmen from a very wide area congregate here for their corroborees, initiation ceremonies, and fights. Rarely indeed does any white wanderer venture this way.

Laurie allowed the troops a two hours' gorge then Larry and Davey became masters of ceremonies. Three spaces of grass were cleared; three pits were dug; big fires were started in them, and stones were placed over the fires. When the fires had burned down to coals, the lumps of meat and legs, with hoofs and all on, were placed on the stones. How the troops chuckled and laughed. Strips of paper-bark were then roofed over and around the meat and the whole lot covered with loose earth. Each improvised oven made a mound three feet high. Then all hands stretched out under their respective shade trees, lazily gnawing scraps of meat. Mules and horses browsed in the rich grass; the warm afternoon dreamed on; Laurie wrote up his patrol notes in the shade of a Leichhardt tree.

For some time I had noticed the grimaces of Nipper, his expressive eyes, his stealthily beckoning finger, and the responses in the big black face of Charcoal, the propitiatory grin of Oomagun, the shy stare of Oombali, all squatting under their tree fifty yards away. I glanced at Laurie; he appeared not to notice anything. I wondered what caused this pantomime. The prisoners had no more stone tomahawks or message-sticks or bones to negotiate the sale of, for we had seen no natives for a week at least. Yet something was on. Prisoners, witnesses, sick, and the women were continually engaged in little personal or group or tribal intrigue. For one thing a rearrangement of domestic affairs was going on among the shock troops, owing to change of conditions, to cir-cumstances, and the opportunities made possible by travel among many people. Mrs Charcoal definitely never wanted to see Charcoal again after jail had claimed him; Mrs Nipper had obviously decided that she could do with less of Nipper; the disdainful Mrs Oomagun, who speaks less than any except by actions, was apparently toying with similar views. According to Davey they had decided that they were sick of the bush and were looking forward to trying a little town life. Though wild as wild cats and without the faintest idea of- what a town was, they were the only ones in the troops now anxious to see Derby. They had made up their minds that they were going to secure new; husbands there. What the prisoners thought of this changed attitude of their wives it was difficult to guess. So it was with the determination not to become involved that I warily approached Nipper.

He squatted forward eagerly. All the others were eyes and ears.

"We go Derby?" inquired Nipper.

"Yes."

"We go longa court-house?"

"Yes."

"We go jail?"

"Maybe."

"We sit down jail little while?"

"Yes, maybe."

A pause, then:

"We come back longa our own country?"

"Yes."

"Wah! Wah! Wah!" they shouted and threw up .their arms in delight. They all nudged Nipper at once, as he was the only one who could speak pidgin-English. Nipper took it for granted that I knew all about the undercurrents of the patrol, or at least some of them. He explained that Charcoal did not care at all what happened to Mrs Charcoal, but that he had another and young wife with a piccaninny, back in the bush, of whom he was very fond. Would he be allowed to return to her?

"Yes."

And Charcoal bared his teeth and threw up his arms with more "Wahs!" of delight. Oombali then eagerly nudged Nipper, his boyish face shining. Nugget also had a young wife back in the bush; he hung on the answer then shouted his delight. Wild man Oomagun thumped Nipper on the back, speaking volubly as he emphasized his points. Nipper nodded importantly then looked up at me.

It appeared that Oomagun had a regard both for Mrs Oomagun and his little daughter, but he also had a still younger wife away back in the bush. Would he be allowed to return to her?

"Yes."

They all chorused the wild man's delight. Then Oomagun's laughing, rugged face changed suddenly to deep concern. Dumbly he showed me a disease, and his eyes spoke volumes.

I told Nipper to tell him that the white doctor in Derby could cure that disease; that it had only just started.

I was very glad then that Oomagun had been captured. That this splendid specimen of primitive manhood who had so rarely seen a white man should be suffering from such a disease, came as a shock. But then, many tainted as he was tainted have never seen a white man. Oomagun was luckier than he dreamed, for he would not now see and contaminate his young wife and friends; he would be cured.

The troops, except the very sick, went to sleep that night in a cheerful mood. A little time in jail would be a wonderful holiday now that they were assured of return to their own country.

"Been cheering up the troops?" Laurie asked, when I rejoined him under our tree.

"Yes, they're all anxious to know whether they'll return to their younger wives out in the bush."

"They'll return all right. They'll only get at light sentence and their absence for a while will save a few lives. They'll get it drummed into them while in jail not to kill and that may possibly save a few more. All the same, I wouldn't like to be in Mrs Charcoal's shoes when Charcoal meets her in the bush again."

Towards sundown, Larry and Davey uncovered their private oven. The meat was done to a turn. And the quantity those two trackers ate was incredible. Then all hands were marched to their bath in the creek, returning loaded with firewood. Renewed chattering broke out as they grouped around their trees, preparing for a feast night. The women scraped the earth from the prisoners' oven, then lifted clear the bark. A cloud of steam and odour of roasted beef done to a turn brought loud "Ahs!" and "Wahs!" from the trees around. The third oven was cleaned up. Davey stood over each oven with a long pointed stick, forking out the big roasts. Men and women were given as much as they could carry, then retired to their trees and commenced eating. And how they did eat!

Laurie asked old Larry how long it would take them to get through.

"Not long," replied Larry between bites. "They eat all night."

I awoke in the middle of the night and some were still munching.

We travelled slowly next day; a big old red bull watched us from the hills. The troops kept pointing out meeting grounds where big fights are staged in the "wet." Several small mobs of wild cattle sped like the wind. Laurie camped early to give the sick a spell. The Big Leper was hobbling along behind, without a sign of complaint.

31
THE LEPER'S RIDE OF MISERY

As we off saddled, Davey said: "You come along me Jack? I show you cave. When me wild-feller man we altogether camp there longa wet. Kill man. Eat kidney fat belonga him. Get ready fight. Secret place. You bring 'em revolver Jack!"

Rather surprised, I did not answer for the moment. Davey waited uneasily. Then:

"S'pose you no bring 'em revolver Jack, more better me bring 'em rifle!"

So I strapped on the revolver. The moral effect of the little weapon is considerably greater than the practical. We waded through man-high grass and down into a black creek where grew a maze of prickly palm. Stooping under drooping fronds we wormed our way up the creek then climbed out into sunlight in open forest. Even here, Davey followed depressions in the ground so that we might not be seen.

"Any wild blackfellows here Davey?"

"Plenty!" he answered with a twist of head and gleam of teeth. "Plenty wild feller all about."

"Suppose they see, they no kill us?"

"Suppose they see revolver, they no try!" he answered grimly.

For several miles nothing betrayed a beauty spot, or anything unusual. Suddenly we were in amongst boulders like tumbled houses; then a waterhole gleamed among palms, hedged by cliffs. Davey pointed to heaps of piled stones:

"Spirit stones!" he whispered. "Dead man he live here; walk longa night-time." Under a sandstone ledge was shelter for a hundred people even through the heaviest "wet." The roof had been white ochred to throw into relief drawings of a male, a female and a baby crocodile. They were well drawn in red and yellow ochre, their internal organs being shown as rounded circles filled with dots. With the crocodile was a little devil-devil man, his small spidery form outlined in red. The drawings no doubt held a world of primitive meaning if one could only have interpreted it. The floor was of clean white sand. In a semicircle facing this veranda-like ledge and six feet higher than it was a large area of bare rock. On this natural stage, explained Davey in low tones, the witch-doctors performed their devil-devil dances. From here, too, set out vengeance bands to carry out the witch-doctors' decrees. Beyond the stage were still, deep pools hedged by cliffs, silvered by a spidery trail of water. Davey now became very hesitant. I waited.

Suddenly he said: "We go back now."

I followed slowly despite his signs for haste, and the more he urgently beckoned the more I lingered. Passing an overhanging rock of ages I stood sniffing in the air . . . and sniffed that unmistakable animal smell of the wild man who has anointed his body with rancid human fat. I dawdled no longer.

The next morning Laurie cut up a pair of his boots for the Big Leper. It was an awful job getting them on his swollen feet. After about two more miles the. man cracked up; the soles of his feet actually began to break away. Laurie called a halt, undid his swag, and took out his pyjama coat and tore it in halves telling Larry to bind it around the leper's feet. The big man looked up piteously, talking in imploring gutturals.

"What he say?" demanded Laurie.

"He prighten you leave him," answered Davey. "He say: 'No more leave me, boss; me prighten bush boy kill him me. This country no belonga me.' "

"Tell him we are not going to leave him; that we are going to take him right to Derby."

We travelled, but by midday the Big Leper was a long way behind, hobbling his hardest to keep up. Laurie called a halt.

"Take the pack off Molly and put it on Kate," he ordered the trackers.

When the leper came up, his feet were peeling away in layers into the bandages.

With a surcingle Davey strapped a blanket on old Molly, the quietest and smallest mule.

"Can you ride?" asked Laurie doubtfully.

The leper gazed at the old mule as if it were some fierce, prehistoric animal.

"Him say him try!" interpreted Davey.

"All right. Tell his lubra to take the halter; she can lead the mule. Now old man, let us see you mount!"

Larry helped him. The leper lifted a long leg over the mule's back, hooked his heel into its side, then desperately climbed up along its neck, just saving himself front tumbling over the other side. His lubra held the halter with arm outstretched in fear of Molly's teeth.

For the remainder of the day the leper clung to the surcingle during this first ride of his life, old Molly obviously wondering what indignity was abusing her back. The lubra experienced a nervous day. When clambering down slippery gullies she kept her arms outstretched behind to push back Molly who simply slid down, butting the woman with her nose. Down several steep pinches the lubra went sprawling, frantically wriggling from under the fat paunch of the mule.

At sundown camp the leper dismounted by slowly rolling off the mule, clinging to its neck. He stood there, gripping the resigned Molly. His limbs had noticeably swollen, bits of skin were showing from what had been bandages around his feet.

"The poor chap stuck it well," said Laurie.

"If the leper had been left behind," I asked Larry and Davey, "would he have been killed?"

"Quick feller!" they replied unanimously. And added that the same fear had spurred the two older lubras who had hobbled so sturdily on behind during the last few days. These and the leper would be a great prize for the wild *munjons*. They would be easy prey.

Night came with a large, golden moon. A lovely, dream-invoking night. The troops were unusually quiet; I thought they glanced apprehensively at our fairly big fire. Out in the grass a mule suddenly snorted.

"Wild *munjon*!" whispered Davey. Mules in the moonlight stood prick-eared, perfectly still.

"Mules smell wild blackfellow!" whispered Larry.

All hands were listening. The strained profiles around the trees told plainly that they anticipated no rescue— rather the reverse.

Again a mule snorted. Charcoal hissed towards the trackers, asking for spears should the *munjons* come.

A wild clattering of horse-bells as every animal stampeded; we listened to their ringing hoofs growing fainter and fainter. But not another sound; and not a spear came.

"Larry . . . Davey," ordered Laurie resolutely, "take rifles and bring back those horses and mules."

Quietly the trackers obeyed; we watched them gliding away. Their rifles gave them the courage of many spears. We kept a sharp look out for the rest of the night.

"It's amusing," said Laurie with a low laugh. "The troops can see much plainer than we, and they won't sleep a wink all night. They'd be the sorriest people on earth if anything happened to us—in this particular country." "Rather a helpless crowd if there was a sudden attack."

"I'd throw the prisoners that bundle of spears and they'd put up the fight of their lives. Each man is an expert."

It was near dawn when the trackers returned with the animals.

Next morning, as we started out, a smoke curled from a hill behind. It was the first signal we had seen since leaving Thompson's. An old white bull, a monster, stamped out of a thicket and surveyed us from only a hundred yards away.

"If he charges," I said, "what a scatter there'll be!"

"See the eyes of the troops!" replied Laurie. "Every man and woman has already selected a tree."

But the old bull quietly regarded us as we passed. An hour later a mob of clean-skins broke cover and with tails in the air set off at a great pace. Larry and Davey were after them at the gallop and jubilation broke out all along the line. A rifle-shot, followed by another, electrified the troops, who pushed excitedly on and presently came up with the trackers. They had shot a young heifer from the saddle. As the beast was being cut up Nipper lifted his head.

"Emu!" he whispered, and pointed with an uplift of his eyes and chin. Presently we heard the faint, curiously throaty call of an emu.

Wonderful ears had Nipper, to hear that distant sound amidst the excitement and noise of over twenty people cutting up a beast. In a few moments the emu came along to stare inquisitively at us.

The cooking-fires were soon burning in a deep depression among rocks near a waterhole. Mrs Oomagun who till now had seemed fed up with the day's march, brightened noticeably when she started on her share of roast meat. They were all very bright, the hard marching day after day was immaterial so long as they had plenty of meat. Only the Big Leper lay like a log. Oombali suffered from awful sores (now partly healed) on both hips where he had rolled on the coals while asleep. The aboriginals are often injured in that way. Dirt and ashes cover their wound apparently without harm; their blood in the course of ages must have become immunized against dirt germs.

As we neared Grace's Knob a thrill of anticipation ran through the patrol; all hands, in between eating, discussed the chances of catching Donkey. None at all judging by Charcoal's guttural laugh and Oomagun's slow grin.

"Theirs is a one-sided reasoning," said Laurie. "They don't take into consideration the fact that we have travelled a long way from Grace's Knob, and will approach it from an unexpected direction. Further, Donkey and Company will probably not expect our return—particularly if they have heard of Allboroo's escape. They will be certain we are away north following him. If they have not heard, which is very improbable, they will think we are well on the homeward track. All things considered, we have a sporting chance of catching Donkey."

The troops were lolling, full bellied, around their fires when Charcoal called out to the trackers that Oombali wanted to tell all about the Worachi murder. As he might have some particulars to add to what he had already admitted, we strolled across. All hands immediately ceased chewing and listened, eyes gleaming from around the tree-butts. Oombali squatted there bashfully smiling, speaking softly as he gazed up. Davey interpreted while all grinned in keen enjoyment.

Worachi, it appears, interfered in Paddy's domestic arrangements, so Paddy suggested to Oomagun and Donkey that it would be a good idea to kill him. They agreed. Being on friendly terms with Worachi, they arranged a hunting-party and started off. At a given signal Oombali threw his arms around Worachi and held him while the others speared him.

Oombali finished his tale then grinned bashfully at the fire. Psychologically, it was the idea then the suggestion that had been responsible for Worachi's death. Put a suggestion into the minds of these people and they invariably act on it.

Big Paddy.

32
DONKEY IS CAUGHT

THE prisoners assured us that we would never catch Donkey. Donkey was a mighty hunter, a great fighting man; he had boasted he would never be taken alive. The "white pleece" would never catch him.

"I like these aboriginals; they have such confidence in themselves," said Laurie as we strolled back to our fire. "It adds zest to the game when you are chasing a first-class man in his own country and he is willing to give you a go for it."

Some old bush instinct woke me that night. I leaned from the blanket and looked around: all was still, the tree leaves drooping as if in sleep. Each fire, faintly flickering, made dimly visible above the grass tops bent knees and portions of bare, black bodies greyed with ashes. But unless a blaze actually gleamed on limb or body it was invisible. A woman sat up and yawningly poked some sticks together; as she sat back she was lost in the night. She reappeared startlingly—Mrs Charcoal in her red dress, the Flame! What crazy urge made her don it now goodness only knows. Almost immediately she threw it off and was at once invisible. There was an apprehensive silence and then—snort of mules, rattle of bells, rumble of stampeding hoofs. Laurie and the trackers were instantly on their feet; the troops were crouching up from every fire. But not another sound, only the rapidly diminishing beat of hoofs. It proved another wakeful night with not even the sight of a flitting shadow.

Next morning the troops rose with their usual yawns, groans and stretching of limbs. As usual, on moving off they tried to hide the meat left over—too lazy to carry it. Grimly the trackers kicked into sight bundles of meat thrown away in the grass. Then the hefty men tried to make the already laden lubras carry it. Laurie quickly fixed things up and away we marched. That afternoon we clambered down into a valley of birds, and camped near big white gums beside a water pool. Davey's sending Mrs Nipper to wash his clothes was sign that we would be at Grace's Knob tomorrow evening. He and old Larry shaved with a blunt old razor, before an appreciative audience of prisoners. When night fell the idea seized Davey to comb the tangled locks of Mrs Oomagun's daughter with the remnant of a comb he cherished. The girl's teeth and the whites of her eyes gleamed as she laughed, but she was otherwise invisible. Night truly takes these people to herself To guffaws Davey broke the remaining teeth of his comb. The child's hair since babyhood had never been washed; had had for its only adornment clay pellets which hardened in the sun.

Next day after rough riding we came out on to a plateau and saw the Big Leopolds fairly close, the Bluff and the big flat top of Mount House looming plainly. That mount is a monument to the fine old wandering naturalist, Dr House. Soon we saw the twin, conical hills named Grace's Knob, so named by that great old explorer Hann. The hills looked surprisingly rounded and smooth under their straw-coloured grass. We rode down on to the flat country and made a crescent course towards the cover of the tall paper-barks along the Isdell. Animals and humans put their best foot forward. Suddenly the trackers reined in; then, leaning searchingly over their horses' necks, branched off.

They had cut the tracks of a hunting party, Donkey and Paddy s tracks among them. But the tracks were several days old; tracks of yesterday were imprinted upon them.

"He's in the locality anyway," said Laurie, "unless signal smokes have warned him. We might surprise him at Grace's Knob. I can leave my sick there and chase him now I know he is in the vicinity. Push on! This is my lucky day."

Through a small gorge we followed the Isdell until it ran out on the plain, then the trackers spread out at the gallop to take the camp in the rear. I followed with the slower patrol.

Donkey had gone. The lined-up natives, old Rattler among them, wore the same sarcastic smile they had when, some two months before, we had galloped this same camp in search of Nipper.

Laurie took it philosophically. At the homestead Bob Maxted, a tall young chap, came out and welcomed us.

"Who are you after?" he inquired.

"Donkey," replied Laurie.

"He was here a day or two ago; must be out in the hills somewhere. Never mind, I'm glad to have company. Come inside; billy's boiling. Let the boys unpack your mules."

"You've got some lame ducks, Laurie," drawled Peter Bextrum as we enjoyed a wash.

"Yes. They'll take some curing too."

"Did you hear about Dave Rust?" inquired Maxted.

"No. We've been bush a good while."

"Well, the abos 'bandicooted' his peanuts. They made sure you weren't doubling back on your tracks, then immediately that Jack Campbell rode away back to Russ's to help Dave back with his little mob of cattle, they cleaned his peanut cultivation right up. Then they raided Dave's cattle, surprised and stampeded them, then speared some. That was the little mob Dave was droving back from Fred Russ's to stock his place. Dave and Campbell managed to get a few back. Haven't heard how many; some still had spearheads sticking in them."

I thought of Scotty Salmon at Walcott Inlet, watching in his dreams his mate droving that tiny mob of cattle to start their new station.

"Have you heard anything of old Felix?" inquired Laurie.

"No. But he must have his mob nearly to Derby by now. Kelvin is with him; you just missed him when you called here. He rode across to give old Felix a hand."

Kelvin Smith was Bob Maxted's partner. They had got a flying start and by all appearances would make good. But what an isolated, lonely life for two young fellows!

While we were talking, Laurie had been thinking. And when he finished the evening meal thoughts developed into action.

"How far away do you say this new missionary, Street, is?"

"About fourteen miles."

"Building a camp?"

"Yes."

"Have you a boy here who knows just where he is?"

"Yes."

"Of course. But you're not going after Donkey tonight, surely."

"It's my chance. By now he probably knows that the patrol is here and will camp here tonight. Thinking he will be safe until tomorrow midday, he will take to the ranges leisurely in the early morning. Almost certainly he is with the natives who are helping Street. The chance of easy tucker, particularly tobacco, will take him there; that's positive as he was here a couple of days ago. He knows I'll be after him in earnest to-morrow; but he doesn't know I'll be waiting at his gunyah with the dawn."

Maxted whistled.

"What a lovely ride!"

"We'll walk when it gets too rough," said Laurie. "Now I'll pack up a bit of tucker in case I miss him and have to follow his tracks."

"In that case we mightn't see you for a month or more," said Maxted. "Tracking Donkey will be like following a shadow."

"Once I see his tracks he's my man!" answered Laurie grimly.

When the camp was all quiet he set out with Davey and the guide.

"I don't envy him his ride," said Maxted. "Still, it is his one chance of catching that bird."

"He'll get him," said Peter quietly. "He has guessed exactly what Donkey will do. He'll be near Street right enough; he can bully him for tobacco. But he'll wake up with Laurie's hand on his shoulder."

Old Peter was dreamily smoking while talking in his slow, drawling voice. Peter loved the blacks. He had spent a lifetime amongst them as their friend and adviser, remaining so despite several narrow escapes at their hands.

Next day late, Laurie returned. sHe had Donkey and Long Paddy and Short Paddy, with Dungart and witnesses. He had galloped their gunyahs at dawn, and had the handcuffs on them almost before they were awake.

These five athletic men were fine representatives of the last of the real stone-age men. Studying them, especially while travelling with them for a time, made it very difficult to believe that their ancestors of 100,000 years or more ago could have been the brute apes that many believe they were. So far as human reasoning from the available evidence can tell, these men were precisely similar to their ancestors many thousands of years before the birth of Christ. Probably the prehistoric man had a brain capable of considerably higher reasoning than our savants have credited him with.

Donkey and his mate in particular had savagely intellectual faces, keen and alert.

33

THE SPIRITS COME AGAIN

CHARCOAL greeted Donkey and his mates with a loud guffaw; Oomagun's deep-lined face was one big smile; Nipper bent forward eagerly, calling out sarcastic sallies; Oombali laughed softly. There was none of the regret such as might have been experienced by white people had their idols suddenly been laid by the heels. Bashfully the newcomers smiled, squatted down, and answered the questions poured upon them.

The women looked on interestedly, Mrs Oomagun without a word. I wondered what was passing behind her dark countenance, for now that Donkey was caught Oomagun's case would assuredly be proved. Almost certainly she was not bothering about that. Mrs Charcoal gazed speculatively; she was pleased even though this latest capture did not rivet the fetters any closer on her hated Charcoal. It gave an air of completeness to see the notorious Donkey on the chain—made the white man's law comfortably inescapable in her eyes. Mrs Nipper was interested only in learning the latest news of her tribesmen and women in the hills. The others and the sick took only passing interest; these men were of other tribes. The Big Leper lay stretched out, taking full advantage of at least one clear day's spell.

Laurie allowed the new arrivals no chance to immediately settle down with the old hands and thus plan problems for the patrol; particularly when he found that old Rattler and his mate had discreetly vanished. Laurie ordered the new prisoners and witnesses to show him where they had buried the body of Worachi. They agreed with alacrity, smiling broadly. Oombali volunteered straightaway; they'seemed to think that now all hands were captured the mere showing of where the body was buried was a joke. Their law is: "An eye for an eye, a tooth for a tooth." All this bother about finding the mere body of a man was absurd. As we filed towards the river followed by the admiring glances of the local tribesmen they were all jokes and gossip. We could guess the big joke, for Oombali and Nipper had previously told us that the bones of Worachi had been taken by his relatives to be buried by his waters.

We crossed the river and there, at the foot of a rocky knoll they showed us a circle of stones about three feet high. Inside were still the paper-bark wrappings in which the corpse had been placed. Standing all around the stones they stared at Laurie, their half smiling expressions plainly asking: "What are you going to do about it now?"

The locality was barely two hundred yards from camp. How often throughout the long march the troops must have chuckled about it. When we had raided this camp for Nipper two months ago the body was still there; every soul in camp knew it. We had camped for several nights quite close to it. Even the piccaninnies had laughed. With a chuckling smile Charcoal said something uncomplimentary about the trackers. Nipper threw back his head and laughed. Old Larry smiled grimly; all were in the net now. Besides, when we rode here first we sought the murderers of Burrin, and they were on the chain now. We knew nothing about the Worachi murder at the time; but the murderers of Worachi, too, were on the chain. In gruff tones old Larry quickly retaliated in the aboriginal for "He laughs loudest who laughs last!" Donkey looked savagely sheepish.

Witnesses were sent for from the camp. They came, and behind them all the tribes-people, standing some distance away. In pantomime the chief actors showed us exactly how Worachi was murdered, placing their feet on the very places where they had walked that day, portraying every action exactly as it had occurred.

Oombali, especially, enjoyed his part for he was the star actor, the cynosure of all eyes. They watched with the keenest interest as he showed how he had thrown his arms around the doomed man and held his body to the spear thrusts. They speared Worachi not because of a woman, they explained now, but because he was an East Kimberley man and though on a friendly visit was still not one of them.

They had left him for dead. But he regained consciousness and managed to crawl back to camp during the evening. There they allowed him to moan his life away: he died just before daylight.

We returned with old Larry in high glee, for now we were really starting for home. Laurie was satisfied too, he had completed a big job.

Next day we said "Farewell!" to Grace's Knob and moved off, thirty-three strong, out on to the Isdell plain, bound for Mount Hart. But a tracking job first. Laurie if possible wanted to catch old Rattler and his particular friend. Rattler had already placed many miles between himself and the patrol since seeing Donkey brought into camp. But a mounted patrol, even though encumbered by prisoners and sick, and having to find food in a country where there is no such thing as a store, is still very formidable, even to an aboriginal encumbered by nothing but his trained body and spears. The aboriginal thinks only of immediate quickness, of the next few moves ahead. The patrol leader sees his man as a travelling or hiding speck in a great maze of country; he has that country mapped in his mind even if it reaches to the sea; he knows, too, that his man is bounded by tribal enmities and friendships, by his partiality for certain food locali¬ties; day by day, slowly perhaps but surely, his actions are foreseen by the patrol leader's far-seeing mind, whose actions hem that man in until he is secured.

The search for Rattler was to cover many miles but was to be swift.

"Ride well ahead when we get a mile out on the plain," ordered Laurie to the trackers, "then Larry ride to the right, Davey to the left. Circle the homestead far out and cut Rattler's tracks."

They did it, while the patrol rode slowly on. Once the tracks were found we put on the pace. Larry leaning over the saddle, his marvellous eyesight detecting those faint traces amongst the grass, even across the perishing reeds of dried-up swamps.

Davey rode out well ahead of Larry then turning cut the tracks away on ahead. Immediately he did so Larry would trot ahead and ride well in advance of Davey, seeking to cut the tracks ahead again. Thus the patrol steadily followed a horseman travelling quickly; time and effort were saved.

That afternoon we shot a cow. Laurie cut portion of the wet hide into moccasins and laced them wet around the feet of a man and woman who were developing sore feet. A splendid idea, for the hide dried into the shape of the feet. In the arid inland the same idea is used to help footsore camels.

Laurie called a halt at the beginning of the Isdell Gorge.

"No hope," he said. "They've beaten the horses. This gorge runs right down to the coast, and the farther it goes the rougher it becomes until the cliffs are six hundred feet high. Impassable for horses. Rattler knows what he is doing. We'll camp here and spell the sick people."

The gorge here had a rugged beauty. It ran between small red cliffs that hemmed in a series of pools infested by crocodiles. Rough bush timber leaned perilously from the plateau above.

At sundown on that particular evening the women were frightened to go for water. Davey had to escort them; they believed the spirits were again travelling with the patrol.

Around the campfires that night the spirit atmosphere reigned: whispers, eyes gleaming towards the shadows, fires merely glowing. The trackers were murmuring by the women's fire.

"The spirits are with them," said Laurie lazily. "Good job too, they won't be so keen to escape. No aboriginal does that on a night when the spirits are around."

Old Larry stood up and walked across, his face very serious.

"Well?" inquired Laurie,

"Ogilla! Spirit people he here!" mumbled Larry.

"He no here," replied Laurie. "You only think him here."

"Him here all right !" insisted Larry. "Black men different; black men know! White man no understan'! Black man know what white man no can understan'!"

Davey came then and in low, earnest tones started explaining invisible spearing to us. Under certain conditions and by the aid of certain influences a man can, they believe, be invisibly speared. Half-caste Joe had said the same back at Merry's. It is a belief common to the hordes and tribes of the Kimberleys, and of certain other localities in Australia. The doomed man feels the wire or glass or bone spearhead in him, but not in the same way as if he had received a spear wound in a fight. Larry said that if any of the natives in the Derby hospital were opened up the doctor would probably find wire or glass inside them.

This invisible spearing belief is most interesting. Some of the desert tribes also believe in it; but as it borders on the supernatural, and is intricate, it would require too much space to explain lucidly here. Briefly: when a man is doomed by the Council of Old Men to die by this particular method, they all go on a friendly kangaroo hunt. The 'roo is speared; they crowd around it. Suddenly all but one draw back and the doomed man finds himself eating alone. The shock prostrates him. He is supposed to be speared then. None can see the act except the man appointed to spear and the witch-doctor, who then puts the gum on that draws the wound together. When the man comes to, the witch-doctor tells him how long he has to live.

But among the desert tribes referred to above is an invisible spearing that is cruelly practical, although the really invisible and this form produce identical results. The doomed man is taken from camp, forced to kneel, then squat back on his haunches, and is held in this position. He generally submits dumbly; hut a powerful man or one crazed by fear may put up a frantic struggle. Straight down by his neck, straight down through the hollow formed by his shoulder blades a very thin, long bone like a very fine knitting needle is forced, right down into his lung. The bone is then withdrawn, the tiny wound closes up and is quite invisible. In due course the victim dies from slow haemorrhage.

Returning to the patrol, Davey explained that the spirit people were really where he spoke, there beside us:

"You can't see him," he insisted earnestly. "He there. Plenty spirit there belonga skeletons."

He shrugged at our incredulity and walked away. Nothing will ever shake these people's faith in mystic beliefs like that—if they are entirely mystic, that is. No aboriginal in Australia has mixed with whites more than old Larry, and yet he believes these things implicitly. Every aboriginal I have ever come in contact with believes them.

Just as we turned in, some owl bird called piercingly and most peculiarly from a tree amongst us: a weirdly commanding sound. The aboriginals instantly knew it was a bird, but to them it was also something vastly different—a spirit that had assumed bird form in order to materialize on earth.

There was not a whisper for the remainder of the night.

Next morning at breakfast Laurie gave careful and detailed orders to Davey. After which, Davey and Monkey stripped naked and for a couple of hours ceremonially oiled and ochred their bodies, completing the transformations with head-dresses of cockatoo and brolga feathers respectively. When Davey grasped spears and wommera it was impossible to recognize in this painted savage the alert, nattily dressed tracker.

Laurie ordered them to follow Rattler's tracks and try to induce him and his particular mate to come in as witnesses. The trackers would follow the gorge, and we would meet them at Mount Hart. If we had passed, they were to follow our tracks.

Davey and his companion Monkey dared not venture into Rattler's country alone clad in clothes.

"Wild bushmen spear us plenty suppose we do!" declared Davey. As he tested the balance of his spears, the very poise of him was all confidence.

The feathers these men wore were of totem birds, and each was eligible to wear the feathers in his head-dress. Rattler and his mate were of the cockatoo and brolga totems. Men meeting wearing feathers were automatically under the protection of the totem represented by the feathers, should they meet people of the same totem. They would not be ambushed, but could be surrounded and given a chance to explain before spears were thrown.

There is strict etiquette in aboriginal law, and it pays the judicious tracker when far distant from the patrol to observe it.

We rode on through a valley with sunlight glinting on red rock, then climbed up over rough divides and there frowned the Leopolds, Bold Bluff, Mount Chalmers and Mount Edgar standing clear. The prisoners and sick gazed rather quietly, for those frowning ramparts brought home the certainty that at last they would really be leaving their own country. The other people had long since left their own country. Across more valleys and ranges and we finally came out on the big Mount Hart valley. It was barely three months since we had been here riding through a sea of grass. The country now looked strangely dry; many of the huge grass patches were quite bowed down while the rest were fast turning straw coloured. Under some species of grass were green shoots; such grass the cattlemen love. The rock-coloured ranges stood out boldly, all sun splashed. I felt sure the mules and horses recognized them.

One morning just after sunrise we rode through Gardiner's Gap, beautifully cool and quiet, the sun only splashing a wall of rock here and there. We emerged from the gap on to the Mount Hart country with its low grassy hills splashed with black outcrops of basalt. When passing between two abrupt conical hills Larry saw a black head bob down far up in the grass. Larry galloped around the hill while the patrol trudged on. We were passing the hill on the other side when we saw Larry come over the top and ride zigzag down. It looked utterly impossible; I expected man and horse tc come rolling, rolling down.

Larry got his man. He turned out to be Charlie, a Mount Hart stockboy, a leper. Felix Edgar had been taking him in with the cattle to Derby and the doctor. But the boy had run away, returned to Mount Hart, picked up his spears, called to his lubra and dog and was making for the wilds.

Laurie convinced him that if he came in with the patrol the white doctor in Derby might cure him; whereas if he persisted in taking to the bush he would certainly die.

Surlily, he consented to join in with the patrol.

"I'm glad to see his lubra coming also," said Laurie as we rode on. "Probably she has leprosy too, poor beggar."

34
INTRIGUE

WE arrived at Mount Hart to be welcomed by the smiling Dick and Toby. They had come straight bush from Walcott Inlet and awaited the patrol, determined to get to Derby. Little Dick immediately inquired whether we had "bullick" in our tucker-bags.

Old Felix Edgar was absent in Derby, but a homestead lubra gave Laurie a letter. In it Felix stated that Big Paddy had broken out, creating panic in the camp. Then had snatched up his spears and taken to the bush, vowing vengeance on white and black alike.

"I'll have a job to get him if he really does mean business," said Laurie. "Oh, well, it's all in the game." Davey and Monkey had appeared at Mount Hart that morning, so the stock-boys informed us, hot on the tracks of Rattler. Smokes had warned him of the coming of the patrol and he had vanished the evening before.

Davey and Monkey had wolfed a meal and set off immediately on Rattler's tracks.

"They've had a great walk already," I said. "They must have covered a considerably larger area of country than we have, since leaving them at the Isdell."

"They'll get him!" replied Laurie confidently.

Laurie granted the sick several days' spell, fortunately for the patrol; for the evening before we left Mount Hart Davey walked triumphantly into camp with Rattler and his mate. He exhibited another wild and woolly specimen, white-feller name Paddy. Paddy stepped forward grinning widely; his huge feet grew toes that a gorilla might have envied. Paddy by tribal law had been ordered to take possession of Worachi's bones and pass them on to Tim to be taken away to be buried beside his waters. Paddy wished to tell all about the bones and in return wanted a trip to the "white man Derby."

"Are you going straight to Derby from here, Laurie?"

"Pretty well; on a different route though; through bush to Napier Downs station, then straight across country to Kimberley Downs. By going to Napier. I have just a faint chance of running into that band of Oobagooma outlaws. The unexpected sometimes happens in this game. The distance is the same, so I won't lose by it, whether or no."

The patrol stepped out bravely on the homeward stage. Nipper strode out like a jack-in-the-box, very important in that he had been to jail! He must answer more and more questions as each day brought us nearer civilization; must describe yet again just what life in jail was like, particularly as to a tobacco issue. Horses and mules put their best hoofs forward knowing well that they were on the homeward track. Three mules easily carried all our possessions now. Laurie had seated sick people on the others, though with difficulty, for the sick feared the animals. The Big Leper still clung to old Molly, his woman leading the mule much more confidently.

Among the shock troops there had, for some time, been an indefinable air of something doing. If Davey had ever shown any slight preference at all to the women, it was towards Mrs Oomagun: it was she mainly who had done his washing and carried his few treasures. But this morning it was Mrs Nipper who proudly carried Davey's belongings, while Mrs Oomagun lagged behind with her child and a scowl. Mrs Charcoal walked without looking to right or left, and for some puzzling reason wore her scarlet dress.

"Mrs Charcoal looks 'very proper,' " remarked Laurie. "I wonder what she's up to?"

"She looks dignified, and Mrs Oomagun looks like a thunderstorm."

"Yes. Probably because Mrs Nipper is carrying Davey's sweat rag. I wonder if old Larry has been up to something."

"Why?"

"Well, when we get to Derby Nancy will learn that the shock troops have travelled with the patrol. She will put nothing past her husband, especially when quick accusation might form a welcome cloak. Larry is an innocent old dog, but feels worried, knowing his little wife. I believe he is hatching something to prove his *bona fides*. We'll see before we get to Napier Downs. I have an ' idea, too, that Mrs Charcoal is casting her eye on Toby." "But he's a woman-hater."

"They all fall," answered Laurie wisely.

The patrol made good time winding among the hills. The grass seeds had all been blown away by time and the wind. It was a pleasure to ride through ever-changing country even though the green had gone off the grass. We camped at the Dromedary—two hills resembling a camel's hump.

That night after the evening meal an unusual quietness fell upon the troops. Then Larry and Davey with Toby and Mrs Charcoal came to our fire. From all the little fires eyes gleamed towards us.

"Toby wants to marry Mrs Charcoal," explained Larry. "He wants you marry him belonga her."

"But Mrs Charcoal is married to Charcoal!" exclaimed Laurie.

"No matter. Charcoal arright. He say marry him arright; he finish longa Mrs Charcoal; no more want her."

"But tribal?" inquired Laurie.

"Tribal arright," nodded Larry.

"Well I won't," said Laurie decidedly. "What is more, I can't. Now you go straight to Charcoal and tell him that I will send Mrs Charcoal straight back to her own country if he likes, or I will make Toby leave the patrol." Larry looked surprised, but he obeyed. Charcoal spoke volubly, gesticulating with his arms as if violently throwing away his words. Larry returned to us quietly grinning and with no little satisfaction explained that Charcoal wanted the marriage to take place; he wanted to get rid of Mrs Charcoal at all costs, if only to save himself the trouble of killing her when he returned from jail. Larry looked across at Charcoal and repeated his interpretation in aboriginal. Charcoal nodded vigorous assent, with an all embracing smile and expressive eyes inviting Laurie to carry on with the business.

"I'm blessed if I will," declared Laurie. "They can make their own arrangements."

Then turning to Toby:

"You clear away out of this!"

Toby walked away with Mrs Charcoal, almost hand in hand.

"What do you mean by letting Mrs Nipper carry your things?" demanded Laurie of Davey.

"I look after her for Nipper!" answered Davey in surprise.

"Oh, do you," said Laurie. "We'll see about that!"

He got up and we walked across to the prisoners' fire. Laurie put it straight to Nipper. He asked him which he preferred: his wife sent back bush, or with him to Derby.

Most emphatically with him to Derby, declared Nipper in pidgin. He had arranged with Davey to look after her while he was in jail. When he came out, he was going to enjoy a spell in Derby making new spears and picking up a lot of iron. Mrs Nipper would then be handy in carrying the iron and anything else he picked up, back to the bush.

We walked back to our fire, except Davey, who answered some eye-signal from the women. Laurie turned on Larry:

"Well! I suppose you have made some arrangement about Mrs Oomagun, you scroundrel."

Old Larry shook his head in alarm. "No more! No more! Carbine look after Mrs Oomagun!"

"Well I'm blessed! What does Oomagun say?"

"Arright! he please. Mrs Oomagun carry back things longa bush when he and Nipper come out of jail."

"I see. So Davey knew Carbine was going to look after Mrs Oomagun?"

Larry grinned.

"He don't know yet," he replied softly.

You don't mean to say he wants to look after the two of them?"

He been think so," said Larry with a smile.

'H'm. Carbine is the other tracker at the police station," explained Laurie to me. "Larry, you arranged all this so that Nancy would not think you had been playing up!"

No more, assured Larry earnestly. "They altogether make it up together. I do nothing."

"You convince Nancy of that if you can," said Laurie grimly. "And what is Charcoal going to do when he comes out of jail? If he gives Mrs Charcoal to Toby then he will have no woman to carry his things back to the bush."

"He stealem young lubra from Derby," explained Larry simply.

"Oh, will he! And Donkey?"

"He stealem young one too."

"We'll see about that when the time comes. Go on, get back to your fire, you old scoundrel."

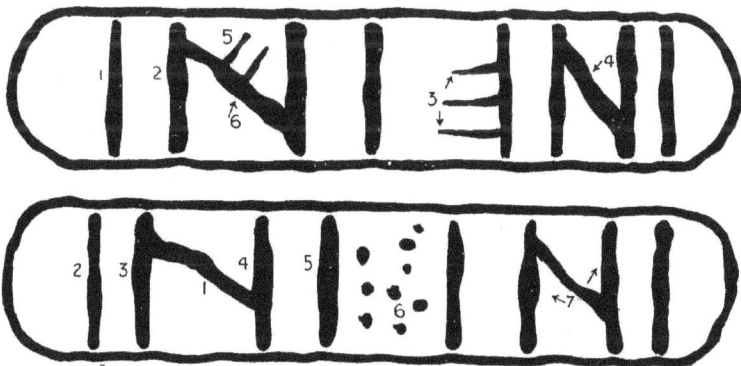

AUTHOR'S DRAWING OF A MESSAGE-STICK FROM THE ISDELL RIVER TRIBE DESCRIBING THE KILLING OF WORACHI
(This stick was passed around among the tribes as we would pass around a newspaper.)

Above: 1. Whisky wanted to spare Worachi, but 2. Marmadu (Donkey) said he was a very strong warrior and swore he would kill him and eat his kidney fat. 3. Moby, Womerun, and Ardgat warned the hunted man that the killers were close upon him and advised him to hide in Parrywarri Creek. 4. Parrywarri Creek, where Worachi hid in vain. 5. Twin hills of Grace's Knob, by 6. Isdell River where Worachi was killed.

Below (Reverse side): 1. Jack wanted to kill Worachi in the Creek, but Ardgat (George) stopped him. 2. Marmadu (Donkey), 3. Dungart. 4. Oomagun. 5. Oombali killed him but now have big trouble with Worachi's tribesmen. 6. Turkey Creek warriors who have sent word threatening vengeance. 7. They say they will fight Oomagun's men near the dead white-man Conlon's station.

35
DERBY

NEXT morning we rode among quaintly-shaped hills that, as day wore on, appeared as bold granite domes rising straight from the flat earth. The troops marched bravely on, Mrs Charcoal in the Flame treading demurely in Toby's footsteps. Presently he turned and handed her young Dick. She carried the boy while Toby graciously took over his spears and the lady's bark water bucket. A little later he returned the water bucket. Mrs Oomagun marched glowering at Davey's back. Davey was whistling in great trim: Mrs Nipper still carried his prized possessions.

We crossed the Barker River, now a string of water-holes, crossed Red Bull Creek, and camped. Toby walked away to cut firewood, the new Mrs Toby following him. Toby cut a big heap of wood and piled it on the lady. Without a murmur she carried it back to camp, and Toby walked away whistling, carrying the tomahawk.

At sundown the dingoes commenced howling; the bush seemed alive with them, their blood-curdling howls rising mournfully from those great domed shadows.

While Laurie was making certain the prisoners were secure for the night, Davey came to me. He wished to trade a pubic shell for tobacco—three sticks. Davey had bought that shell from a bush black six weeks ago. It was, till now, the only curio he did not wish to trade. It was a pearl shell, polished and nicely ground down to shape. Painted and befeathered, with this big shell dangling from his belt a warrior would look the real hero when dancing in corroborees in Derby. I bought the shell, but wondered why Davey wished to sell it at the last moment, especially as he received a daily tobacco allowance. Of course, his obligations to the ladies might have cut heavily into that.

At breakfast next morning old Larry suddenly called out: "Mrs Oomagun! She run away!"

Every one stopped eating, dark eyes gazed towards Laurie. He smiled.

"She's a free agent," he said. "She can come or go as she pleases. But I wonder why she came all this way and then ran away!"

As the horses came trotting into camp the prisoners called out the news and grinned at Davey's crestfallen face. (He had gone for the horses at daylight.) Charcoal and Oomagun led a hearty laugh.

"Why he laugh?" inquired Laurie.

Larry grinned:

"Davey losem new wife."

"But he was going to look after Mrs Nipper."

"He like Mrs Oomagun best. He lose tobacco too!"

"Tobacco?"   .

Larry, with an owlish grin, explained that last night Mrs Oomagun had prevailed on Davey to sell his pubic shell to me, and demand three sticks of tobacco. And now she had gone—with the tobacco. Davey had lost his shell, tobacco, and woman all at the one blow. How the women were enjoying the joke! What hurt Davey was the blow to his pride. He squatted silently to breakfast, frowning at sundry giggles, nudges of elbows, and the smiles on the prisoners' big black faces.

Probably the lady, watching the camp from among the long grass and trees, was expecting the trackers to seek her at any moment. She could have been caught with ease. She dare not leave the shelter of the creek with its big trees, for behind her was a lightly-wooded plain upon which she would have been seen long before she reached the sheltering hills. It would only have meant a light canter to have caught her, let alone a tracking job. I wondered if she really wished to get away.

"I'm glad she's gone," said Laurie. "She's not really necessary as a witness whereas the others are. And old Larry will have one little problem less to explain away to Nancy."

The patrol was soon in the picturesque Napier Range: a ragged barrier of spires and pinnacles and broken walls, but only a few hundred feet high.

We witnessed a touching love scene as we marched. The late Mrs Charcoal marching demurely in the rear, even behind the Big Leper. Toby marching ahead of the lady carrying nothing, while she in her red dress carried young Dick astride her shoulders, her bundle strapped under her arm, a bark water bucket in one hand, Toby's spears in the other. Throughout the day she was Toby's shadow. When we rode by, she plodded on with downcast eyes, the modest maiden, no longer the Mrs Charcoal of the patrol.

In the afternoon we rode out on to a large, well-grassed plain, and saw in the distance the red roofs and windmill of Napier Downs homestead. The animals set up a great pace; the troops all stared at this white-man station, a forerunner of new and exciting scenes to come.

An air of scrupulous cleanliness was all around the little iron buildings. A quietness too, crows down by the killing-yards hardly squawked under a brilliant sun. The manager, Harry Bannon, was away mustering, and the place was all locked up.

We hurried on to Hawkestone bore. Near by, two red sandstone rocks rose one hundred and fifty feet from the plain. This was to be our last bush camp. Wearily we unsaddled at sundown; the little fires were built; billies* were put on; a grey bower bird came along and watched operations.

It was a cold night, the smoke from the fires rose like a veil to the trees. In a cold dawn we awoke for the last march. Ash-covered men and women on their elbows poked the fires together; sleepy-eyed women filled the billy-cans; the sick groaned and moaned, as they kicked the cold and cramp out of their stiffened limbs. We all welcomed breakfast and sunrise. Mules and horses were brought into camp; then a quick packing up. The Big Leper's lubra (she was a girl with a woman's face) put the blanket and surcingle on her man's mule, and he mounted without a word. Laurie gave the order to march. The trackers moved off, then the prisoners, then witnesses, then the shock troops, then the sick followed by the pack-animals. Birds were whistling their early morning calls; the sun was big and round and red. The last march had started. We crossed the Lennard. We had had to swim it nearly three months before; it was now only a chain of waterholes.

Laurie hurried on ahead. He wished to ring up Sergeant Pike and the doctor in Derby; he wanted to hire the mailman's motor truck, and so save the troops a sixty- mile walk from Kimberley Downs to Derby.

At Kimberley Downs Mrs Thompson made us very welcome. Laurie had missed his young wife by a day. She had been on a visit with Nurse Connell and had stayed nine days watching for the patrol from the crest of Mount Marmion. Laurie secured the mail-truck.

The troops all stared at what Nipper described as a "cart that would go without a horse or anything." We had to push it to get the engine going. All hands eagerly put their clumsy weight into it; they imagined we had to push it all the way to Derby. Larry and Davey would stay behind to bring on the horses and mules.

"Come on now, all together, get aboard!" shouted Laurie. The troops rushed the truck. It was the funniest thing seeing them trying to scramble aboard; the trackers had assured them what a wonderful treat they were to enjoy. Laurie had a job, packing them like sardines. It was managed at last and we started off, Laurie at the wheel, the troops holding on like grim death. They just stared at the ground and at the trees whizzing past, silent and frightened. By the time we arrived at Meeda station they were growing used to it. There would come a laugh with a bump; grunts and laughter as we skimmed past tree or anthill. When we reached the main road Laurie let her out.

The troops all shouted as a 'roo hopped across the road; they yelled when we nearly ran down a cow. It was a race to beat the sunset. The older women and the sick clung tightly to one another. Hard to tell whether they were frightened, amazed, or just taking in the staggering surprise of the timber flying by and the wind whistling in their ears.

We arrived at the native Lazarette just before sundown. Here the sick were sorted out. It was a silent parting All stared at their new home. One old warrior mumbled for his spears; Laurie gently told him he would not need them any more. The Big Leper was the last of the silent ones to file through the gate.

Just at sundown we bowled along to the police station and into the yard. Sergeant Pike greeted us. So ended the patrol, after twelve hundred interesting miles.

THE FIRST MOTOR RIDE OF THEIR LIVES

FINALE

IN Derby it was learned that Bunch-'em-up Gardiner had died in Felix Edgar's arms at Yabagoody well. Several days later, five of the lepers escaped from the Leprosarium. Crossing a mangrove-shaded creek that night a crocodile took one unfortunate. The others were tracked and caught within twenty-four hours by Larry and Davey.

The prisoners were tried and acquitted, much to their astonishment. They eventually made back to their own country— except Nipper; he was found to be a leper. However, as soon as he tired of the Leprosarium, he escaped and no doubt is roaming his beloved hills again. Davey unlawfully entered the Leprosarium to visit a, lady friend and Laurie placed him under arrest. This hurt Davey's dignity and he deserted, taking with him Mrs Nipper. Probably he now roams with Nipper, as wild again as the hills, at the sacred ceremonies with his own blood brothers, chanting to the rising moon upon the waterfall of Charoo.

Dave Rust and Scotty Salmon failed at their Mount Elizabeth venture and are now again at their old love, Karunjie. Good luck to such battlers. Felix Edgar was forced to abandon Mount Hart; he died of fever in Broome hospital some months ago. So Mount Hart has gone back to the wilds again after breaking the hearts of two grand pioneers. Fred Merry is going stronger than ever. One of the roaming doggers, Anderson, has since been speared.

Old Larry is still going strong in Derby, but his little wife Nancy has developed leprosy.

ETT IMPRINT has the following ION IDRIESS books in print in 2024:

Prospecting for Gold (1931)
Lasseter's Last Ride (1931)
Flynn of the Inland (1932)
The Desert Column (1932)
Men of the Jungle (1932)
Drums of Mer (1933)
Gold-Dust and Ashes (1933)
The Yellow Joss (1934)
Man Tracks (1935)
Over the Range (1937)
Forty Fathoms Deep (1937)
Madman's Island (1938)
Headhunters of the Coral Sea (1940)
Lightning Ridge (1940)
Nemarluk (1941)
Shoot to Kill (1942)
Sniping (1942)
Guerrilla Tactics (1942)
Trapping the Jap (1942)
Lurking Death (1942)
The Scout (1943)
Horrie the Wog Dog (1945)
In Crocodile Land (1946)
The Opium Smugglers (1948)
The Wild White Man of Badu (1950)
Outlaws of the Leopolds (1952)
The Red Chief (1953)
The Silver City (1956)
Coral Sea Calling (1957)
Back O' Cairns (1958)
The Wild North (1960)
Tracks of Destiny (1961)
Gouger of the Bulletin (2013)
Ion Idriess: The Last Interview (2020)
Ion Idriess Letters (2023)
Walkabout (2024)

www.ingramcontent.com/pod-product-compliance
Lightning Source LLC
Chambersburg PA
CBHW021228090426
42740CB00006B/427